BORIS Th. SOKOLOFF, M.D., Ph.D., Sc.D., is an eminent research physician, specializing in cancer. Born in St. Petersburg,
Russia, in 1893, he graduated from the University of St. Petersburg
and served with the Russian Army during World War I as a
physician. He was a member of Russia's Institute of Science and
head of the Department of Experimental Medicine, Lesgaft University. Since his escape from Russia in 1920, Dr. Sokoloff has been
connected with some of the most advanced cancer-research institutions of Europe and America: the Pasteur Institute in Paris,
the Rockefeller Institute for Medical Research, the Cancer Institute of Columbia University, and Dr. Leo Loeb's Department of
Pathology at Washington University Medical School. For nine
years he has been Director of the Bio-Research Laboratory, Florida
Southern College, engaging in certain phases of cancer study. .
Nationally known for his work in experimental cytology and
pathology, he is the author of many books. Among them are
Cancer: New Approaches, New Hope (1952); *Science and the
Purpose of Life* (1950); *The Miracle Drugs* (1949); *The Story of
nicillin* (1945); *The Civilized Diseases* (1944).

THE WHITE NIGHTS

Other Books by *BORIS SOKOLOFF*

1952 *Cancer*

1950 *Science and the Purpose of Life*

1949 *The Miracle Drugs*

1947 *Jealousy, a Psychiatric Approach*

1945 *The Story of Penicillin*

1944 *The Civilized Diseases*

1941 *Unconquered Enemy (Cancer)*

1939 *Middle Age Is What You Make It*

1937 *Napoleon: A Medical Biography*

1936 *The Achievement of Happiness*

1935 *Vitality*

1934 *Man's Bio-Dynamics*

1933 *Death of Simon*

1932 *Doctor Garine (Introduction by Theodore Dreiser)*

1932 *Edward Beneš: a Biography*

BORIS SOKOLOFF

THE
WHITE
NIGHTS

*Pages from a
Russian Doctor's
Notebook*

THE DEVIN-ADAIR COMPANY · 1956

NEW YORK

PUBLISHER'S NOTE

The White Nights is the story of the author's participation in the events of the Russian Revolution. It does not purport to be a full history of the period. The episodes and the states of mind of which it tells are highly interesting in themselves, and in the publisher's opinion they are as important and as relevant for our time as they were in the turbulent days of 1917. Some occurrences of which Dr. Sokoloff writes are still in controversy, and a few persons who took part in them will possibly disagree with portions of his account. However, the author's journal, on which the book is based, is supported by documentation quoted in the footnotes. Dr. Sokoloff, incidentally, wrote two extended articles on the Russian Revolution which are included in the *Archives of the Russian Revolution*.

To Alice

AUTHOR'S NOTE

The events described in this book took place during the turbulent years 1914-1920, when the Russian intelligentsia were fighting desperately for democratic ideals. They are events which the author witnessed and in which he actively participated. All the names are identical, a part of historical records, except the names of personal friends of the author, which have been changed in order to protect the lives of their relatives who might be behind the Iron Curtain.

BORIS SOKOLOFF

CONTENTS

THE WHITE NIGHTS

Chapter 1

INSTEAD OF
INTRODUCTION

Twice a week, after classes, I would hurry through the snow-covered streets of St. Petersburg. The winter days were short and, by four in the afternoon, semidarkness engulfed the icy sidewalks. Stumbling through the deep snow, I would run almost as if possessed, afraid of being late for the reunions at my history teacher's home. I had been flattered by his invitation to join his "student parties," where, as a rule, only the older high-school students were present. For me, a youngster of twelve, the discussions at Chaskolsky's home were a revelation. They opened up a new world of ideas.

The long dinner table was covered with plates of sandwiches, a quietly boiling samovar, hot tea, and jam. Two dozen boys of various ages, some seniors, avidly absorbed every word uttered by our professor and no less hungrily consumed the sandwiches and pastry. He called these reunions

3

"an education in democracy." To me, they were more than this. My whole personality, my philosophy of life, my concept of the human race and of myself as a part of it received a sound foundation there. The beliefs and ideals with which I was imbued there were to remain forever a part of my being.

Chaskolsky, without political party but a man of progressive aspirations, was what might be called an "idealistic democrat." To him, democratic ideals and principles were more than a political system. They were a religion. He believed that once democratic principles were introduced on an international basis, everlasting peace could be achieved. He regarded every suppression of human rights as an insult to man's intelligence, for democratic principles were, he insisted, inbred properties of the human race. Whether he was discussing the democracy of Pericles, or the events of the French revolution, or the American Bill of Rights, he repeatedly argued that democratic freedoms were indispensable premises to economic progress.

An associate professor of history at the University of St. Petersburg, Chaskolsky also taught history at my gymnasium.[1] To him, the history of mankind was a never-ending

---

1. A Russian classic gymnasium of my time had nine grades: one preparatory and eight others. It was not coeducational. Boys were admitted to the preparatory grade at the age of seven, but often they were a year or two older. Graduates of the gymnasium were admitted to a university without taking entrance examinations. Only those students with high marks, however, were allowed to enroll in a medical school or in the Institute of Technology and similar specialized schools. For data concerning education in Russia prior to the Communist revolution, see *Russian Schools and Universities in the World War* by Ignatiev, Odinetz, and Novgorotsev, Yale University Press, New Haven, 1929. There was a marked advance in the educational system between 1908 and 1914. According to these authors, "It was estimated that in order to provide all the children of school

struggle between democratic ideals and antidemocratic doctrines and trends. "This fight will go on for many centuries to come," he warned us. "But don't worry, my friends, the final victory will be with democracy."

He was an anti-Marxist. He discussed with us the work of Karl Marx and read pages from *Das Kapital* and other publications of the German economist. Impartial and open-minded as he was, Chaskolsky was, nevertheless, very critical of Marxism, as a doctrine denying the role of individuality in the social and economic progress of man. He was devastatingly critical, in particular, of the party newly formed by Lenin. "Bolshevism is a reactionary movement which rejects all democratic principles," he said, and he advised us to study Lenin's writings carefully. "It is the old antidemocratic movement under new slogans."

Thanks to this "education in democracy," when I entered the university at the age of sixteen I had already formed my political opinions, and these I never have changed. Nothing that has happened or that has been written or said since the days of my youth has even slightly affected my profound belief in democratic principles, my antagonism to Marxism as a dialectical, unscientific doctrine, or my conviction that Lenin's bolshevism was a reactionary movement.

An encounter occurred at that time that was to leave a strong impression on me.

In my senior year at high school, I took a short trip to

---

age with an education by 1922, it was necessary to establish 317,-000 schools. Of this number, Russia had in 1908 less than 100,000. During six years of intensive educational activity, Russia recorded a gain of 49,458 schools. The total enrollment in 1914 was nearly 7,500,000 children of both sexes." This educational progress was interrupted by the Communist *coup d'état*.

Europe during the summer vacation. While in Geneva, I decided to stop at the Library of the Société de Lecture and glance through some old books. When I asked for a certain volume, the librarian replied that it was already in use and pointed to a man who was seated by the window, engrossed in reading and surrounded by books. There was no one in the place except this man, the elderly librarian, and myself. The man had a large, bald head, reddish, graying beard and mustache, and broad shoulders. I noticed one other detail. Although it was a sunny morning, he was wearing rubbers, and his trousers were turned up to the calf. I asked him if I might borrow the book I was interested in.

He glanced at me with hostility from under lowered brows. His eyes were narrow, Tartarlike. He grunted.

"Take it." Then he added, "A useless book."

"Why useless?" I asked, rather timidly.

"Slush, drivel, this Rousseau of yours. Now take Robespierre—there's a man for you. Follow his example. He knew what he wanted."

"He wanted power," I injected.

"Of course, he wanted power. Power over the masses."

"The masses should govern themselves," I protested.

"Humbug. The masses are either sheep or scoundrels. They must be guided with an iron hand."

"I beg your pardon. Doesn't man fight for his ideals, for his rights, for his individuality?" I asked, indignant.

"Nonsense! Man fights only for bread."

"But what about love?" I cried with alarm. "Doesn't man love his fellows?"

"Ha! Ha!—you're a simpleton, my boy. Society is based only on struggle. Love just gets in the way. It's a fairy tale for children and fools like you," he said with irritation.

"Yet it is love that has guided the progress of humanity."

He burst into laughter. "The history of the human race is controlled only by economic factors. Class war, hatred between the rich and the poor, between the capitalists and the workers, is the moving force in the social progress of mankind." He made a gesture to indicate that the conversation, of which I have recorded only the main points, was over.

"Who is this man?" I asked the librarian when I returned the books I had borrowed.

"He calls himself Lenin. I don't know his real name," she answered.[2]

Years later, in 1916, in St. Petersburg,[3] I climbed the interminable stairs to the fifth floor of an old house at Number 23 Tverskaya Street. Having read in the morning papers that Alexander Kerensky, who not many months after was to be the leader of Russian democracy, was gravely ill, I had decided to pay him a visit, or at least to find out his condition. I had never met him before.

The small, simply furnished apartment was crowded with people, coming and going. There were members of the Russian Parliament—the Duma—artists, workmen, scientists, students, and several physicians. The most popular man in St. Petersburg was lying in his bedroom, recovering from a kidney removal. He was pale and feverish, yet smiling at his visitors and full of vitality.

Every minute there were telephone calls, answered by his

---

2. "All day," wrote Lenin's wife, "Vladimir Ilyich [Lenin] sat in the library, but in the evenings we did not know what to do with ourselves." *Vospominaniya [Reminiscences] o Lenine*, Nadezhda Krupskaya, Gosizdat, Moscow, 1926, p. 134.

3. St. Petersburg was renamed Petrograd after the beginning of the war. Still later, in 1924, it became Leningrad. To us who were born there, it remains old St. Petersburg always. Throughout this book, I name the city according to the period of which I am writing.

wife, inquiring about the condition of the "man of courage," so called because he had addressed to the Czarist government words no other man dared speak. His speeches in the Duma were events in themselves. Leader of the Labor party, which had but eleven representatives in the Duma, he had succeeded in making his group the most active in the Parliament. As an orator, he was extraordinary. Listening to his ever-simple but sincere and ardent words—words calling for the rights of men—people wept. It was not only the words themselves that touched men's hearts but the manner in which they were spoken. Living always under the threat of arrest and persecution from the Czarist government, this man staunchly defended the principles of freedom in which he believed.

I entered his bedroom when my turn came. He smiled at me. "I hope you will recover," I mumbled. "We all need you. We, the youth of Russia, need you to build the future."

"Thanks," he answered. "I will get well."

Only one year later, this man with only one kidney took the heavy burden of trying to save the democratic government of Russia from Communist domination.

While a freshman at the university, I joined Kerensky's Labor party. But politics, in the strict sense of the word, never attracted me. During the years that followed, I took no part in politics, giving all the time I could take from studies and scientific research to "constructive activity," participating in the cooperative movement, teaching in night schools for adults, and becoming closely associated with the University of Lesgaft, an institution organized along the pattern of the Sorbonne.

During the years 1905–1914, there was in Russia an ever-growing movement for democratic ideals. This was fought not only by the Czarist government but by the Bolshevik party as well. In labor unions, in cooperatives, in educational institutions, the Bolsheviks tried hard to stop the growing influence of the democratic parties. All this took place long before the October *coup d'état* by the Communists in 1917.

Late in 1916, I was mobilized and sent as a physician to the southwestern front. I remained there during the February revolution, when the Czarist government was overthrown and the coalition democratic government formed. The coalition's goal was the convocation of the All Russian Constituent Assembly, scheduled for October 1917. I was present during the events of October, when the Communists seized power. Although the election to the All Russian Constituent Assembly took place in November 1917, when the Communists were already in power, the majority of elected deputies belonged to the democratic parties. I was elected on the Labor party ticket from the southwest army district. I did not want either the nomination or the election. I was not a politician. And so, against my wishes, I became involved in the dramatic fight for the Constituent Assembly. Being nominated chairman of the military commission of the Assembly, I was in charge of the defense of this institution against the Communists, who dissolved it on January 5, 1918, by armed force. My arrest was ordered but I escaped to Kiev and returned to the front, which was in a state of disorganization.

In the summer of 1918, a new military front was formed on the Volga by the democratic parties, with the active support of Czechoslovakian legions. The All Russian Constituent Assembly met in Ufa this time, without the Communist members, and we were all requested to come there. It was an interesting experience for me to travel through a Russia under Communist domination, twice crossing the Soviet frontier before I reached Samara from Kiev. Eight months later, I arrived in Paris by way of Siberia, Japan, and China and was present at the Versailles Peace Conference.

A large part of Russia was in the hands of the Communists, but several regions were still free from their domination. North Russia was headed by a friend of mine, Nicholas Tchaikovsky, an old-time leader of the cooperative movement. The Red Cross was sending supplies to Archangel, and I joined a Red Cross unit as a physician. By the end of 1919, I was again in Russia, in the north, working as a physician on the Vologda front. In the early spring of 1920, a reshaping of the North Russian government took place. I was named Secretary of Education, but my administrative activity was very brief indeed, for, under pressure of the Red army, it was decided to evacuate the army of North Russia.

The small ice-cutter on which I was a passenger was unable to break through the ice and reach Norway, its destination, and I was captured by the Communists in the White Sea. A local Soviet condemned me to death, but at the last moment an order arrived from Moscow to send me there for interrogation. In Moscow, I was condemned to death for the second time and transferred to Boutyrki Prison.

After one hundred and twenty-two days in Boutyrki Prison, I was called one day to the warden's office. I was sure that the last minutes of my existence had come. But, to my amazement, the warden told me I was free to go anywhere I wanted. Much later, I learned that Nicholas Morosoff, President of Lesgaft University, had intervened on my behalf, begging Lenin to "save the life of a promising young scientist."

I returned to Petrograd and to my scientific activity at the Institute of Science, where I was appointed Director of the Laboratory of Experimental Medicine. After several weeks in that city, it became apparent to me that continued existence under the oppressive Soviet regime would be intolerable, and I decided to escape from the country. I happened one day to meet Olga Kerensky, the wife of the former Premier, on one of my regular visits to the House of Scientists. She and her two sons were hostages of the Communists and expected any day to be sent to Siberia or liquidated. I persuaded her to join me in my adventure, and we succeeded in escaping, in September 1920.

I returned to scientific activity, and my political career was over. I received a research fellowship at the University of Brussels, Belgium. After several years of research, first in Brussels and later at the Pasteur Institute in Paris and at the University of Prague, I was invited by the Rockefeller Institute for Medical Research to come to New York and work there on cancer. I arrived in the United States in 1928, and in due time took my citizenship papers.

I was soon to become perplexed and greatly disturbed by the attitude in American intellectual circles toward Russian communism. When, on many occasions, I talked with Theodore Dreiser, with Heywood Broun, and with many other writers or professional men, I found them blinded with admiration for the Soviet regime. It was utterly hopeless to explain to them that their concept of Russia past and present was entirely wrong. They believed every word of Communist propaganda. They were ignorant of the fact that the Czarist government was a relic of the past, in its death throes long before its existence was ended, and that its influence upon the intellectual and spiritual life of the Russian people had long been lost. These admirers of Russian communism ignored the well-known fact that there was in Russia an enormous group of people, the intelligentsia, democratic in their aspirations and way of life, idealistic in the extreme, and that in large part it was made up of the common people, the sons and daughters of peasants and workmen.

To the American intellectuals, inspired by clever Communist promotion, there was nothing but darkness until Lenin and his comrades took power in Russia. Yet, in many ways, Russia prior to 1917 had become more democratic in spirit, more an intense believer in democratic principles than many countries of today where democracy is well established. The inner life of most Russian universities was freer of restrictions on liberty of thought, belief, and speech than is that of many Western universities today. To the American intellectuals, admirers of the Soviet, Russian communism was a revelation, a highly progressive revolutionary movement; while to us, who knew its true nature, it was a reactionary, antidemocratic movement which had turned Russia back to the despotism of the past. They did not realize, they did not want to see that the Communist movement was directed not so much against the conservative elements of Russia as against its democratic progressive elements, and that the victory of communism actually meant the complete destruction of the intelligentsia as such and the annihilation of democracy.

When I would open my mouth and try to say a few words against communism, I was called a "White Russian." Dreiser frequently called me this. To him, the term "White Russian" was a synonym for "reactionary." It was soon to be replaced generally by the term "fascist," applied to anyone who criticized Soviet Russia.

After fifty years of neocommunism, during which those under its sway have grown in number from a small group of fifty-odd persons [4] to about 800 million, there still persists a

---

4. Lenin (whose real name was Vladimir Ilyich Ulyanoff, also spelled Ulianov) came of a well-to-do family and originally was a member

friendly attitude toward the movement on the part of certain American intellectuals, in spite of all that is known about it.

---

of the Russian Social-Democratic party. The first congress of this party took place in Minsk, Russia, from March 1 through March 3, 1898. It was at the party's second congress, July 17-30, 1903, in Brussels, that the "Bolsheviks" and "Mensheviks" had their birth. Lenin was chiefly responsible for this break-up of the Social-Democratic party into these two antagonistic factions. He became undisputed leader of the Bolshevik faction. The Russian word *bolshe* means "more." *Menshe* means "less." The real difference between the two factions lay much more in their tactics than in their doctrines. Lenin's attitude was dictatorial and was described by Plekhanoff, leader of the Mensheviks, as "Bonapartism" (*Iskra*, 65, 1904). Even in that early day, Lenin manifested a genuine hatred for liberals and radicals who, although sympathetic to the cause of bolshevism (like today's fellow travelers), had not fully accepted his doctrines and had not joined his party. "We must utilize them as much as we can," he wrote in 1904. "But never should we enter into cooperation or union with them." The fight between Bolsheviks and Mensheviks continued unabated until the end of 1917, when Lenin seized power in Russia and liquidated most of the Mensheviks. Lenin's party was officially called the Social-Democratic Bolshevik party and the movement was known as "bolshevism" until March 6, 1918. The names then were changed, respectively, to the Communist party and communism. However, as early as April 17, 1917, Lenin, in his famous "April theses" delivered to the members of his party in the Tauride Palace, proposed abandoning the name "Bolshevik" (or "Bolshevist") party, which he never had liked, and urged that it be changed to the Communist party. (See *Lenin*, Hutchinson, London, 1947, p. 115.) The term "communism" hardly applies to the movement initiated by Lenin, for this movement is actually *state capitalism* in its extreme form. In speaking about Russian communism, the term "neocommunism" is more appropriate.

For the sake of clarity and consistency, the terms "Communist" and "communism" are used throughout this book instead of "Bolshevik" and "bolshevism," except in quotations from speakers and writers.

There must be some answer to the paradoxical fact that extreme individualists, as are many intellectuals, who value their freedom above all else, nevertheless give support to this utterly anti-individualistic and antidemocratic movement. Perhaps the answer can be found in the events of 1917, when an aggressive minority, numbering less than two percent of the population, was able to triumph over the democratic government. It is about these events that this book is written. It is written with much hesitation, with sorrow and grief, for it tells about the tragic inability of democracy to cope with communism in 1917.

This book is not a historical treatise. It is a recollection of small, often insignificant events of that epoch, composed from the pages of a notebook. I do not remonstrate with democracy for its weakness. In a sense, I sympathize with it for its weakness. I have tried to understand the nature of the "illness of appeasement" by describing the human side of that tragedy, which already has become the world's tragedy.

I have sought, through telling the story of my experiences, to put my finger on the essential factors of this illness, which long since has spread throughout the world. The appeasement of 1917 is the appeasement of today. It has corrupted the intellectual circles of the United States, Europe, and Asia as profoundly as it did the Russian intelligentsia of my time.

Chapter 2

THE DEATH OF LINDE

I EXAMINED the patient. He was a young soldier, not more than twenty, with a childish, moonlike face, and very blond. He was semiconscious and running a fever of about 105 degrees. Abruptly I said to the nurse:

"Write: Typhus complicated by hyperpyrexia. Possibly, hemorrhagic nephritis. Check his blood and urine."

The nurse had recently been assigned to our hospital and it was her first case of typhus. But her face remained immobile, as if she were unconcerned about the contagious disease.

"Yes, doctor."

Something in her voice told me that she was deathly afraid but was trying earnestly to conceal her feelings. I took the samples of blood and urine myself.

"Where did they bring him from?"

15

She checked her notes and replied, "From the 443rd Regiment." I was disturbed by this information. The regiment was part of the 111th Division, which had recently been transferred to our XIII Army from the northern front. Epidemics of typhus were ravaging the area where the regiment had previously been stationed.

"Who is the regiment's chief physician?"

"I believe it's Dr. B.," the nurse informed me. This again was bad news, for Dr. B. was a young physician only recently graduated from the Samara Medical School. He had had no experience with infectious diseases and had admitted as much.

I shrugged my shoulders and grumbled: "I must go to the front and talk with him about this case. Call him and tell him I will come to his unit shortly."

The hospital was in a small town called Rojitsche, partly destroyed by fire and bombardment. Only a few houses remained intact, and these were occupied by the personnel and patients of the hospital. The inhabitants of the town, largely Jews and Lithuanians, had been evacuated many months before. One or two shops were still selling cigarettes and candies. The streets were unpaved, and red-gray dust, raised by army trucks, penetrated the hospital rooms and covered floors and beds with a thick layer. The windows in the surgery room were kept closed as a protection against the dust, and during the hot summer months it was unbearably uncomfortable to operate there.

I lived in railroad cars that had been transformed into a luxurious laboratory unit by the Red Cross. Everything was at my disposal for clinical testing. The laboratory was big and bright, with enormous windows, a special animal room, and a small library. The second car contained living quarters for me, my assistant, the nurse, and an orderly. There was also a cozy little dining room and kitchenette, which made us the envy of the army medical men. We moved with the army and were in charge of any epidemics that might break out. We worked in close association with the XIII Army's general hospital, housed not far from our unit.

My train was located near a railroad bridge on the banks of the river Malta. Swift and narrow, with reddish water, this river had been the scene of the bloodiest battles between Russians and Germans, many months before I arrived. Now the front, about ten miles away from Rojitsche, was quiet, and only local skirmishes were taking place here and there. Very few wounded were brought to the hospital. Most of the patients were routine cases of infection or battle fatigue. Now and then a German plane would circle around the hospital and drop a bomb or two, but this was our only distraction. The nearest town, Lutzk, was about fifteen miles away and our only communication with it was by horseback or ambulance. It was not a pleasant trip and we seldom went there, or to Rovno.

The doctors and nurses attached to the hospital spent endless evenings playing bridge, and I, a sad exception to the general rule, took long walks along the banks of the river. Deeper into the country were small farms and ranches with cherry gardens and orchards and fields sowed with wheat or oats. Men and women worked every day in the fields, silently, as they had done for generations, apathetic toward the war which was so close to them and yet so distant. They read no newspapers; no mail was ever brought to them, and they had but the vaguest, though uneasy, notion about the events which were brewing in Petrograd.

Getting into the car one day, I called my assistant, Carl Schelling. He was a young man of German extraction, an experienced bacteriologist of exceptional preciseness and enchanted by science. Science was a religion with him, and he visualized himself as an obedient and devoted servant of its rituals. Nothing unconnected with science concerned him. When I announced to him that the Czarist regime had been overthrown and that the democratic coalition government under Prince Lvov was elected, he calmly said, "What of it?" and resumed the discussion about the latest work on yellow fever. He frankly admitted that the discovery of *Stegomyia fasciata,* a mosquito which is responsible for the transmission of yellow-fever virus, excited him much more than the victory of the democratic parties over the monarchists.

This promising young scientist was killed that same autumn when a German plane made a direct hit on our train. The laboratory was completely destroyed, Carl was fatally wounded, and I escaped with scratches. It occurred shortly before my departure for the north.

But on this peaceful morning, we were free of any dark premonition and we discussed the testing of the specimens I had brought him to prove typhus infection. Carl was very enthusiastic. "I will try to make a culture of *Rickettsia prowazekii,* and of course the agglutination test. I hope I succeed." I did not want to disappoint him. The test was a pure formality and was needed only for our hospital records. But he was so eager to perform a good job that I raised no objection to his making all possible tests. We were ready for luncheon when my orderly announced that Captain Linde wanted to see me.

"Linde?" I exclaimed. "Impossible!" But here he was, walking into my room with his usual calmness.

There were five of us, childhood friends. A peculiar group of youngsters united by mutual interest in science and music.

There was no intimacy, no deep friendship or attachment among us. We knew very little about one another's family life or personal problems. We never discussed, never even touched, the inner sanctum of our thoughts and feelings. There was even a certain detachment among us, an abstraction in emotion. And yet, one night a week, with almost religious faithfulness, we would gather at my home. We discussed the latest books. We debated the neovitalism of Hans Driesch, the evolution theory of Goldschmidt, Lossky's intuitivism. We often disagreed, but our arguments were restrained and dispassionate. And after I had served supper, we played music for two hours or more. Two members of the group were violinists, one a cellist, and one a pianist; I was the only listener. At midnight, never later and rarely before, we would go for a walk, continuing our discussion, which was so abstract and yet so vital to every one of us. After taking them to their homes, I would saunter for an hour or more along the banks of the Neva River. And for the next seven days, we would see little if anything of one another.

The Neva was silent and motionless in her stern glacial bondage, and the quay was covered with foot-deep snow. Infrequent passers-by in long, heavy fur coats walked slowly, like puppets moved by an invisible force. The pale, hazy face of the moon, the distant ringing of church bells, the soft creak of fast-running sleighs created a sense of detachment from life, of unreality. Are these slowly moving figures alive, I wondered, or are they ghosts who have come back to us from the past, enjoying the winter fascination of our river, their river? That stranger standing there, in frozen immobility, contemplating the boundlessness of the snowy river shroud, is he truly a living being, or is he a turbulent wanderer unable to find peace even in the immortality of his soul? It might be Moussorgsky, thin and short, with long curling hair, small nose, and protuberant, expressionless eyes. Does he still love humanity passionately, as he loved it when he was alive? Does he still believe, as he proclaimed shortly before his tragic death, that in the course of time we Russians will be able to say the final word on general harmony, on the brotherly communion of all nations in accordance with the law of the Gospel of Christ?

But the passers-by would move away, frightened at my approach. The illusion broken, I would return home.

We all were St. Petersburgians, by birth and by aspiration. We all had graduated from the same high school, located only a few blocks from my home, where I was born and lived until the war. Each of us chose a different profession, or, as we called it, avocation. Linde was a mathematician *par excellence*. "Like Napoleon," he would say, "I like to read logarithms. I enjoy them." Serk was a poet, specializing in English literature, a writer of promise. As a student at the University of St. Petersburg, he published several short stories, forceful and masterfully written. Vassiliev, realistic in his attitude toward life, practical and tenacious, was enrolled in the Institute of Communications and was studying to be a railroad construction engineer. Demidoff, a student of law, was an orator of dynamic personality while still a junior at the university. And I, in turn, a medical student and physiologist, worked steadily to become a specialist in cancer.

We never called each other by our first names or even, as is the Russian custom, by the first and father's first names. We used only the family name. It was not customary, but then again, our group of youngsters was an unusual phenomenon even for the St. Petersburg of that epoch.

I had not seen Linde for more than a year, but I had read a good deal in the papers about his dramatic army career. He was stationed in the capital, as a sergeant in the Semenovsky regiment, just when the February revolutionary movement had gained momentum. At the most critical moment, when the Cossacks and police had fought the insurgents to a standstill and had gotten the upper hand in the streets of Petrograd, Linde appeared at the head of the Semenovsky regiment and turned the tide in favor of the democratic revolution. He was acclaimed a hero of the revolution. In one of his rare letters to me, he gave a vivid picture of these events:

"I don't know what happened to me. I was lying on a couch in the barracks and reading a book by Haldane. I found it an interesting treatise, somewhat confused and poorly balanced. I was so absorbed in it that I didn't hear shouts and roars coming from the street. A wild bullet broke the window glass near my couch. I was furious. 'What the hell is going on there?' I asked my comrades. 'Look out the window,' they suggested. I looked. It was a mess. The Cossacks were firing on defenseless and unarmed crowds, striking people with their whips, crushing the fallen with their horses. I was shocked, as if hypnotized by this terrifying picture so different from the state of mind which had been mine when I was analyzing Haldanism. And then I saw a young girl trying to evade the galloping horse of a Cossack officer. She was too slow. A severe blow on her head brought her down, down under the horse's feet. She screamed. It was her inhuman, penetrating scream that caused something in me to snap. I jumped to the table—it was a large oak table—and cried out wildly, 'Friends! . . . Friends!' It was a matter of only a few minutes before I was surrounded by hundreds of servicemen, perplexed and surprised. 'Long live the revolution,' I shouted again and again. 'To arms! . . . to arms! Let's take arms and drive away the Cossacks. . . . They are killing innocent people, our brothers, our sisters! . . .'

"Later they said there was something in my voice that made it impossible to resist my call. As in a fever, I ran to the regimental depot, took a rifle, distributed hundreds of rifles to other soldiers. 'All out on the street,' I cried. 'Follow me. . . .' They followed me without realizing where or in the name of what cause they went. They simply ran after me. . . . Our regiment had at that time about six thousand enlisted men. They all joined me in the attack against Cossacks and police. We killed a few of them. The rest retreated. I led my regiment to the barracks of the Preobragensky regiment, which joined in. By night, the fight was over. The revolution became a reality. The Czarist government was overthrown. . . . And I, well, I returned the same night to my book by Haldane."

Not for long. As soon as the coalition government was formed, he was commissioned in the rank of captain and sent as a deputy political commissar to the XIII Army. That was the last I had heard. And now here he was, the same Linde, tall, powerfully built, very blond and handsome, the image of an ancient Viking.

"What wind brought you to this God-forsaken hole?" I asked him, inviting him to our dining room.

"Troubles," he answered curtly. "The 443rd regiment refused to obey orders to occupy the first-line trenches. The regiment is infiltrated with Bolsheviks."

"We have no Bolsheviks in the XIII Army," I remarked.

"No," Linde agreed. "Your army is in good shape, but the northern section of the front is demoralized by Bolshevik propaganda. The regiment was transferred from Vilno."

I told him about the typhus case and my need to go to the front. We agreed to drive together. Linde explained to me that he was a sort of political "exterminator" visiting the military units infested by Bolsheviks. "I expose them and destroy their nests as fast as I can," he smiled, and added, "not always successfully."

"How do you accomplish this?"

"Not with a hot iron or a gun, only by the force of my personality," and he smiled again.

We talked about St. Petersburg and our friends. I wondered where they were.

I learned from Linde that Vassiliev was transferred to the XIII Army and was the commander of an armored company stationed not far from Lutzk.

"I met him only last week in Rovno," Linde explained. "He is an ardent anti-Bolshevik and an enthusiast of our democratic government."

"And you are not?"

"Well, yes, of course. . . . Democracy is an excellent, vital idea. But democracy is something that should be defended and fought for."

"But it is being defended."

"It was. They fought hard in the past for the idea of democracy, for freedom, for all freedoms. But now that they've achieved their goal, well, they've become soft, yes, too soft, unrealistic, they don't see the danger to their very existence."

"Do you truly believe, Linde, that the Bolsheviks are a real threat to our government?"

"I do. . . . They are a small minority but they are well organized and very active. They infiltrate all the important central institutions, including our Department of the Army. They dominate the railroad workers' union, the arsenal, the Navy, the police. You'll find a small but active nucleus of Bolsheviks in every important organization."

"But haven't you talked with Kerensky and other members of the government?"

"I tried, but it's hopeless. . . . Petrograd is a madhouse. Everyone talks and talks. . . . Endless speeches, usually passionate, often convincing. A gigantic oratory, fantastic in its dimensions, that is the capital today. You'd think the speech-restraining center in the brain had suddenly been removed by the revolution. Kerensky, Miliukoff, Tchernoff, and hundreds of others are plunged in watery oratory, day after day. . . . And the Bolsheviks are hard at work."

"So the front is really the best place to be?"

"That's what I've found."

I was ready to agree with him.

Soon after luncheon, we left for the front in Linde's car. The road was deserted. The fields, uncultivated for three years, were covered with wild-growing shrubbery. Here and there a lonely farmhouse, minus windows and doors, stood as a sad reproof to the absurdity of war.

For a long time Linde drove in silence. Then suddenly he began to talk. His voice was warm and friendly and there was an emotion which I had never before felt in it.

"Do you remember our evenings? I never told you how much good they did me. They gave me a belief in mankind, in man, in Russia. . . ." Abruptly changing the subject, he said, "You know, I never finished reading that book by Haldane. I didn't like it. His concept of the 'wholeness of the organism' seems naïve to me, a feeble attempt to revive the old materialism. . . . In fact, I'm glad I didn't have a chance to finish reading it. . . ."

He turned into a side road and in a few minutes we arrived at the headquarters of the 110th Division.

A young aide-de-camp met us. He saluted and informed us that General V., division commander, was expecting Linde.

We entered a large, comfortable tent and were introduced to the general. He was a tall man with gray hair and short white mustache. There was no friendliness in his face as he shook Linde's hand. I noted a slight hostility on the part of his staff officers also.

"Captain Linde," he said, "the situation in the 443rd regiment is out of control. It's an outrageous situation."

"Is it so serious?" asked Linde.

"I'm afraid it is. Two months ago, my division was in perfect fighting condition. But they sent me reinforcements from Petrograd which included a lot of scoundrels. Very soon the trouble started. When we arrived here, the 442nd and 444th regiments were assigned to the front line and moved in promptly. Now it is time to replace them with the 441st and 443rd regiments. The 443rd has flatly refused to take their positions. It's open mutiny. They elected a regimental soviet composed entirely of Bolsheviks. Two days ago, during the night, my armored cars were demobilized. Their engines were smashed. I have no way of enforcing my orders and punishing the mutineers."

"How many Bolsheviks are there in the 443rd regiment?"

"I couldn't give the exact figures. About 50 or 60. No more. But they control the whole regiment."

"Have you tried to talk with them?"

"Captain Linde," the general replied sarcastically, "we in the army do not talk with mutineers. We give orders, and if they are not carried out, we court-martial the offenders. . . ."

"Of course, General," Linde answered conciliatorily. "Of course. I understand that. But has Colonel G. tried to find out what they want?"

"What they want! They want immediate peace with the Germans. They wounded the Colonel's aide-de-camp. They threatened to kill all the officers. They drove them away, the bastards. . . . But I requested an armored company from Lutzk. I expect it any moment. And then I'll show this riff-raff how costly it is not to obey my orders. . . . I'll teach them a good lesson. . . ."

For a minute or two there was silence, finally broken by the calm voice of Linde.

"General, I would like your permission to visit the mutineers."

"You don't need *my* authorization, Captain," coldly answered General V. "You need *their* permission to talk with them. But I warn you, it's hopeless—and dangerous. But it's up to you. . . ."

"With your permission, I would like to go there. . . ."

General V. shrugged his shoulders, turned to a staff officer, and briskly said, "Lieutenant Safronov, conduct Captain Linde to the 443rd regimental headquarters." And, shaking hands with Linde, he said almost warmly, "Good luck. And be alert."

Safronov was no more than 22, with an open face and charming smile. I liked him at once. We went to the car and drove along a road full of ruts and hollows. "The regimental headquarters is only about five miles from here," Safronov remarked. "Do drive very slowly." He informed us that he had been a student at the Institute of Technology when he was drafted by the army. He had already been wounded twice, but not seriously, and was decorated with the Cross of St. George for bravery.

"I know all about you, Captain Linde, and I admire you. I read about you. . . ." he said to my friend. "It's a terrible thing, what the Bolsheviks did to our division. We're all ashamed. . . . Do you really intend to talk with them?"

"Certainly. . . . I have to go. It's my duty. I was sent here to keep up morale. We must avoid any bloodshed," Linde replied.

"May I . . . may I . . . go with you . . . please? Perhaps I can protect you. I am armed. . . ."

Linde smiled. "Of course . . . but *I'm* not armed. In circumstances like these I don't believe in guns. . . ."

"But they are brutes, complete fanatics. . . ."

"We shall see. . . ."

A large group of officers met us when we approached headquarters. They were all armed, some with revolvers, others with rifles. Colonel G., the commander, was among them. He shook our hands in a friendly spirit.

"Captain Linde, I must beg you not to go any farther," and he indicated with his hand a large crowd of soldiers, some of them lying, some sitting, on the lawn near the camp, not more than a thousand feet from us.

The moment they saw our group, the gray mass of soldiers began to stir, rising from the ground like a gigantic prehistoric animal. As if expecting some action on our part, and as if preparing for defense or attack, they gradually took an almost military formation. They divided into two groups. One, scattered and amorphous, contained the larger part of the regiment. The other, small but compact like a mainspring, aggressive and menacing, formed itself on the right flank of the crowd. They held rifles with bayonets fixed. These were the Communists.

"Thank you, Colonel," replied Linde, "but my duties give me no choice. I must go."

"Then five of my officers will go with you," G. declared. "I insist."

"All right, but they must follow me at a distance," said Linde.

Slowly, our small group of eight began to move, Linde a

few feet in the lead, the rest following. At first he headed in the direction of the tight group of Communists. When we were close enough to see their faces frozen in expectation, he suddenly turned to the left and walked toward the large mass of soldiers. He walked faster and faster, and soon he was no more than fifty feet away.

"Don't follow me any farther. Remain here," he ordered, and in a few minutes he was facing the regiment.

"My friends," he said, and his voice was loud and clear and calm but vibrant with strong emotion. "I have come to you from our government, the government of democratic Russia. The February revolution gave you freedom. It will bring you prosperity and peace, it will give you everything that you have dreamed about. But, friends, we must have patience. We are at war. I know that you and you, every one of you, wants peace. But do you want a shameful peace? Do you want to become slaves of our aggressive enemy, the Germans? Do you?"

"No, no," the crowd shouted.

"No. I knew you would say no. You are brave and honest citizens of our great country, of our democratic Russia. I call for patience, a little more patience. An honorable peace will soon be achieved. It is for you and your children that you must, I repeat, you must obtain an honorable peace."

"Yes! Bravo!" the crowd cried.

"It's men like you and me, who come from simple folk, who made our country free. Friends, long live democratic Russia!"

The crowd responded warmly to his appeal. Hundreds of voices shouted, "Long live democratic Russia, long live Kerensky, long live Linde!"

But while Linde was talking and was so masterfully gaining the confidence and sympathy of the crowd, I noticed that the group of Communists was slowly moving in his direction. Now they were no farther than twenty feet from him. They held their bayonets as if ready to attack. Three soldiers, more determined than the others, were in the lead. "Look!" I seized Safronov's hand. "Look over there. They'll charge any minute now."

Safronov took out his revolver. "Yes. . . . Oh, my Lord!"

But Linde did not seem to see them. "In the name of the democratic government of Russia, I call on you to obey the order to go to the trenches. . . . I call on you to do this. . . ."

"Yes! Yes!" shouted the crowd. "We shall."

"Swear in the name of democracy. . . . Swear . . ." but he did not finish the sentence. A Communist drove his bayonet into Linde's back. At the same moment, Safronov fired. The murderer was killed instantly, his rifle falling to the ground beside his body. For a moment the attackers stopped. But one of them, who was behind their now-dead leader, swiftly covered the few yards that separated him from Linde, who was now half-sitting, half-lying on the grass. The soldier raised his bayonet. He charged upon Linde, his face full of hate and determination. My poor friend tried to protect himself, grabbing at the bayonet with bare hands. Again Safronov fired, but this time he missed. His bullet struck a man in the crowd, and the attacker, indifferent to the firing, struck my dying friend again and again. The mass of soldiers, who only a few moments ago had welcomed and applauded Linde, remained immobile, panic-stricken. Not one of them came to Linde's defense, not a single man in the crowd of two thousand protested against this merciless and brutal killing of a defenseless man, who had been acclaimed a hero of the Russian revolution.

Some of the Communists started to run in our direction,

holding their bayonets ready for a charge. At this moment, when the lives of our small group were hanging by a thread, someone in the crowd shouted:

"The armored cars! The armored cars are coming!" They were magic words. The advancing Communists turned and fled like wild rabbits, disappearing in the crowd. The killer, holding the rifle in his hands, its bayonet red with blood, hesitated for a minute, then followed his comrades.

Linde was still alive. He was bleeding profusely. The grass around him was stained with his blood. He opened his eyes, looked at me, and murmured "How idiotic . . . I knew . . . I'd be killed. . . ." He died before I was able to bandage his wounds. He had received more than thirty bayonet stabs. Safronov was crying like a child. The soldiers, now deeply moved, their faces sad, surrounded us. One of them whispered, "He was a good man. . . . God bless his soul."

The armored cars arrived. The soldiers of the 443rd regiment were ordered into formation. Rifles were examined, bayonets checked. Everything was in perfect order. There was no trace of the killer and not one of the soldiers was ready to admit knowledge of the killer's name. Among the officers who followed Linde, none was able to identify the murderer. The soldiers of the 443rd regiment, now meek and docile, went obediently to their front-line trenches that evening. I returned to Rojitsche without having had a chance to see Dr. B. and discuss the typhus fever case.

Three days after Linde's death, four more cases of typhus were admitted to our hospital. The situation seemed grave; it required drastic measures. The records showed that all affected patients were from the 7th company of the same regiment. It looked like an epidemic. I requested the doctor to send the whole 7th company, with their belongings, to

Rojitsche. They arrived the same day, about 200 servicemen altogether, and I ordered the complete disinfection of their tents and belongings.

Since typhus is transmitted from man to man by the body louse, which is infected with the viruslike germ of typhus fever, our goal was to eliminate all the lice which infested the men of the 7th company. Carl Schelling, my assistant, was excited. He wanted to collect live lice and isolate *Rickettsia prowazekii* from them. He proudly showed me the slides he had made from the blood of the first typhus patient. "His blood was swarming with *Rickettsias*. They're so small you can detect them only with a special staining."

I warned him, "Remember Prowazek's tragic end. . . . Be very careful when you try to find infected lice." Dr. Prowazek was a German bacteriologist who died from typhus fever while experimenting with the parasites. But Carl was deaf to my warning. Truly a scientist, he disregarded all danger and eagerly looked through the soldiers' coats for the priceless lice. He did catch dozens of them but was not successful in finding the ones with *Rickettsias*.

Our disinfecting train was a marvel of perfection—it was said that the Red Cross had spent a small fortune on it. One car in the middle of the train served as a reception room, where the soldiers took off their uniforms and underclothes. These were immediately transferred to the washing-disinfecting car. The stripped men were then directed to the bath car, where there were hot and cold showers and a barber shop for those who needed shaves or haircuts.

A part of the bath car was converted into a *banja,* or hot-air bath, which has been used by Russians from time immemorial. High on the shelves, in a temperature of 130° F., the men baked as long as they were able to tolerate the terrific heat. In the next car, they were given fresh linen and clothes and sent to the examination room which was located in the car adjoining that. Here they underwent a thorough examination. I was looking for a petechial rash, characteristic of typhus, which appears as a rule from seven to ten days after contagion. As the examination proceeded, I came across five suspicious cases, and these were promptly admitted to the hospital.

When I was approaching the end of the inspection, a soldier whom I was checking arrested my attention. There was nothing tangibly peculiar in this large, powerfully built northerner except a slight animosity in his attitude toward me. He was neither rude nor impolite, but was distinctly arrogant. I looked at him. His face was an ordinary one, with narrow eyes and low forehead. But the expression was sullen and stonelike.

His pulse was fast, temperature normal. I looked again at his face and had the strange feeling that I had seen him before. I tried to remember. Suddenly I realized that he was the man who had bayoneted Linde to death. I clearly recalled him now; the face was engraved in my memory. Yes, I was in the presence of a killer. For a moment I did not move. He stood before me, also unmoving. Then, with an effort, trying hard to control my voice, I said: "You may go. . . . Next." I rapidly completed the examination of the rest of the 7th-company soldiers.

I was confronted with a difficult situation, calling for extreme tact. That this soldier, whose name was Ivan Buschakov, was the killer, I felt no doubt. And it came to my mind that Dr. B. had warned me, "The 7th company is thoroughly infested with lice but also with Bolsheviks." And he added, "Be careful, old man, lice and Bolsheviks are both dangerous, so I have heard." Investigation had revealed that it was the men of this company who were Linde's attackers.

I called my orderly, Ilya. He was one of the most fearless men in our army. He had served for three years in a shock brigade, was decorated several times for bravery, and after being gravely wounded was assigned to my hospital. I explained the situation to him. "I'll take care of this scoundrel. Don't worry, sir."

And he did. He checked his revolver, called Buschakov, and told him that we suspected him of being infected with typhus. He asked him to enter the bath car, which was by now empty and dry. He locked him in and, finding a machine gun, set it up before the door of the bath car. Then he reported to me. "Sir, it's up to you," he said. "Shall we kill him?"

"No, no, of course not. I will call regimental headquarters." But before I was able to make the connection with Colonel G., two unexpected visitors entered my car.

One was my friend Igor Vassiliev, who for the last two years had been the commander of an armored company attached to our army. The other was Boris Moisseinko, whom I knew only slightly. He was Kerensky's personal political administrator at the headquarters of the XIII Army. An affable and soft-spoken man, he was a typical representative of the Russian intelligentsia of Chekhov's period.

"So Linde was murdered," Vassiliev gloomily remarked the moment he saw me. "We came to investigate this case."

"I understand that the murderer was never caught," said Moisseinko.

"Abominable mismanagement on the part of the regimental commander," injected Vassiliev.

I hesitated a moment, then told them about Buschakov.

Vassiliev jumped from the chair and roared: *"He is here? Hand him over to me!"*

Broad-shouldered, of medium height, with dark hair, Vassiliev was a man of enormous physical strength. As a senior in high school, he had astonished us with his incredible feats. One of his routine demonstrations was to lift with one hand a husky youngster weighing 170 pounds and throw him high in the air. But he never, as long as I knew him, misused his strength. Mild and good-natured, he was loved by all his friends and colleagues, always ready to help them in their troubles. But now Vassiliev was in a state of uncontrollable rage.

"*Where is he?*" he shouted.

"In the bath car. Locked in," I answered.

"Let's go."

"Stop, Vassiliev," interrupted Moisseinko. "We must keep within the law."

"To hell with the law, you soft-hearted politician. . . . I want to meet him. . . . I'll . . ."

There was no restraining him. He ran from my car. We followed him. He ordered Ilya to open the door and mounted the steps leading to the bath car. Moisseinko, Ilya, and I, with four officers of the 7th company, followed.

The bath car was fully lighted. Buschakov was sitting on a bench in the corner of the car, smoking a cigarette. When he saw us, he slowly, perhaps too slowly, rose. He said nothing. The expression on his face was stony.

Vassiliev approached him and watched him for a long time, as a tamer watches a wild animal which he intends to subjugate to his will. The silence was unbearable.

"Buschakov," said Vassiliev at last. "Buschakov, why did you kill Linde?" He spoke very slowly, and there was menace in his deliberate speech. There was no answer. Buschakov maintained silence, in which, however, there was arrogance, a challenge to us all.

"I interpret your silence as an affirmation. I know you are afraid. You Bolsheviks are yellow when you are cornered.

You are brave only when you murder an unarmed man."

"I am not afraid. . . ."

"Oh, you're not, you yellow dog!" Vassiliev's rage was rising fast. He slapped the other's face. But, instead of retreating, Buschakov hit my friend a strong blow on the jaw.

"That's better," roared Vassiliev, "much better. . . . Now we can fight. . . . All of you," he shouted, turning to us, "go away. Give us room." We obeyed.

The fight began. I will never forget it as long as I live. It was utterly savage and brutal; all rules were completely disregarded. It was a fight for life. Both were men of great physical strength. Both were inspired by hate and anger. Both fought as if demons possessed their souls and bodies. Blow after blow fell on my friend's head, but each hard hit seemed to make him only stronger, more violent, more savage in his merciless attacks on his enemy.

"You yellow dog!" he roared. "Your dirty killer!" Vassiliev knocked the other down on the floor. "Get up!" he cried, "get up and fight like a man!" But the moment Buschakov arose, Vassiliev knocked him down with such force that he remained unconscious on the floor. Blood flowed from his nose and mouth, and he was breathing heavily. We hoped the fight was over. But it was not.

Vassiliev lifted the man in the air and threw him with all his might into the corner of the car. And again, and again, for how many times I cannot remember, he repeated the act. The floor was slippery with blood. "Vassiliev, stop!" cried Moisseinko. "You've killed him. . . ."

"Not yet, not yet . . . go away, you milksop!" Then he slapped the face of the prone man, again and again. Hard and brutally. And suddenly he stopped.

"He'll survive . . . but he'll never forget this beating. You may send him to the hospital now, and then court-martial him." Washing the blood from his face and body, he added calmly, "That's how democracy should deal with the Bolsheviks. You numbskulls don't understand that they respect nothing but brute force. Let's go, Moisseinko, we don't have to go to the front. This lesson will teach every Bolshevik in the 111th division how to behave." And, smiling, he shook my hand. "I apologize for the mess I am leaving your beautiful *banja* in," he said, and he departed with Moisseinko.

"There's a man!" pronounced Ilya. "He certainly can fight. . . ." He told the male nurses to take Buschakov, or what was left of him, to the hospital. Vassiliev was right. While Buschakov recovered from his injuries, he talked a good deal about the fight. "He was a devil," he said. "Better to die than to fight again with that demon."

Brought before the court, Buschakov admitted he was a member of the Communist party and that he had been ordered to kill Colonel G. But when Linde unexpectedly appeared before the regiment, the Communist nucleus decided to kill him instead. Buschakov was condemned to death and was executed before a firing squad in the old fortress at Lutzk. I was not present at his execution, but Dr. B. told me that he died without a word, and with the same frozen expression on his face which he bore when I had examined him.

It was three long years before I had news again of Igor Vassiliev. I was at the front, this time in the north. I was in a Red Cross railroad hospital unit on the Archangel-Vologda front. The fighting line was very narrow, not more than five hundred feet wide. On both sides of the railroad were impassable swamps and heavy forest. In winter, everything was covered with deep snow. The Red army trenches were about a thousand feet from our hospital, and on a sunny day the Communists and their movements were clearly visible. In the winter, small patrols, ours or those of the Red soldiers, occasionally scouted the vicinity of the front line, penetrating a mile or two into the forest.

On Christmas Eve, the coldest I have ever experienced, Vassiliev suddenly arrived. He was the same exuberant and flamboyant person, gay and amusing, full of witty jokes and exciting stories. We spent Christmas Eve together. He recounted his life of adventure and fighting in the civil war with General Denikin's forces and other southern armies. He was wounded twice, but he said, "I survived, for better or worse." He had come from Paris to Archangel for a short visit, bringing ammunition for the northern army. Igor still was unmarried and unattached. "I love life too much to be married. . . . Life is movement, never-ending movement, a bubbling ocean of emotions. And marriage is a motionless pond overgrown with molds." We drank champagne and vodka, and he sang gypsy songs in a pleasing baritone. We stayed till morning, lost in reminiscences of student life and of our hopes and dreams, which were shattered so abruptly by the October *coup d'état.*

The next day he was restless. "Let's go scouting in the forest," he said. I protested. I told him that it was full of wolves and bears and that we might meet the Red army patrol. "Nonsense," he insisted, "that's what I'm looking for . . . a skirmish with the Reds." And so we went, armed with rifles and guns, and small axes to cut the branches. The snow was dry and hard and we skied fast, faster than I expected. In no time we were deep in the forest. We were a mile or so from the railroad when we heard voices and saw a small hut, apparently an outpost of the Red army. It was heaped with snow. We saw it too late. Two soldiers ran in our direction with rifles in their hands. I stood stupefied, unable to decide what action we should take. When the Reds had come close to us, Igor fired twice. Without uttering a word, both soldiers staggered and fell to earth with a thud. Small streams of blood trickled down their faces and congealed in the icy morning air.

"Excellent hits," laughed Igor. "Both of them through the right eyes."

"Why did you kill them?" I angrily demanded.

"You're crazy," replied Igor rudely. "You're a softy. There was no choice. They would have captured or killed us. This is a civil war. The cruelest kind of war. Let's run. Their comrades will soon be after us. We have a chance of reaching our outpost before they can kill us."

But in the turmoil of the skirmish we had lost our direction.

We heard voices, angry and excited. "They're after us," Igor said, and he laughed. "This is fun." He was feeling very gay, while I was most unhappy about the whole adventure, which was looking very dark. "Follow me," he ordered. He hastily dug a trench among the venerable pines and covered it with branches. The voices were near. There were five Red soldiers: "Look," said a voice, "tracks . . . Let's follow them." The soldiers were no more than fifty feet from us.

"Hey, you, down there!" cried Igor. "Don't stand still there, you'll catch cold. Come up here where we are." They moved about excitedly, startled by this unexpected call.

"Who are you? What are you doing here?"

"Your friends, hurry up. We're frozen."

The Reds still hesitated. Then, "Come on, comrades," said one, "they're frozen. . . ."

Igor looked over the edge cautiously, placed his rifle on a large branch, and pulled the trigger. The first soldier stopped and fell with a muffled groan. Four shots followed in quick succession. Three agonized cries echoed the shots. One soldier escaped unhurt. Igor was indignant. "I missed him. . . .

Inexcusable," he said, as we jumped out of the trench and ran to the fallen Reds.

Three lay dead, and one was moaning in pain. We leaned over him. He had a young, weak, beardless face.

"Comrades, brothers, spare me . . . don't kill me," he moaned.

Igor looked at me. Did I seem to him compassionate? Certainly. Kindly disposed? Yes. He took out his gun and, as though irritated by my unspoken protest, fired at the head of the wounded boy.

We had lost our way. For three long hours we traveled through the forest and still we had not reached the railroad. The short polar day was at an end. It was bitterly cold. Our hands, feet, and faces no longer ached. There was no habitation in sight, no abandoned hut where we might take shelter from the penetrating northwest wind.

We decided to stop and make a fire. The moon was almost insupportably bright over the forest. The pines were covered with a heavy, moist mantle of snow, bluish in the moonlight. We gathered dry branches and built a fire, hopelessly small, which was unable to warm us.

"My left hand is frozen," announced Igor. It was, indeed, and was already swollen. I was distressed, but Igor only smiled. "You take life too seriously, my friend. Let's dig a lair in this blessed snow." We did. Exhausted and half-frozen, we soon were asleep.

On the third day of our flight, we came to the shores of the White Sea. We were fifteen miles from my hospital and four or five miles from the nearest village, Laevka. Instead of going east, we had stumbled northeast.

The sea, very narrow at this point, was covered with huge masses of ice from the polar regions, pushed slowly south by a northeast wind. In their haste, the monster icebergs collided noisily and angrily, as if in a mad fight for existence. "They act like men," Igor murmured.

We sought shelter behind a huge, snow-covered rock and sat down to smoke. We were safe, or were we? Igor's frozen hand was causing him intolerable pain and had become bluish-black. "It's gangrene," he remarked.

"I'm afraid it is," I answered unhappily. Only a miracle could save his life. As if reading my thoughts, he asked, "Would immediate amputation save me?" I nodded.

Igor looked at me with his customary sardonic smile and took off his fur cap. He drew a clean cloth from his bag and cut the string of his knapsack with a knife. Then, baring his swollen arm, he asked me to bind it tightly above the elbow with the cord. Plunging his arm into the snow, he withdrew it rapidly and, with a movement quick as lightning, chopped off his coal-black hand with one stroke of the axe.

The thick blood flowed freely in large streams and stained the snow a crimson red as it fell.

"Please tighten the tourniquet, and dress the wound for me." Igor's voice betrayed neither pain nor weakness. I was feeling faint, near to collapse, but I did as he requested. We were on the move again, and by the end of the day we reached the village of Laevka. Vassiliev was immediately transported to Archangel.

I never saw him again. But, years later, I heard that he was with the Chinese Nationalist army, assigned to their engineering corps, constructing railroads somewhere near Burma. He was still unmarried and unattached, according to the nurse who had seen him there.

Chapter 3

DOCTOR BETVUGIN

ALL was quiet on the front. Days went by, monotonous, regular, unvarying. Autumn was there, in brilliant yellow, with occasional musty rains and multitudes of singing frogs. Free from daily routine work, I plunged into the scientific research I had begun before I was drafted into the army. The potential immortality of living cells! The topic had attracted my attention while I was still a student at the university. I read with avid interest about the work of American scientists and tried to duplicate it. Was it possible to keep tissue alive after removing it from a living organism, from a frog, a mouse, or even a man, provided favorable conditions were created for it? And, if so, how long would these cells continue to live outside the body? For days, or months, or forever? When I read the report by Ross Harrison of Yale on his pioneer work in cultivating cells outside the organism, I was excited. Here was a method which might give us the answer to the eternal problem of death and life. If only we could succeed in taking tissues from an old man and keeping them alive for years after his death! This would revolutionize all our concepts of biological phenomena. It would prove that our body consists of immortal cells and that death is the attribute of a defective organization in higher animals and men.

Immediately after graduation I joined the staff of the National Institute of Science. The head of this privately supported organization was Dr. Sergei Metalnikoff, an internationally known biologist, who, after the Communist counterrevolution, moved to Paris and was elected a member of the Pasteur Institute. He was an unusual man. Kind and sensitive, he was completely engrossed in scientific research. He was a man of vision and encyclopedic knowledge and had the tenacity and persistence without which no goal in scientific research can be achieved.

An intimate friend of Dr. Alexis Carrel, he enthusiastically endorsed my plans for the investigation of so-called cultures *in vitro,* or cultivation of living cells in test tubes, outside the organism.

I was appointed head of this new department. It was a poorly paid job. I hardly made ends meet, but the work was exciting.

"Why should we start with frogs or chicks?" asked Dr. Metalnikoff when the laboratory was ready for operation. "Let's take a few forward steps. Let's work with human tissue."

In the Oboukhov Hospital, with which I was associated, an elderly patient was dying from cancer. I asked his permission to take a small piece of tissue from his abdomen. He agreed willingly. Removing the tissue under perfectly sterile conditions and placing it in a saline solution, I brought this priceless specimen to my laboratory. My assistant, a young girl named Anna, gave her blood. I cut the specimen into many small pieces and placed each of them on a specially made hollow glass slide, adding blood plasma. Covering them with small glasses to preserve sterile conditions, I put them in a thermostat at 97 degrees Fahrenheit. Would the tissue grow? Would it stay alive?

I waited two days, impatiently, and seemed headed for a great disappointment. There was no growth, no sign of tissue movement. I waited another two days. This time, under the microscope, I noticed small filaments of cells pushing out from all sides of the cultivated tissue. I ran to Dr. Metalnikoff and cried, "They're growing!"

And they were. This tissue, taken from a dying man, remained alive and grew steadily after this unforgettable day. It continued to thrive for many years after I left Russia and came to America. My last news about this piece of human flesh came in 1942, when my associate, Dr. Strelnikoff, who replaced me as the head of the laboratory after my departure, wrote: "Lopuchin's flesh is still alive." Lopuchin was the name of the man who had donated his flesh for this experiment.

We continued our investigation on a large scale. We cultivated human flesh of various origins: nervous, muscular, epithelial, with the same results. They grew, some fast, some slowly, but always steadily and unabated. In no time, our laboratory became known as the outstanding center for the new work on preserving life. Years later, Dr. Metalnikoff received a Pasteur Prize for his book *Immortality*, which was based on this work. We proved to our own satisfaction that potential immortality is an attribute of all living cells—yet this discovery did not alter the bitter truth that the human organism, consisting of immortal cells, is in itself mortal.

And now, in my little laboratory at the southwestern front, I was trying to renew my old investigations, taking advantage of the lull in battle.

One September morning, when I was checking the culture of freshly prepared human flesh, I was rudely interrupted by a violent knock on the door. I hadn't time even to say, "Come in," when Dr. George Betvugin, the chief surgeon, entered. He was very brief. "I shot her," he said calmly. "Please go and see if she is alive, I don't want to look at her . . . living or dead." And he left abruptly.

Six months before, when we were informed that Betvugin was assigned to the hospital as chief surgeon, I had been quite puzzled by his transfer. His reputation as a brilliant surgeon was firmly established. His association with the Moscow Medical School, where he performed the most daring operations, about which I read in medical journals, entitled him to an assignment to any large military hospital. Instead, we learned that he was coming to our obscure front-line mobile unit. It was strange. It was inconceivable. With his arrival, our bewilderment only rose.

We were all in the dining room, chatting and drinking tea after luncheon, when a handsome stranger entered. He was striking in appearance, tall and slender, with a blue-black Van Dyke beard and short mustache, graying dark hair, and light blue eyes. Meticulously dressed in an elegant uniform, with expensive breeches and shining spurs, he looked like one of His Majesty's Hussars. He remained silent for a minute or two as if searching for someone in the room.

"Oh, no!" a woman's voice exclaimed. Turning to the end of the table, I saw the head nurse covering her face with her hands.

"What's this all about?" I asked. Then I turned to the stranger. "Did you want to see someone?" I asked rather rudely.

He smiled and said, "I beg your pardon for this intrusion . . . but I am assigned to this hospital."

"To this hospital?" I repeated.

"Yes, as chief surgeon. I am Betvugin."

The moment he pronounced his name, a chair went down with a bang and the head nurse rushed from the room. Dr. Betvugin seemed to ignore her conduct. "I apologize for disturbing your meal," he continued, still standing.

I introduced him to our personnel, and he courteously made a turn around the table, shaking hands with everyone. He was very cordial, and asked questions about our work. He presented a strong contrast with us, in our shabby khakis and worn shoes.

"He looks like a prince," my nurse whispered to me. And he did look like a prince from a fairy tale.

On the evening of Betvugin's arrival, when I was ready to go to bed, Ilya announced that the head nurse would like to see me. "She is very disturbed, she is crying."

Helen von T . . . had only recently been assigned to the hospital, but she had already gained the admiration and liking of our entire medical staff. The surgeons were very pleased with her ability as a surgical nurse. Experienced, and a hard worker, she was ready to help out any nurse in her duties. The patients had only the warmest praise for her kind and friendly attitude toward them. "She is an angel," they would say. In fact, she did look like an angel, with her beautifully shaped, fine face and light blond hair. Tactful and reserved, she took no part in any gossip, this common affliction of hospitals. All the young medicos were in love with her and tried in vain to make dates with her. She was an ardent reader, and more than once she asked me for medical books. Apparently she belonged to a well-to-do family, but neither I nor anyone else knew much about her past. "She is our enigma," the young surgeon Polevitzky would say, again and again. "Let her remain so." And here she was, sitting in my room and crying bitterly.

"I must leave the hospital at once," she murmured miserably.

"Why?" I asked her.

She made no answer.

"Because of Dr. Betvugin?" I persisted.

She nodded.

"Do you know him?"

"Yes, he is my husband. No," she corrected. "We are separated."

"How long have you been married?"

"For three years."

"He seems to be a very charming man."

"Oh, yes. He is, but . . ." And, stumbling at first, but becoming gradually more animated, she told me the strange story of her relations with Betvugin. Her father had been a criminal lawyer of some distinction, a man of high cultural standing, but a very domineering personality. "He was a despot, and he ruled our family with an iron hand," she said. He adored her, his only daughter, but he was overexacting in his demands. He reduced his wife to a state of horrified subjection. "She never dared to express her own opinions or wishes. She was very unhappy, my poor mother, and I loved her so much. She trembled in my father's presence and was afraid to make a move or say a word. When I was ten, she killed herself by taking poison. She died in my arms."

Although Helen was too young to understand the intricacies of her parents' relationship, she learned later, from her mother's diary, which she found hidden in an old trunk, that at the bottom of her father's morbid attitude was the eternal story of jealousy. It appeared that her mother had been in love with a young doctor, a poor country practitioner, but her parents forced her to marry a well-to-do lawyer, much older than herself.

"Did her father change after his wife's suicide?" I asked.

Helen was crying now. "Only for the worse," she said. All the concealed passion of an aging man, she told me, was now directed toward her. To him, she was the personification of his dead wife, whom he hated and loved so insanely. She was not permitted to meet any young people, or to go to any parties or even to school. He engaged private tutors and kept her with him all the time that he was free from his profession. "I knew he loved me . . . but I hated this man who killed my mother."

When she was seventeen, her father became ill with an intestinal infection that required an immediate operation. Dr. Betvugin, already a famous surgeon, was called in. Her father died soon after the operation. "And I, well, I had fallen in love with the doctor." On his advice, she enrolled in the nursing school at the Moscow Hospital. After two years of courting, Betvugin married her.

"Had he been married before?" I asked.

"Yes . . ." there was hesitation in her voice. "Yes, he was. His wife died a few months before our marriage. I don't know the cause of her death." During their six-months' engagement, Betvugin was very considerate of her. "He was enchanting, the most charming man, gay and easy-going. He tried to anticipate my wishes and please me in every possible way. He gave me every freedom. . . . And it was this that I most appreciated in him. He seemed so different from my father. And my life during these six months was very happy.

I was happy for the first time in my life. I breathed like a human being again."

But it ended overnight, after their marriage was consummated. Betvugin's true nature was evidenced now. Like her father, he manifested extreme possessiveness, and his jealousy was like madness. She was deprived of all freedom. She became a slave of his possessive love, she was his property. She was shattered by the unexpected change in her husband.

"It's not easy," she told me, "to describe my feelings. Of course, I was in love with him. . . . But something was broken in me, in my feelings toward him. I was in revolt, complete revolt. At night, lying by his side, I was distressed by a painful sensation that my father was alive again and was in bed beside me. My hatred for my father had all come back, but now it was directed toward the man I had loved and admired so tenderly only a few weeks before. Perhaps it was my fault. Perhaps in my own mind I exaggerated his possessive attitude. Perhaps I had a complex about my freedom. . . . But this feeling was stronger than myself."

She became morose and silent, she said, and often was irritable with him. She avoided his embraces. She refused to go out with him. She stayed away from him. Their relationship disintegrated. Unable or unwilling to understand her reactions, he accused her of infidelity. He pursued her, constantly demanding emotional responses. They quarreled often. He was sharp, rude, and threatening; she, silently resentful, embittered, and withdrawn. Once, in a mad rage, he slapped her face. The next day she left him, taking a few belongings. "I went to Petrograd and accepted the assignment to this hospital. Here I was happy again. I found peace of mind. . . . But now, here he is again. . . ."

"But do you still love him?"

"I don't know. In some strange way I missed him when he was not here. But now that he's here, I'm in such a state of confusion and unhappiness that I simply cannot live any more. I admit, I often admit to myself, that it's all my fault. . . . But what can I do?"

I was in no position to offer any solution. Here was another case of a poorly adjusted person paying with married unhappiness for mental wounds inflicted in childhood.

"I will do what I can," I told her. "It might take a few days before we can get permission from headquarters for your transfer. In the meantime, stay in your room if you wish. Have your meals there. I will place you on the sick list." Then, a little ashamed of the severity of my tone, I added, "We all like you very much. . . . We will be very sorry to have you leave us. Good night, Mrs. Betvugin."

I had no opportunity to talk with Betvugin the next day as I had intended. Several wounded servicemen were brought to the hospital and he spent the whole day in the operating room. Helen was absent, apparently in her room.

Betvugin thrilled us with his extraordinary skill. We all were ready to concede his ingenuity as a surgeon. The brilliance of his technique in gastrectomy was particularly astonishing. When he operated on servicemen with abdominal wounds, we could hardly restrain ourselves from gasping. He was fast, efficient, precise. In one very grave and seemingly hopeless case of abdominal shell wound, he surpassed himself by performing a complicated gastrectomy and colorectostomy. The man, half dead, was saved.

But no less surprising was Betvugin's peculiar insistence that every patient admitted to the hospital should have his appendix removed. It was more than a conviction with him. It was an obsession. We accepted his fancy with amused tolerance at first. But after he had performed ten or more appendectomies for no reason whatsoever, I was obliged to question him on his peculiar attitude.

"Why do you remove the appendix when there is no sign of inflammation?" I asked him.

"The appendix, dear friend, is an atavistic attribute," he replied. "Its presence affects man's mentality. It incites his bestial instincts. The appendix should be removed from anyone, young or old, healthy or ailing. In my department in Moscow," he proudly remarked, "not a single patient escaped appendectomy. I preserved all removed appendixes in formalin for posterity. Of course," he continued, "I really prefer to perform a clean-cut appendicostomy, using a McBurney incision. But, of course, it is impossible to operate on everyone in this manner."

I pointed out to him that in the army hospitals only proved cases of appendicitis were, as a rule, operated on. He dismissed my statement lightly and continued with his routine appendectomies. Soon this became a source of friction between him and the other physicians. Again and again he would return at luncheon or afternoon tea to his beloved topic. He tried to persuade every nurse and orderly to consent to the removal of his appendix.

"Is your appendix removed, Doctor Betvugin?" Schelling once asked him.

"Why, no, of course not," he said smiling. "Why should it be? My appendix does not affect my mentality. My mind is beyond any physical influences. It is above them. Of course not . . ."

A few years later, in 1926, when I was in Prague, I read a speech delivered by Betvugin at a medical meeting in Moscow. By that time he had become an important personage in the Soviet Health Commissariat. "The appendix," he announced, "is a bourgeois atavistic attribute. There is no room for it in the Proletarian Republic. We must free ourselves from this ignominious relic of the capitalistic regime. . . ."

Now and then, news would reach me that Betvugin was in great favor with the luminaries of the Soviet regime. Much publicity was given to his operations on this or that Communist leader or leader's wife. A Moscow physician whom I met at a scientific meeting in Budapest told me that Betvugin was the top man in Soviet medicine. He was living in unusual luxury, even for a Communist favorite. "He has two cars, and horses," complained the doctor, "and a large house occupied by himself and his new wife, a former ballerina of pre-Soviet fame. I visited him one day. A butler, a real butler, opened the door for me. . . . Well, that is the paradox of life today in the country of the proletariat." But apparently Betvugin was careless toward his connections in Communistic circles, for he soon disappeared. Nobody knew what had become of him. There were rumors that he was "liquidated" or had been sent to Siberia.

As the days went on, Betvugin succeeded in appeasing his wife. Helen no longer stayed in her room. She carried on her duties as before, and spent a good deal of her time in the operating room assisting her husband. At meals she sat next to him, silent and subdued, yet smiling at his jokes and small talk. On several occasions, when I was taking my usual evening stroll along the banks of the Malta, I saw them out riding, intimately, side by side.

"He's conquered her again, the brute," bitterly remarked Polevitzky, our young medico. "It won't last long. . . ."

One evening, when I was engrossed in examining slides of growing tissues, Betvugin entered my room.

Courteously, he asked my permission to talk with me. "I'm

a little drunk," he apologized, "but only a little. I have an un-controllable impulse to talk with you. I know you don't like me. . . . Well, frankly, I don't like the kind of people you are. But I like you personally. Are you surprised?" Indeed I was.

"There are two kinds of people in this vast world of man-kind," he began, smoking a cigarette. "One kind, and to this you and your friends belong, are strangers to any strong, uninhibited emotion. They know nothing about overwhelm-ing passion. They transfer their weak, diluted emotions to their brain and transform them into vague, confused ideas. They monkey with ideas, with the mental sensualism of a eunuch. They multiply them, they complicate them. They find their happiness, if this is happiness, in a multitude of impotent, barren ideas. Strong, determined action is foreign to them. One might call them intellectual sensualists. Even in science, which, of course, is by itself a fertile field for ideas, they achieve nothing. They are unable to accomplish any-thing beyond publishing endless articles and papers which are a demonstration of their emotional impotence.

"And there are men of another kind. Fortunately or un-fortunately, they are in the minority. At least in our beloved country. They are men of action, of a simple, clear idea. They like two and two being four and not, as Turgenev described it, five. They are capable of immense passion, for they trans-fer their simple idea into emotion. It is men of this type who create empires, who incite revolutions, who move the world.

"I know what you want to say," he interrupted, before I could utter a word. "I know you're going to call my atten-tion to our revolutionaries who killed the Czar, who made the Revolution. . . . But, old man, this was nothing but a ges-ture, the apotheosis of their emotional impotence, self-glorification through a superb sacrifice of their lives. But who cares about the sacrifice, or their lives?

"I am not a politician," he said. "I don't care about politics, or about revolution or monarchy, in fact. But I admire a man who is inspired by a single idea, who knows what passion is, a passion which can crush and annihilate everything that stands in the way of reaching his goal.

"I am not a psychologist, certainly not, but I do feel that there is something in man, in his constitution, which makes him either a sensual intellectual or a passionate man of action. But—please don't interrupt me—there is still too much alcohol in my blood . . . I might forget what I want to say . . . but . . . yes, I did not come to see you to discuss the human race. I intended to tell you a story about my friend. An amusing story. I hope you disapprove it . . . I don't need your approval, old man.

"I had a friend," Betvugin went on, "a brilliant surgeon. Yes, he was a genius in his field. Nobody surpassed him in the art of surgery. He was a man of unusual determination. As a boy, he had decided to be a surgeon, and nothing but surgery interested him. As I say, he was a man of a single idea. One morning he was called to visit a patient, an old man with acute appendicitis. At the patient's home, a young girl met him. Was she beautiful? No matter. But when my friend met her in the hall of this gloomy house, he knew at once that she was his woman, that as long as he lived she would, she must, belong to him alone. A passion of incredible force rose in him. It was more than a passion. More than love. It was an obsession. While he was examining the old man, my friend clearly realized that this girl would never belong to him as long as her father was alive. She was the property of the old man. She showed this in a multitude of little words and actions significant to an observing man such as my friend was.

"Well, what would you do if you were in my friend's place? Nothing, of course. You might cry and torture yourself by the hopelessness of the situation. But not my friend. He was a man of action, inflamed by passion. He ordered the old man transferred to the hospital. He prepared him for an immediate operation. He opened his abdomen. Yes . . . there was nothing seriously wrong with the old mule except an infected appendix, slightly deformed. For a brief, yes, very brief second my friend hesitated. Or did he? His hand moved involuntarily and the scalpel made a hole in the infected appendix.

"Now here is a perplexing observation," Betvugin continued. "My friend did not decide to cut into the appendix. He did not condemn his patient to death. His ethics would not have permitted him such professional abuse. His hand moved as if it were directed by an uncontrollable force. His scalpel was pushed by a power belonging to his subconscious mind. This was an accident, my friend tried to convince himself. But *was* it an accident? You, my learned friend, might try to solve this psychological puzzle . . . if you wish." And he laughed.

"But this was only part of his problem. The girl was free after her father's death. But my friend was married to a woman who meant nothing to him. Only his wife stood between him and his goal. She was an ailing woman. She complained of uterine bleeding and uteralgia. He brought her to the hospital and examined her in the presence of a nurse. He could clearly see a small ulcerous growth on the cervix of her uterus. There was no question in his mind but that this was a carcinoma. She could be saved by an immediate hysterectomy. My friend opened his mouth to say, 'Carcinoma of the cervix. Hysterectomy.' Instead, he dictated to the nurse, 'Benign fibroma.' And, in saying these words, he realized that someone not himself was speaking. Someone else was making a false diagnosis which would cause his wife's gradual death from cancer. What force made him a liar? What power directed him to betray his professional honor? Or was this also an accident, a *lapsus linguae*? That is up to you to decide, old man. . . . Well, this was the story about my friend that I wanted to amuse you with. . . ."

Betvugin got up, lighting another cigarette.

"Why did you tell me this disgusting story?" I asked angrily.

"Why? No reason at all . . . old man." As he was going out of my room he turned and said, "Or perhaps I wanted to impress upon you that you should not interfere with my relations with Helen. It's not safe. . . ." And he was gone.

I was so revolted by Betvugin's conduct that I immediately made a record of his story, trying to remember his exact words. I decided to send this report to headquarters the following day.

It was early the next morning when Betvugin announced to me so rudely and dramatically that he had killed his wife.

Actually, he had not killed her. I found her in her room, semiconscious and bleeding profusely. Her wound was serious but not fatal. The bullet had gone through her left shoulder, missing the heart by a few inches. No bones were injured, and after proper treatment she was given a sedative.

While on the operating table, she remained silent and depressed. She said but a few words to me, and did not mention her husband or the accident itself. Two hours later, I visited her again and found her stronger and in a better mood.

"It all started," she told me, "when he asked me to leave

the hospital and return to Moscow with him. I refused. He was in a rage, the like of which I had never seen." He told her boldly that she belonged to him, that no power in the world could take her from him. He was ready, he said, to commit any crime to keep her with him. He was menacingly aggressive, and still she refused to submit to his wishes. And then, suddenly, he took an automatic out of his pocket and fired twice. "I was prepared to die. . . . I wanted to die. It was all so hopeless . . ." It was a miracle that she lived.

I tried to find Betvugin but was informed that soon after the shooting he had left Rojitsche with all his belongings. As soon as Helen's health improved, she was transferred to a Rovno hospital.

The night before her departure, our medical personnel gave her a party. It was a warm, friendly affair, with many emotional outbursts on the part of our young physicians. "You're an angel!" cried Polevitzky in exaltation. "Pure and divine and beautiful. . . . But the devil possesses your soul —the devil, your husband." He kissed her hands and begged her to be his wife. There was much drinking and dreaming and endless toasts to Russian women and their fates and their devotion to unworthy men. Helen sobbed and made a confession in very Russian fashion: "I like you all. . . . I was very happy here." After her departure, life in the hospital returned to its day-to-day calm, to work and bridge and political discussions.

One morning in Nice, ten years later, as I was making the rounds of the patients at Saint-Roch Hospital, I was stopped by Dr. Louis Prat, the chief surgeon.

"Your compatriot, a Russian surgeon," Prat said, "I cannot remember these Russian names, is going to give a demonstration of his appendicostomy technique. It is said he does it in three minues. *Viens, mon vieux.*"

I went. The operating room was full of young surgeons and interns.

"He brought his nurse with him," announced my friend Cartotto to me. *"Et comme elle est belle, parbleu!* No wonder he performs miracles of surgery."

In silence we waited for the unknown surgeon. Like a stage performance, I thought. And it was indeed dramatic when Betvugin appeared, followed by Helen. Both were striking in white blouses; he, almost gray, and she, so radiantly young, enchanting, and superbly beautiful and elegant.

Dr. Prat introduced me to them. Betvugin hardly expected to meet me there. But if he was displeased, he did not show his feelings. Amiably he shook my hand and remarked to Prat in excellent French: "We are all friends."

He had not changed much. Except for more gray in his dark hair, he was the same. Arrogant and handsome, self-possessed and authoritative, he played his role of top man in surgery to perfection.

The patient was ready for the operation when Betvugin arrived. He slowly washed his hands, and while putting on the gloves he gave a brief lecture on the technique he was using. Again he resorted to his old theory, which apparently pleased his audience, that everyone must have his appendix removed promptly. Psychosomatic medicine was not yet known, but there was nothing wrong or complicated about the postulate that the appendix, whether healthy or inflamed, might affect the mind. In fact, this postulate appealed to the hearts of the young surgeons listening to Betvugin's talk; they were always on the lookout for new victims of their imperfect skill. What a great new field of surgical activity this elegant Russian promoted, they thought. There are more than a hundred thousand appendixes to be removed in Nice alone. What unlimited potentialities!

"Dear colleagues," concluded Betvugin, "the appendicostomy, if properly performed, requires about twenty minutes. But I have reached such a superbness of technique that I am able to complete it in three minutes. . . . Please check the time. . . . One, two, three . . . I begin." No doubt his technique was superb. His hands moved so fast, the incisions were so precise that the operating knife seemed a part of his hand.

He finished triumphantly in two minutes and fifty-five seconds. "It is a record," he announced proudly. "Thank you very much, gentlemen, for giving me the opportunity to make this demonstration." And he promptly left the room, followed by Helen, while his audience remained in perplexed prostration.

"What a man!" Cartotto said, shaking his head sadly. "What a surgeon!"

Only Dr. Prat, one of the leading surgeons of France, failed to be impressed by Betvugin's performance. "Your compatriot should go on the stage," he sarcastically remarked. "Yet there *is* something inhuman about him." I said nothing.

The same evening, as I was strolling along Les Promenades des Anglais, I saw Helen sitting at a table in the Hotel Negresco. She was alone. She waved, inviting me to join her.

"Where is he?" I inquired.

"I don't know." She was irritable, almost angry, and slowly, as if with effort, she said, "I hate every minute I am with him. . . ."

"But you are still with him."

"I am. . . . I've tried lots of times to escape him. He always follows me. . . . I was very happy when he went to Moscow and married another woman. I felt free again. I felt myself. I moved to Paris and worked there at the hospital; in fact, I enrolled in the medical school. And then, six months ago, he appeared in Paris, from nowhere. . . . I prayed for his death at the hands of his friends the Communists, whom he adored so much. And yet he is here. . . ."

"How did he escape from Russia?"

"I don't know. I don't know anything about him, or about his present or past associations. But they don't concern me. . . . What's important to me is that I'm hopelessly involved with him. . . . Hopelessly."

"But he loves you."

"Yes, yes," she said angrily, "and that's the whole trouble. If he'd only stop loving me. I hate him, with my whole body and soul. I want him to be dead, once and forever."

"You shouldn't say such things . . . yet, I understand your feelings."

"Yes, it's terrible, I know, but it's true. I cannot help it, I cannot. One day I'll hit the bottom of despair and kill myself. I hate him as if hate were the most precious thing in my life. I increase my hate by adding more and more accusations against him. When he hits me, I enjoy it, because it helps my hate. And yet, part of my soul belongs to him. It's madness. I know he's a scoundrel, and cruel and eaten with pride as only the Lord creates such creatures. I'm his slave . . ." and she broke down.

"Here he comes," I whispered to her.

Gay, debonair, Betvugin came to the table.

"Well, it's nice to meet you, my friend, after so many years. How have you been? Still looking in the microscope and trying to solve the eternal problems of life and death?" He sat down nonchalantly. "What do you drink? Vermouth? The drink of the petit bourgeois. . . . I prefer champagne. In

Moscow it became my daily beverage. Yes, they gave me the best champagne available in Russia. . . ."

"And in Siberia," I interrupted, "did they give you champagne also?"

He smiled, and his eyes gave no answer to this impertinent question. Unable to hide my anger, I abruptly left the table, saying a curt good-bye.

I was unable to forget Helen, in her misery and despair, and a strange premonition impelled me to look for her again, as if I could give her peace of mind. During the next ten days, I searched in vain. Again and again, I walked by the Hotel Negresco and back and forth on Les Promenades des Anglais. I visited the casino many times, and other bars where one might expect to meet them. There was no trace of Betvugin or Helen, and I decided they had left Nice.

Ten days after my talk with Helen, I was stopped in the lobby of Saint-Roch Hospital by Dr. Cartotto. "Have you read the paper today?" he asked excitedly.

"No, not yet. I've had no time to look at newspapers."

"Read this," and he pushed a newspaper in my hand. "Look. What do you say?" On the front page was a picture of Betvugin, and I read that the noted Russian-refugee surgeon was killed by his wife, Helen, in a hotel in Beaulieu. It was an open-and-shut case of murder and suicide. She was as dead as he was. No notes were left. The motive behind this tragic murder was unknown. The story said that, according to the hotel clerk, they seemed the most happily married couple in the world. The paper carried no picture of Helen. They had not found one in their luggage. Even in death, he remained faithful to his ego.

Chapter 4

INDIVIDUALISM VERSUS
STANDARDIZATION

Wₕₑₙ I entered the University of St. Petersburg at sixteen, I was anxious to find the answers to the multitude of questions which troubled me. In spite of my youth, I was, without suspecting it, already impregnated with blind yet forceful faith—not in God or Providence, not even in human nature, but in the supremacy of science. I was a victim of sciolism, the superficial thinking which is the common affliction of modern man and the first step toward modern materialism. For, at bottom, what is materialism if not pride of intellect?

As I look back on my university days and try to understand the birth and phenomenal success of communism in Russia, I cannot but feel that a contributing factor was the mechanistic trend in the universities of my time. In almost every natural-science course that I took, I felt this undercurrent of materialistic philosophy. Whether I was listening to a professor of embryology, an anthropologist, or a physiologist, I sensed the tendency to simplify the phenomena of life. Without explicitly saying so, they intimated that sooner or later we would know everything about the essence of the vital life processes. Some would even quote Francis Bacon and agree with him that man's domination over nature was proof that he understood it. And Democritus was nearer to their hearts than Aristotle or Plato.

For the universities of the pre-Soviet period were actually the educational centers, the birthplace, of the intelligentsia. This word "intelligentsia" was little used outside Russia. It had a special significance which hardly can be properly understood by anyone not living in Russia at that time. Webster defines the word as: "intellectual or learned people taken as a class, in contrast to the illiterate." This interpretation is not correct, for it does not touch the essence of this word as it was generally used in Russia.

There was also in Russia a word *intelliguent*, which did not correspond to the word "intellectual" as used in other countries. The work "intellectual" is usually applied to a man who believes in the power of intellect, and who is apt to submit his emotional life more or less to that power. The Russian word *intelliguent* applied rather to the general intelligence than to intellectual inclinations; much more to humanitarian tendencies than to the power of intellect. One would apply the word *intelliguent* to Chekhov but would not use it in regard to Karl Marx or Lenin, who were essentially intellectuals.

The Russian word *intelligentsia* was introduced in practice by the writer Boborikin in about 1860. He applied it to the group of liberals who were preoccupied with the idea of helping the people and making their lives more tolerable. Nicholas Mikhailovsky, the leader of Russian democratic idealism, gave a clearer definition of this word. "We can say," he wrote, "with a clear conscience that we are the Intelligentsia. Because we know a great deal, we think about many things. Our profession is science and art and literature. . . . Our hearts and minds are with our people, from whom we have become detached by our education. We are in debt to the people. And this fact serves as the basis for all our activity." Mikhailovsky, as well as many other Russian writers and philosophers, definitely considered the intelligentsia a class. Berdyaiev thinks it is a superclass: "The intelligentsia is that part of mankind in whom the ideal part of the human spirit has conquered class restrictions."

The Russian intelligentsia were both idealistic and democratic in their political beliefs and way of life. They were highly individualistic. Individualism was the basis of their philosophy; they attributed great importance to the perfecting of personality.

A feeling of social responsibility bordering on what we could call a sense of "social guilt" was characteristic of the Russian intelligentsia. The desire for material comfort and economic success was foreign to many of them. True enough, some were in comfortable circumstances, others very poor, but there was a peculiar similarity in their attitudes toward life. Often they avowed an idealism that was too extreme, an altruism too accentuated, a desire for sacrifice too pronounced. And their disregard of material accomplishment was very close to complete lack of interest in their standard of living.

In their professional life, however, many were good lawyers or teachers, excellent engineers or scientists, able physicians or surgeons. Few were good businessmen. They were, as a rule, impractical. They lacked realism even in politics. They lived entirely among ideas and ideals; they dreamed about a new world, but they wanted freedom most of all. They were unquestionably humanitarian and utterly Russian in every respect. A smoky room, a table loaded with samovar and plates of sandwiches, and groups of twelve or fifteen men and women of various ages were typical of an evening assemblage of the intelligentsia in St. Petersburg or some other town. For hours they would discuss the eternal problems of mankind, problems which never will be solved.

The universities were educational "mills" for the intelligentsia, the centers of Russian humanitarian idealism. The influence of the universities upon youth was enormous. Yet, with the beginning of the nineteenth century, a materialistic trend gradually crystallized there. The economic materialism of Karl Marx and the mechanistic tendencies of natural science produced a deep influence upon some students.

This new concept soon became a powerful force in the political life of Russia and the whole world. But then an open revolt against the "technologism" of natural science developed in the universities. The revolt was led by a group of young associate and assistant professors, some of whom later became internationally known for their work in experimental biology.

I remember vividly the introductory lecture by Dr. Eugene Schultz, associate professor of embryology. It was a violent attack on the mechanistic trend in biology. "You are impressed," he said, "with the work and statements of Jacques Loeb, this modern prophet of crude materialism in biology. You are ready to follow his lightheaded theory of the physico-chemical nature of the living organism. You are only repeating the ill-fated example of the Iatromechanistic theories of the seventeenth century. There is no essential difference between what Jacques Loeb teaches and what Giorgio Baglivi postulated." And he explained to the large audience, composed of science students and faculty members, that, according to Baglivi's theories, the organism was a "box of tools," the teeth serving as scissors, the stomach as a bottle, the intestines as sieves and the veins as pipes.

Schultz gave a fascinating picture of this constant struggle between the mechanistic and vitalistic trends in natural science, stressing the fact that all the vitalistic theories which had been offered were reactions against mechanistic thinking. He told us that it was Thomas Sydenham, the greatest physician of his time, who revolted against the Iatromechanistic theories of Baglivi and others. Sydenham exhorted his students to throw these fallacious theories overboard. In his practice, his teaching, and his writings, he called on them to go back to Hippocrates and to be faithful to his spirit. And Sydenham was only one among many "rebels" against the theory that the organism is a machine.

Schultz vividly described to the attentive audience the remarkable work of George Ernst Stahl, who urged the biologists to go back to Aristotle. In his *Theoria medica verva,* Stahl wrote: "It is never repeated often enough that the groundwork of life is activity, not matter . . . for matter in itself is only passive and indifferent to all activity, and is simply distributed and coordinated within some form or structure. Bear this in mind." Stahl's brilliant disciple Bochat developed his ideas and theories further. And after them came the men who made history in biological science, men like Claude Bernard, Johannes Muller, C. F. Wolff, C. F. Blumenbach, J. V. Uexkull, Hans Driesch, Jennings, and many others.

Schultz's lecture was only one of numerous attacks on mechanistic science. Gurvitch, Losskyi, Metalnikoff, and many others tried to stop the growing power of materialism, inspired and promoted by leaders in natural science and economics. With the fall of the democratic government, which was actually composed of elements of the idealistic intelligentsia and was their creation, there was no room for men like Schultz and Losskyi. Some of them became exiles from Soviet Russia, others were annihilated mercilessly.

The scientific center of Russian materialism was Dr. Ivan Pavlov's laboratory. There, research on human and animal behavior was conducted under the leadership of the famous physiologist, and there the extreme doctrine of "objective psychology" was born.

Pavlov's Wednesdays were renowned; they always attracted a large number of his faithful disciples and students. They almost were a sect, a scientific religion whose master, teacher, indisputable leader was Ivan Petrovitch Pavlov. On these Wednesday afternoons at the Institute of Experimental Medicine, the basic problems of Pavlov's teaching were the chief, perhaps the only, subject of discussion. I vividly remember one of these Wednesdays when an "unwelcome outsider" abruptly asked Pavlov if he believed in psychology and its place in medical science.

"Psychology?" replied Pavlov sarcastically. "Psychology is invented by unscientific men. There is no room for psychology and the subjective method of investigating the mental activity of man. It is physiology which will give the answer to the puzzling problems of mental activity."

"Do you mean that all the mental processes of man are nothing but physiological manifestations of the brain?" The persistent stranger was clearly antagonistic to Pavlov's teaching.

"Of course," grumbled Pavlov with irritation. "Of course; by studying the higher nervous activity in man, we will gradually come to know everything about his so-called psychology."

"Does this mean that you agree with Setchenov that thought is nothing but an inhibited reflex?"

In mentioning the name of Ivan M. Setchenov, the stranger touched the soft spot in Pavlov.

"Setchenov was a great man," Pavlov angrily remarked.

"Was he?" the stranger demanded, also raising his voice. "I do not think so, Professor Pavlov. He was a narrow-minded man who was unable to grasp the complexity of mental activity." And without another word the stranger walked out of the room.

"Who is that imbecile?" shouted Pavlov.

Dr. I. A. Orbeli whispered the name in Pavlov's ear.

"I knew," smiled Pavlov, "that he must be one of those neovitalists." I later learned that it was Dr. Gurvitch, an outspoken antimaterialist.

About two years after the Communist party overthrew Kerensky's democratic government, Lenin paid a visit to Pavlov's laboratory in the Institute of Experimental Medicine at Petrograd. The meeting of these two men took place in October 1919. It was not publicized and, except for two of Pavlov's closest associates, no one was informed of this unusual visit. Dr G. P. Zelenyi, who was present at this meeting, made a transcription. He permitted me to read it and to copy its essential points. This was shortly before I left Soviet Russia.

As usual, Lenin was blunt and direct. He avoided all preliminaries.

"How can human behavior be controlled?" he asked Pavlov.

"I don't quite understand your question," was the answer.

"We are building the new world, the world of communism. You are not a Communist?"

Pavlov shook his head. He was not a Communist at that time and he never joined the party, even when he was declared a "hero" of the Soviet Republics.

"That's not important. Important is the fact that I want the masses of Russia to follow a pattern of thinking and reacting, along a Communistic pattern. All of them."

The idea seemed absurd to Pavlov, but he listened in silence.

"There was too much individualism in the Russia of the past. Communism does not tolerate individualistic tendencies. They are harmful. They interfere with our plans. We must abolish individualism."

"But this is an enormous task. Individualism plays a great role in the lives of the Russians," remarked Pavlov.

"Nonsense. Man can be corrected. Man can be made what we want him to be."

Pavlov took time to answer. He did not want to antagonize the all-powerful ruler of Soviet Russia.

"Do you mean that you would like to standardize the population of Russia? Make them all behave in the same way?" he asked.

"Exactly . . . That's what I want, Ivan Petrovitch, and you must help us."

"In what way?" Pavlov was perplexed.

"By your studies of human behavior. Nothing else. Just scientific research along your own lines."

And Lenin began to develop his idea that human behavior should be controlled by proper education. To the astonishment of Pavlov and Zelenyi, he knew a good deal about the work of Pavlov's school on conditioned reflexes. He was explicit, even if not always scientifically exact.

When Lenin was a young man and was in the process of formulating his theories of dialectical materialism, he searched for biological data which would confirm his ideas. He came across a book by the noted physiologist Ivan M. Setchenov, which had been published in 1863. This book, thirty years old, was *Reflexes of the Brain*. In it, Setchenov stated that thoughts arose as a result of inhibited reflexes, that the whole psychic component actually represented a bridge between receptor and effector.

"Thought is nothing," he wrote, "but an inhibited reflex, or a reflex which has lost its last part. . . . All movements known in physiology as voluntary," he declared, "are reflex in the strictest sense of the word." In other words, man's mental activity and psyche were reduced by Setchenov to reflexes of a purely physiological nature. Although Lenin did not grasp the intrinsic reasoning of the physiologist, he fully understood that Setchenov refused to admit the existence of soul or psyche and considered man's mental activity to be a sort of electromechanical device. This was the type of scientific evidence for which Lenin was looking, and he found it.

When it was published, Setchenov's book caused great excitement among the Russian intelligentsia, and he was immortalized by Ivan Turgenev as Bazarov, the hero of his novel *The Fathers and the Sons*. It was from that time that the term "nihilist" was applied in Russia to anyone who, like Bazarov, refused to admit the existence of the soul.

The moment Lenin referred to Setchenov's work, Pavlov became animated and took a more active part in the conversation. For he considered Setchenov his precursor in the theory of reflexes. Soon the conversation turned into a lecture on "neurism," the theory which was the basis of Pavlov's studies. Pavlov's lecture to Lenin continued for almost two hours, occasionally interrupted by a question from his listener.

Pavlov explained that the term "neurism" was introduced into practice by his professor, Dr. Botkin.[1] "We call neurism a physiological concept which tends to extend the influence of the central nervous system to possible large fields of the organism's activity." The central nervous system, he said, makes a unit of the organism, by coordinating and directing all its functions. The nervous system has a predominant, almost exclusive, role in all that man does, voluntary or involuntary. The brain, and the brain alone, serves as the essential substratum for higher nervous activity, for man's mental processes, moods, emotions. When man is sick, something is wrong with his brain function, Pavlov said. Cancer, diabetes, gastric ulcers, even infectious diseases might be traced to the brain.[2]

"Our school is in complete disagreement with the concept of Western physiologists like Muller, Virchov, or Needham." And he went on to outline the difference between the two schools. To the adherents of neurism, the personality of man, his pattern of acting and reacting, is merely the product of individual experience during life. It is the end result of man's

---

1. *The Collected Works*, I. P. Pavlov, AN, USSR, 1951, v. 1, p. 197. See also *The Teaching of I. P. Pavlov and the Pathological Physiology*, A. G. Ivanov-Smolensky, AMN, USSR, 1952, pp. 120, 121. See also "Reflex Activity of the Organism under Narcosis," *Archives of Pathology*, 15, 1953, USSR, pp. 77-81.
2. "Emotions and Laws of Higher Nervous Activity," V. S. Deriabkin, *Journal of Higher Nervous Activity*, 1(6), 1951, p. 889. See also *The Experimental Investigation of Higher Nervous Activity*, V. P. Protopopov, AN, USSR, 1950. See also "The Effect of Overstraining of the Central Nervous System on the Development of Experimental Leukemia," N. O. Rauchenbach, E. M. Jarova, and M. P. Khokhlov, *Archives of Pathology*, 14, 1952, USSR, pp. 23-31.

adaptation to environment. This experience is based on the formation of conditioned reflexes, and the association of these reflexes in the brain. According to neurism, then, natural instinct, heredity in general, plays only a secondary role in man's behavior and his personality pattern.

"Does this mean that hereditary factors can be overcome by proper education?" asked Lenin.

"Under certain conditions—yes. They can be overcome, I believe, and we have a good deal of experimental evidence that conditioned reflexes can abolish unconditioned reflexes, or, as they are called, natural instinct.

"The European physiologists, of course, defend the idealistic concept of man's behavior," Pavlov continued. They adhere to the so-called cellular principle. They consider the living organism as an entity, the properties of which are predetermined by inheritance and embryonic development. The organism, according to them, only partly depends on environmental conditions. They are wrong."

And Pavlov explained how he and his associates had found that external stimulus, which forms the conditioned reflex, is of prime importance. The same conditioned reflex can be induced and formed in humans of very different personalities. This is in direct contradiction with European teaching, he admitted. According to them, the organism's reactions depend on the specific properties of the organism itself, its chemistry, its physics, its individuality. "They overstress the importance of the organism's individualistic characteristics— we minimize its importance. We attribute importance to the outside stimulus, or, if you prefer, to environment. They accept a dualistic point of view in their interpretation of psychic phenomena. We don't."

"That's fine. Excellent," exclaimed Lenin. "That's exactly what I wanted to know. You are a materialist, as we are?"

"In my research, I am." Pavlov did not amplify upon his carefully reserved statement. However, it was said that privately, outside his scientific activity, not only was he not an atheist but he was a deeply religious man.

This meeting between Pavlov and Lenin was the take-off point for the Soviet government's gigantic project of controlling human behavior, of standardizing the personality patterns of the Russian people. It was actually a war on individualistic drivings, on that Russian individualism of which we had been so proud in the past.

The practical consequences of this meeting soon became evident. Pavlov's laboratory was turned into an oasis, "untouchable" by the Soviet Cheka. And neither the bourgeois origin of the scientists nor their political aspirations, not even their counterrevolutionary past were significant as long as they were taking part in the work on neurism. They were left in peace, unafraid of repressive measures.

Several of Pavlov's disciples were appointed as heads of physiological laboratories and institutions in other cities, where work was at once directed along the line of neurism. New laboratories were organized for the purpose, and financial support was given by the Soviet government to this vast project.

Individualization versus standardization! That was the important point, more important than the political and social differences that were to arise in the forthcoming struggle against Soviet totalitarianism. To the Russian intelligentsia, the proper and full development of man's individuality was the basis for a progressive development of human society. The Russian Communists accepted a crude materialism as the basis for their social experimentation. Their political concepts caused them to reject the significance of individualistic trends in man. By decree, they simply left no place for individuality in their social system.

Yet, individuality reigns in the living world, from the lowest and simplest organism to the highest and most complex. No other quality of living matter is more powerfully manifest. As long as living matter is actively alive, individuality is present. When, however, living matter is in a state of degeneration and decay, it tends to lose this characteristic.

In the experiments I had conducted in association with Professor Metalnikoff, even the simplest animals, like the infusoria, manifested a high degree of individuality in their reactions, reflexes, and anatomy. No two living cells in the same body are absolutely identical. Everyone is familiar with the fact that no two fingerprints have ever been found to duplicate each other. No human organs have ever been found to be exactly the same. This elementary law of living nature is completely disregarded by the Communists. They believe that the masses of men can be standardized and deprived of all individual manifestations. They stubbornly assert that, by sheer power of educational propaganda, they will be able to subjugate people and make them into robot-like machines which think, act, and react in the same pattern. They use Pavlov's "neurism" as a scientific basis for their biological theory. They reject and condemn every scientific work which contradicts Pavlov's hypothesis.

When the Soviet government came to power, neurism became the official scientific doctrine. For, it was argued, if man's behavior can be reduced to a chain of conditioned reflexes, the behavior of the population can be standardized. How earnestly the Soviet leaders take this problem, one may see from what has recently been taking place in this respect.

From June 26 to July 4, 1950, an extraordinary scientific congress took place in the great auditorium of Moscow University. More than 1400 delegates—physiologists, biologists, pathologists, and psychiatrists—were present. This congress was called "The Scientific Session Dedicated to the Problems of the Physiological Teaching of Pavlov," but its actual aim was of much farther reaching significance. The goal was to promote a scientifically elaborated control of human behavior.

The essential elements of Pavlov's teaching served as the basis for this government-dictated movement. Pavlov's postulates were accepted in their simplified and extreme forms. The behavior of man is the product of his environment. Man can transcend his heredity and transform his environment. That is, although he is controlled by his environment, he can rise above it and alter it, an absolute contradiction. And since man's thoughts and ideas are nothing but a chain of conditioned reflexes, elaborated during childhood and adult life, man's personality and behavior can be controlled by proper education. By conditioning his reflexes, man can be "standardized," can be made to think and act according to the pattern required by the Soviet government. Thus, the whole population of Soviet Russia and, in fact, of the whole world can gradually be transformed into "standardized" masses, thinking and behaving in complete uniformity.

The scientists, physiologists, and psychologists who disagreed even slightly with "superneurism" were denounced at the Moscow congress as "enemies of communism," and some were deprived of their positions at the universities. Even men who were formerly associated with Pavlov, like the academicians I. S. Beritaschvili and I. A. Orbeli or Professors H. A. Rozhanski and P. K. Anokhin, who deviated in their work from the official line of research, were proclaimed "bourgeois lackeys."[3]

These four physiologists were among many others accused of individualistic trends in their work, the purpose of which was supposed to be the elimination of individuality.

Attacks on the "heretics" of neurism did not abate with the closing of the Pavlovian congress. The issues of the *Soviet Journal of Physiology* of the 1950s are full of articles denouncing one or another physiologist.

Lenin's dream of standardizing the non-Communist population of Soviet Russia, of transforming it into millions of robotlike men, educated in the same pattern of reflexology and deprived of all individuality, men who would follow the Communist theories without protest, fight, or question—this dream has not been abandoned by the present rulers of Russia. Anyone who believes that the basic property of all living beings is individuality, any scientist who knows that evolution is impossible without individuation, might be perplexed by the absurdity of this dream. Yet it is being put into practice on a gigantic scale unknown in the history of the human race.

Much has been said and written about Soviet Russia and the political and economic activity of the Communist party. Yet, the most important aspect of communism has somehow escaped public attention: its relentless fight against the individualistic tendencies of subject people. Russian communism is the most extreme and extraordinary form of anti-individualism that has ever existed in our civilization.

----

3. "The Decree on Academician I. S. Beritaschvili," *Journal of Higher Nervous Activity*, 1(2), 1951, pp. 145, 146. See also "The Decree on Academician L. A. Orbeli," *ibid.*, 1(3), 1951, pp. 307-309. See also "The Decree on Professor N. A. Rozhanski," *ibid.*, 1(5), 1951, p. 645.

The fight between individualistic principles and materialistic standardization, which by now has culminated in the complete suppression of all independent scientific thinking in Soviet Russia, was only in an embryonic stage when I was at the university. The extreme materialists were still in a small minority as compared with the student body at large. We, the youth of those days, still enjoyed freedom of opinion, and individualism was the basis of our ideological drivings.

Chapter 5

THE BROTHERS PYATAKOFF

O<small>NE</small> day a group of medical students and interns were chatting in Dr. Ivan Pavlov's laboratory while waiting for the professor to begin his demonstration. It was during my internship, and I was spending a good deal of time there, although I was far from being a disciple of his. The conversation turned to premonition, not a very popular subject with Pavlov's followers. The majority did not believe there was any scientific foundation for admitting the existence of a "sixth sense," and only one of those present objected—and rather timidly—to the denial of "this vital factor in human life," as he phrased it. This was Dr. Nicholas Rogestvensky, an able physiologist, who remarked that he himself had been having a recurrent premonition, a very strong and persistent vision. "I distinctly see myself opening the door of an elevator and falling down into the dark abyss of the elevator shaft," he told us. "While falling, I hear my wife calling out, 'Don't use the elevator. It's broken.' The strangest thing about this vision is that I experience it not in my dream but when I am still half awake. It's not a dream," he said, seeing the skeptical smiles of his colleagues, "but more like a real vision."

We took his story very lightly, and we jokingly advised him to avoid using elevators and to walk up and down stairs.

Some six months later we were all invited to a party at the home of one of our colleagues, who lived on the sixth floor. The party was gay, and it was late in the night when we left together. We were all in high spirits. We rang for the elevator, which was of a rather primitive type. Nicholas, while discussing with us one of Pavlov's recent experiments on dogs, opened the door and stepped forward. At that very moment our host's wife shouted, "Don't use the elevator. It's broken." Nicholas fell three floors, landing on the top of the elevator car. He survived the fall, but suffered broken legs and arms and a serious brain concussion. He was in bed for ten months or more, undergoing endless operations, but he gradually recovered and was able to return to his scientific work.

When Pavlov was told about this strange premonition, he brushed it aside. "An obvious coincidence . . . There is no such thing as premonition," he crisply remarked.

It is hard for us biologists and medical men to accept the existence of a "sixth sense," which cannot be measured or proved by orthodox methods of investigation. Yet, when one of us undergoes an experience such as Rogestvensky's, we are willing to admit that science might be wrong and that there is much in man's mind and perceptions which we know little about and never will properly understand.

Precisely for this reason, the following events of September 29, 1917, became engraved in my memory—so deeply that they influenced to some degree all my future concepts of human life. In a sense there was nothing extraordinary in the fact that a lone German bomb should have made a direct hit on my laboratory car. It was tragic—tragic beyond human comprehension—that the bomb should have killed my friend and assistant, Schelling, and completely destroyed two cars. It was even less understandable that I should have escaped death by a tiny fraction of a minute. It was all an accident of war, of death and destruction, of survival and escape. But there was another quantity in the events of that day that I still cannot account for and cannot reject as being of no significance.

I remember it as clearly as if it were yesterday. I was lying on my couch, half asleep. I became conscious of a loud noise from a plane. The sound was deafening and gave me the impression that the plane was only a few feet above my railroad car. I distinctly saw the face of a German pilot, although my eyes were closed. And then I heard Ilya yelling, "Here it comes . . . Lord save us!" and someone murmuring, "Schelling is killed."

I jumped from my bed in a panic and raised the window curtain. It was early morning. The only sound was the singing of birds. There was no commotion in our train, no noise other than snores from Schelling, asleep in the next room. Was it a dream, a nightmare? Possibly so. Quite probably. But the minute I begin to review the circumstances, I am obliged to admit that certain elements contradicted its definition as a dream. For, during the entire time of my dream-vision, I was cognizant of the ticking of my table clock, clear and unquestionable.

Whatever role my subconscious mind might have played is of secondary importance. The fact remains that, six hours later, we were discussing with Schelling a microscope slide of a tissue taken from a patient's femur. We agreed that it was a case of fibrosarcoma, a hopeless malignant growth. Schelling was preparing to show me another slide when I interrupted our discussion by going to my room at the other end of the car for cigarettes. Suddenly I heard the noise of a plane. The moment I reached my room, there was a terrific explosion and something hit me hard on the head. I lost consciousness.

Polevitzky's voice reached me in my semiconscious state. "He is alive."

"Poor Schelling is dead." This time it was Ilya speaking.

Schelling was dead. Silently we stood at his grave while the village priest delivered his obsequial prayers. Who guides man's destiny, I wondered. Mere seconds had separated me from the same tragic fate as my friend. Was it pure accident that his life was ended so abruptly, or was this destined long in advance by the Supreme Power? My thoughts were interrupted by Ilya, who was coming with a tombstone. He had found it somewhere in Lutzk and succeeded in engraving Schelling's name and the date of death. World War I was ended for Schelling as well as for the Russian people. We were entering bloody, chaotic civil war, the global significance of which no one could foresee. We still were living in the world of illusions and dreams created and nursed by our idealistic background. We had not the realistic pragmatism of the older nations of Europe.

In my student days, I would often take my meals at the university's self-service cafeteria. Open until eight in the evening, it was a meeting place for students. Here and there, one would find a group ardently discussing philosophical and social problems—and consuming hot tea, for which there was no charge. I often suspected that many students spent a large part of the day in the cafeteria instead of attending classes. A registered student was not obliged to be present at his lectures. The examination was all that counted. (The registration fee for a semester was twenty-five roubles, or about twelve dollars. A student could take any number of courses without additional charge. And so the cost of higher education in Russia was very low then, and anyone, however poor, could be graduated from a university or medical school. Consequently, a large percentage of the students came from the lower and middle classes.[1] As a rule, the aristocracy sent their sons to special educational institutions such as the Imperial Lyceum or the "Pravoved School," a law school which prepared young men of the gentry for government positions. At the university, we enjoyed complete freedom of speech and belief. And nobody interfered with our behavior as long as it did not affect the course of academic life.)

Often, while taking meals at the cafeteria, I would notice a certain man who was always surrounded by a group of students. He was about thirty and had the face of a thinker. Large, dark eyes, an immense forehead, long, gold-brownish hair, and a strong mouth. He wore a woolen shirt, Tolstoy fashion, with a belt. He spoke very slowly, often without finishing his sentences. Now and then, one of his listeners

---

1. "The student bodies of Russian universities were democratized by the influx of the 'rankless' elements. Over 50 percent of the students earned a living completely or partially, doing largely tutorial work, while in certain universities the percentage was much higher. University scholarships and all sorts of financial aid from different organizations were quite prevalent, enabling a wide social variety to attend the institutions of higher learning." *Russian Schools and Universities in the World War,* Ignatiev, Odinetz, and Novgorotsev, Yale University Press, New Haven, 1929, p. 385.

would ask a question. He took his time answering it, as if trying to find a clear-cut formulation for his thought.

"Who is that man?" I inquired of my neighbor one day.

"We call him the Socrates of the Neva," was the answer. "He's an old-timer. I believe his name is Chester. Apparently from a Russified English family."

"There are Chesters in the textile business in St. Petersburg," I remarked.

"Possibly he's one of them. I don't know. He was a successful lawyer, they say, and something happened. He left his profession and entered the university. He was graduated from the Imperial Lyceum, I think, and then took up philosophy. I often saw him at Losskyi's seminar on Kant. He's a brilliant man, but he looks a little eccentric to me."

"How long has he been at the university?"

"I don't know. He was here before me, and I'm a senior. So he must have been here at least five years now."

"Perpetual student?"

"Apparently."

I approached the group at Chester's table. He was discussing the morality of man.

"Man has a soul. We all agree upon this," he was saying.

"Not all of us," someone injected.

"We all must agree upon this," Chester stubbornly repeated. "I make no definition of the soul. It's something in the seat of man's normal waking intelligence and moral character."

"A vague definition," a listener remarked.

"Not so vague as it appears to you. Every one of you feels the presence of the soul. It is in you, whatever it is; by virtue of it we are denominated wise and foolish, good and evil. . . . We should not concern ourselves with either speculative or empirical psychology. We must be concerned only with a common principle of epistemology and ethics."

His voice was deep and there was hypnotic power in it. The words meant little. They seemed of secondary importance. The man who uttered them was a man of passionate, unshakable belief. Yet he was not preaching. He did not attempt to impose his own ideas on his listeners. He did not even try to convince them, but only spoke from the heart. His attitude toward the group was friendly, even gentle, yet somewhat detached.

"Are you a follower of Leo Tolstoy, Chester?" someone asked.

He shook his head.

A student sitting at his side, apparently a faithful follower, answered for him. "Of course not. Tolstoy seeks in moral ethics an escape from his inner personal conflicts." He was almost indignant. "He has a standard morality for everyone. We do not promote or defend any generalization in this respect. Man must find his own soul. He must recognize the moral virtues inbred in it. For all men are basically good. If they do evil, it is because of insufficient knowledge of their souls. Their ignorance misleads them. For this reason we are strongly opposed to any imposition of another person's will and opinion on his fellowman. Every man must find himself, through understanding his own soul."

"But man is weak," said the student who had first spoken, probably a Tolstoy follower. "He is full of the devil, he must be guided by a right and moral man."

"Tolstoy," returned the second student, "does not appreciate the significance of individuality and its role in the moral development of man. He has a false estimation of good. Yes! There is much *acrasia* in the lives of men, much weakness. But moral weakness and wrongdoing are always involuntary, a reaction against the suppression of individuality, of man's soul. Man never does evil because it is evil. He does it in spite of its evil nature."

"Does this mean, Chester, that you are opposed to any form of tyranny, political, religious, or social?" someone asked him.

"A tyrant is a monster of wickedness," again replied the second student. "He is the source of all evil in this world."

I hurried away to my laboratory class, for which I was late, but decided to meet and talk with this unusual man. Several weeks passed before the opportunity arrived.

It was late on a July evening. A white night, slightly foggy. I wandered along the banks of the Neva, enjoying the aimlessness of my walk. I descended the stony steps leading to the water. I wanted to be closer to it. I knelt down and put my hands in the water. Only then did I notice the figure of a man sitting on the steps.

"I knew you would come," he said. It was Chester.

"But you don't know me." I was perplexed.

He remained silent, as if I had not spoken.

"I wanted to meet you," I murmured.

"I knew that. . . . You have a restless soul. But the time will come. . . . You will find yourself, as I found myself."

"How . . . how?"

There was no answer. We sat in silence for many minutes, he immobile, eyes closed, as if in a somnambulistic state, his breathing hardly perceptible. Suddenly, he opened his eyes, as if waking from a coma. He murmured:

"I saw you standing on a sidewalk. It was Moscow. You were in a British khaki uniform, very dirty and torn. Your hair was long, very long. You were smiling and looked happy. You recognized me and made a slight movement with your hand as if greeting me. I was walking in the middle of the street, which looked to me like Tverskaya Street, with a group of people. They were all sad, and some were crying. We were surrounded by guards, a dozen men in strange uniform with a red hammer as an insignia. . . ."

"A most peculiar dream," I remarked. Was he joking?

"It was not a dream," Chester said gravely. "It was a vision. Occasionally I have these strange moments of vision, or, if you like, premonition. In such moments I lose all contact with my surroundings. My 'sixth sense' becomes extremely sharp."

"Your premonitions . . . are they always fulfilled later on?"

"Always." He was firm. I was incredulous. "You will see," he said.

This was in 1910, when I was a freshman at the university. Ten years later—it was July 1920—when I had just been released from Boutyrki Prison, I was standing on a sidewalk in Moscow, in an enchanted mood after four months of confinement. I was about to cross Tverskaya Street when I noticed a group of prisoners, encircled by Chekists, walking along the street. Apparently they were headed for a Siberian prison camp. In the first rank was a tall, erect man. He dominated the group of scared, unhappy prisoners with his calm, untroubled attitude. He turned his head in my direction and smiled. I recognized Chester. He was unchanged. Clean-shaven, in the same Tolstoy-style blouse, hatless, his hair long and golden, he seemed perfectly detached from his surroundings. Instinctively, I raised my hand to salute him, but cut the gesture short. It was not quite safe to welcome him in the presence of the Chekists.

"I'm not crazy," he said smiling, as we sat on the Neva steps. And he looked at me tenderly. "Some men apparently are endowed with this ability to foresee events. A most distressing ability," he added. "But let's go to my rooms and have a bite."

He lived on the bank of the Moika River. His two-room flat was simplicity itself, very clean, bare, and neat, to the point of austerity. A few straight chairs, no armchairs, several shelves loaded with books, no pictures on the walls, a small desk with tidy files. I noticed many books on criminology and criminal law.

"I was a criminal lawyer," he informed me, as he prepared tea and sandwiches. "I had rather an extensive practice. Then I began to think. It was a slow process, but finally I decided to give up my practice and devote myself to finding the truth about human existence. When I defended murderers, who were always victims of their conflicts with the world around them, I found that I was very ignorant about human nature and men's motivations and urges. One of my clients was a rich man who had lost his fortune in speculations. What did he do? He killed his wife and two children and attempted to kill himself. He survived and was brought to court. Absurd behavior. And there was an older man, jealous of his wife. He suspected her of infidelity. He killed her. Incredible nonsense. Men of this kind were completely without common sense or any proper evaluation of life. Modern man has lost all sense of true values, a sense which was strongly manifested in the Age of Illumination in ancient Greece. This is why I decided to give up my practice and dedicate my life to the knowledge of self.

"I donated my fortune to public educational institutions, because simple habits are essential for man's true existence. Modern man is beset by utilitarian drivings. He is never happy. He always excites his inner conflicts, and his individuality is handicapped."

"What do you do for a living?" I asked.

"I teach mathematics in a school for adults."

"Have you ever had a premonition about the future of Russia?" I dared to inquire.

"No. My visions are always associated with my own life."

"And what do you know about your future?"

"Several times I have had the same vision. I kill a man."

"You kill a man!" I was horrified. "With your philosophy? With your self-understanding?"

"Perhaps a contradiction *ad absurdum*. At least in my vision. But the circumstances of my becoming a murderer are excusable."

"Are there any circumstances that excuse murder?" I protested. Instead of answering my question, he told me his premonition.

"I'm a prisoner in a labor camp, working on the construction of a railroad somewhere in the north. It is winter, and everything is covered with snow except the narrow strip where the road is being built. Our road gang is composed of all sorts of people, old and young, men and women. They all appear faceless to me except two: the commandant of the camp and a young girl. I have never met her, or any girl like her. She was a complete stranger to me, yet she was already a part of me, I mean in my vision. I was returning to the camp one night after work and heard a cry for help from the commandant's cottage. I went in and saw the brute trying to rape this girl. My hands suddenly swelled, became gigantic; they filled all my vision and they strangled the commandant. It was terrifying, my enormous fingers pressing into the neck of that savage."

"And how does your vision end?"

"It doesn't go any further. It just ends with my strangling the commandant of that mysterious labor camp."

In 1932, a prisoner who had escaped from the Soviet labor camp near Segozero in the Kem River region told me that shortly before his escape from the camp, Chester had been killed by the Chekists for murdering the commandant. He did not know the circumstances, but it was rumored that the Socrates of the Neva had defended a girl prisoner from an amorous assault by the Chekist.

I witnessed another remarkable instance of extrasensory perception at the Oboukhov Hospital in Petrograd. A middle-aged physician there by the name of Loutouguin performed miracles of premonition. On many occasions, he predicted the death of patients who, from all clinical evidence, should have survived the minor surgery they had undergone. One day a healthy-looking young woman was admitted to the hospital with mild appendicitis. Her temperature was almost normal and there was nothing wrong with her other than a painful appendix. It was decided to operate at once. But Loutouguin was opposed.

"She will die if she's operated on," he stubbornly insisted.

The chief surgeon dismissed his assistant's "crazy notion." The girl was operated on and died from anesthetic shock, apparently caused by hypersensitivity of the adrenal gland.

Russians in general are not free from superstition, and it was not long before the surgeons of Oboukhov Hospital were asking Loutouguin his opinion on every case scheduled for surgery. It became routine procedure.

In one case, however, he was unable to foresee the future. When he was himself admitted to the hospital for kidney stones, surgery was urgently indicated. Asked what the outcome would be, he hopefully stated that the operation would go well. He died a few hours after the operation, which was recorded as—in medical terms—a success. The cause of his death was internal bleeding accentuated by cirrhosis of the liver.

The strange story of Loutouguin came to my mind when I became involved in the tragic case of the brothers Pyatakoff.

I left the front on the evening of the day that Schelling died. I was headed for Petrograd to report the destruction of my laboratory. On my way to Kiev I stopped off in Lutzk. There I was informed that I had been named by the conservative wing of the Labor party's district committee as a candidate for election to the All Russian Constituent Assembly. The elections in the XIII Army were scheduled for November, and I was requested to return promptly to the front after my trip to the capital. The nomination was wholly unexpected by me. I did not deserve it. To be one of the eight hundred representatives of the 180 million Russian citizens was a task for which I was not prepared. This was the last thing I ever wanted. Thus, against my will, I became a part of the events with whose consequences the entire world is today confronted.

The army rear presented a picture of complete chaos, a striking difference from the front. Trains were jammed with deserters, still armed, often drunk, and the military police were unable to maintain even an appearance of order. Here and there, in small villages and larger towns, the Communists openly accused the democratic government of being "the hanger-on of the bourgeoisie," "the dogs of the international capitalists and imperialists." They called for an "immediate peace without annexations and contributions." They demanded delivery of the "land to the peasants and the factories and plants to the workers." Their speeches made a deep impression on some of their listeners, who wanted to "go home" and take off their uniforms at any cost.

In spite of the chaotic state of transportation, there was an abundance of foodstuffs of all kinds. Everything was obtainable in stores and restaurants at reasonable prices. No hunger, no famine, no economic factors were present which, it so often is said, accounted for the birth of the Soviet regime. But there was an enormous weariness of war and longing for peace. The most stable elements among the servicemen remained at the front, in spite of the chaos. The weak, the cowards, the deserters were eager to listen to Communistic slogans and to follow them as the shortest road to peace and to their homes.

Kiev, the beautiful capital of the Ukraine, was as gay and colorful as ever. It was in a state of animation and excitement, of perpetual festival.

A great crowd, well-dressed and noisy, filled Kretschatic, the main street and the meeting place of Kievlians. Except for the many men in uniform, there were no signs of war or revolution. The open markets along the main street were bulging with fruits and vegetables, with flowers of various shades and scents. Romancing was in the air. Girls and boys rambled together on the broad sidewalks or sat in open cafés.

I stopped at army headquarters, where my friend Dr. Michael Maidansky was in charge of the medical division of the southwestern front. It was a joy to meet this open-minded man once again, after more than a year's separation. He complained to me about "the political naïveté" of the Ukrainian separatists, their selfishness and nearsightedness, which seriously endangered the future of democratic Russia. "These cheap politicians," he said, "refuse to send bread and other foodstuffs to the East. They are criminals, and yet they claim to be liberals and believers in democracy. . . . A funny interpretation of that great word . . ."

I mentioned that I was going to visit the Pyatakoffs. "A most peculiar family," he said, and he told me something of their history. The elder Pyatakoff, head of the family, had died several years before. He was a self-made man, a foreman at a small sugar refinery. He built his own refinery and developed it into the largest in the Ukraine, becoming one of the richest men in Kiev. "He was one of the few millionaires in our city. Perhaps a multimillionaire." The old man lived very modestly, however, and left a huge fortune in trust to his three children.

"The eldest son, Nicholas, is carrying on the father's business. The second brother, Gregory, became a militant Bolshevik and has been in jail more than once. He hates his brother, and the hatred is mutual. I've heard," Maidansky explained, "that Gregory's bolshevism is much more emotional outburst than logical conviction. A sort of escapism. I know very little about the youngest son, Michael."

"He's my friend," I inserted. "He's the one who asked me to visit his family when I go through Kiev."

I had first met Michael Pyatakoff in the zoological laboratory of the University of St. Petersburg, while I was still a junior. He was my neighbor at the working table. Very tall, well over six feet, with long, light blond hair, a mustache and beard, he looked a typical Chekhov hero. He was very silent and an excellent worker. I knew that he was the son of a highly religious father, and I was quite perplexed by his materialistic beliefs.

"Well," said Maidansky, "watch your step and don't run into Gregory. I met him only the other day in the public library, and he must still be in the city. Incidentally, when he's in Kiev, he stays in the family home. I assume, to annoy his brother. . . ."

And so I went to visit the Pyatakoffs.

Dr. Maidansky drove me to their house and left me. "Be careful. . . . The Pyatakoffs are political dynamite," he warned, and said good-bye.

The street, high on the hills surrounding Kiev, was enchanting. It was strangely quiet under the tall lindens that crowded along the sidewalks. There was no sound, no clamor of voices, no living things visible. Romantically called Under the Lindens, the street appeared to be engulfed in meditation, in a Nirvanistic stage. The Pyatakoff house, large, white, built in colonial style, with marble pillars and two large wings, was silent. It was surrounded by a large cherry orchard and tea-rose bushes.

I rang the bell. There was no immediate response, but after a time the massive door was slowly opened and a very old butler admitted me to the hall. I requested him to announce my arrival to Nicholas Pyatakoff. The butler was deaf and it took me some time to make him understand what I wanted. He asked me to follow him and, walking slowly and painfully, brought me to a large, semidark, heavily furnished room. A few minutes later, Pyatakoff entered. I liked him at once. Very tall, blond and clean-shaven, he vaguely resembled his brother Michael, but was without his sulkiness. Open-hearted, friendly and direct, he impressed me with his sincerity and sprightliness. Here is a healthy specimen of the human race, I thought.

We sat down before a fire and drank Ukrainian wine, brought by the old butler. We talked about Russia and communism, Ukrainian nationalism, his sugar business—which was prospering in spite of chaotic conditions—the latest books by Bunin and Kuprin, his hopes and future plans.

His talk was invigorating, his ideas sound and stimulating. And yet, listening to him, I began to feel as if I were in the presence of a dead man—or one who soon would be dead. It was a most peculiar sensation and had no justification whatsoever. Never had I experienced such a strong intuition, and I hope I shall never experience it again. It was depressing and even frightening. For here I saw, in my imagination, a healthy young man doomed to die. I became so engrossed with this feeling that I no longer heard what he was saying.

"You are distraught," Pyatakoff reproached me, smiling.

I protested mildly.

"Are you going to Petrograd?" he asked.

I nodded.

"Will you see Kerensky? Do you know him?"

"I might. I know him quite well. I might, if it's necessary."

"It is. I have an urgent message for Kerensky, a message of prime importance. I intended to go see him myself, but I can't leave Kiev now. May I depend on you?" he asked anxiously.

I assured him I would deliver his message to the Premier.

Then, with seeming reluctance, he recounted the story of his brother Gregory, who had been converted to communism some years before and become intimately associated with Lenin. "His hatred for our family and all that we are is unbelievable. Yet he retains his rooms in this house and stays here when he's in Kiev. Why? I don't know. Perhaps for his conspiratorial work." Gregory had arrived in Kiev a few days before, he said, in a state of agitation. He had many visitors during this time, and several meetings were held in his rooms in complete secrecy.

Nicholas admitted with some embarrassment that he had become so suspicious of his brother's behavior that he decided to search his room while he was absent. "I'd never done such a shameful thing before . . . but I felt that it was my duty as a citizen of this free country to find the cause of all the agitation."

He found a paper hidden in Gregory's desk. It was a letter, written in Lenin's own hand on a plain sheet of paper, to Gregory Pyatakoff. The letter informed Gregory that the armed revolt against Kerensky's government was planned for October 16 and that he, Gregory, was to organize a group of five hundred faithful Communists, arm them, and bring them to the capital a few days before.

"Here is the letter," Nicholas said, handing it to me.

I gasped in astonishment. "But this letter. . . ." I stammered. "It's fantastic. . . . Yet it's authentic. . . . I know Lenin's writing. It's his." And at once I made my decision. "I will leave for Petrograd today and see Kerensky when I arrive."

Nicholas shook my hands warmly. "Thanks. I am greatly relieved. . . ." I left him hastily, and in the hall I almost collided with a tall, bearded man, almost identical in appearance to Michael.

"Who are you?" he rudely asked me. "What are you doing here?"

I explained that I was a friend of his brother Michael and was looking for him.

"He is not here. . . . I hope you have not seen my other brother? He's a scoundrel."

This man is mad, I thought; what nonsense is he saying? Without answering him, I hurried from this strange house where a multimillionaire's son who was a conspirator against his country and a militant Communist still felt at home and behaved like a pig.

Some days later I read in the Petrograd newspapers that, in Kiev, Nicholas Pyatakoff, director of a sugar refinery and leader of the Liberal party, was bloodily murdered in the night by a group of unknown armed men who had entered his house on Under the Lindens Street. Pyatakoff's rooms were searched by the intruders and his safe and furniture were ransacked. Robbery was suspected, the newspapers said. But I knew better. I knew that it was Gregory who, finding that the letter from Lenin was missing, decided to take the law into his own hands.

Three months later, on January 5, I met Gregory Pyatakoff in the hall of the Tauride Palace, where the convention of the All Russian Constituent Assembly took place. He recognized me immediately.

"How are your brothers?" I asked him innocently.

"My older brother was killed. . . . He got what he deserved," he answered briskly.

Some years later, I learned that Gregory Pyatakoff, at that time one of the top men in the Soviet government, was liquidated by Stalin. I felt no regrets.

In the turbulent years that followed this incident, when I, a laboratory scientist completely engrossed in medical research and alien to political adventures, was thrown by fate into the midst of the civil war; when my life became a matter of day-to-day survival and was filled with perils, I could no longer dismiss premonition lightly. When I was in Moscow's Boutyrki Prison, condemned to death by the Communists and expecting any moment to be called for execution, premonition told me that I would live. And when I decided to make the hazardous trip across Soviet territory to Ufa to attend the convention of the All Russian Constituent Assembly, I embarked with a light heart and a full sense of assurance that I would succeed, in spite of the fact that the odds were a thousand to one that I would be caught by the Communists.

Chapter 6

THE MALADY OF
APPEASEMENT

I ARRIVED in Petrograd on the morning of October 7. It was the October of 1917, which was to change the course of Russian history. It was a cold, brisk day, clear and sunny, unusual for autumn. Riding a tram on Nevsky Prospect, the capital's main street, I saw no signs of the unrest or agitation I had expected. The automat where I stopped off for a snack was jammed with men drinking vodka and eating caviar and salmon sandwiches. Beautiful Alexandrovsky Square, famous for Czarist military parades, was full of animation. Cars and cabs, cavalrymen and marching troops gave the impression of great, well-organized activity. Approaching the Winter Palace, located on the northern side of the square, I was impressed with the number of cars. There were no fewer than seventy of various colors and models parked at the curb.

The Prime Minister's reception room was filled with visitors, all waiting for an appointment with Kerensky. The nice-looking reception clerk shook her head hopelessly when I made my request. "There is a waiting list of thirty-two, and some of them have been waiting three days." I insisted that I had a message of prime importance, but in vain. "Sorry," she said, "I cannot help you."

An army general standing nearby, with many military decorations on his chest, condoled with me: "It's easier to get into heaven than to obtain an audience with Kerensky."

Suddenly I remembered that a schoolmate of mine, Boris Flekkel, was one of Kerensky's administrative secretaries. The receptionist announced me to him. In no time he came down and brought me to his richly decorated office, apparently a former czarina's reception room.

I showed Lenin's letter to Flekkel. He was not surprised at all. "The situation is very grave, I know, but HE doesn't believe it. He doesn't want to believe it. His party leaders don't believe it. . . . They're all perfectly sure that the Bolsheviks will never even attempt to seize power. Naïve. Childish. But true."

"But Kerensky is not a stupid man? He's a politician of long standing and experience," I protested.

"It's a sad story," continued Flekkel. "He's a changed person. He shrinks from reality when it's unpleasant. No, there's no sense in your seeing Kerensky. He wouldn't pay any attention to your warning. You might only irritate him. And, anyhow, he's too busy now with the pre-Parliament's session. I think he's leaving in a day or two for the front. It's hopeless. . . ."

"What shall I do?" I cried in despair.

"Frankly, I don't know. There are a few men who might listen to you. Kishkin, Tchaikovsky, Plekhanoff . . . but they have no influence, or very little, with Kerensky. You might go and see Colonel Polkovnikov, military governor of the Petrograd district," Flekkel added. "He's in charge of the defense of the capital. But I'm afraid you'd be disappointed meeting him. However, give it a try. I'll make an appointment for you. His office is on the south side of Alexandrovsky Square."

Flekkel, very small as a boy, with blue-black hair and vivid dark eyes, was one of the best pupils in our school. He became involved in the Socialist movement very early and joined the Social-Revolutionary party. He studied law and was graduated with honors from the University of St. Petersburg. An army private when the February revolution occurred, he was assigned to Kerensky's staff. There was great sincerity and conviction in him and very little of the politician. He admired his chief, and yet he had the courage to acknowledge the Prime Minister's inability to cope with the tragic situation. He remained in Petrograd after the fall of Kerensky's government and was killed a year later by the Communists when he tried to cross the Samara front.

Absorbed in my thoughts, I was entering Alexandrovsky Palace when a deep voice abruptly stopped me.

"What are you doing here in this bedlam of the Russian revolution?" I turned my head and saw a tall, strongly built officer. At first I did not recognize him. After a moment I realized it was Boris Savinkoff in the uniform of an army colonel.

I explained my mission and the trouble I was having in trying to get some action on Lenin's conspiracy.

"It's hopeless, dear friend, utterly hopeless," he consoled me. "I don't understand what has happened to all our revolutionaries. . . . Where is their active spirit of the past?

Their courage and prompt action? Where is it? It disappeared the moment they took over the government. Lenin and company should have been arrested long ago. . . . I insisted . . . I begged Kerensky. . . . No response . . . I wash my hands of the whole business. . . . Everywhere the most appalling appeasement . . ."

"Not everywhere . . ." I protested.

"Everywhere in our party . . ."

And he left as abruptly as he had come.

Savinkoff was a legendary figure in the Russian revolutionary movement. Hated by the Bolsheviks, he in turn hated them with a passion approaching madness.

Many books and stories were written about him and his fight against the Czarist regime. The Russian youth of my generation were fascinated by his superhuman audacity and courage, his ability to meet the most difficult and apparently hopeless situations with exceptional equanimity. To us, he was a hero, the personification of an idealist-revolutionary and modern gentleman-adventurer, almost a superman. He was a writer and poet of unusual brilliance and talent, yet a man of action *par excellence*. I met him on one or two occasions when I was still in high school, and later on, when he became a member of Kerensky's government.[1]

Ten years after our brief encounter in Alexandrovsky Palace, I was to meet Savinkoff again, under quite different circumstances. I was visiting the famous Monte Carlo aquar-

---

1. Boris Savinkoff served as a political commissar with the Seventh Army until July 30, 1917, when he was appointed Deputy Minister of War. In connection with General Laurus Kornilov's revolt against Kerensky's government, Savinkoff was dismissed one month later and replaced by Colonel Verkhovsky.

ium and strolling through the Casino. Distractedly, I was observing the roulette wheels and the gambling crowd, when my attention was attracted to a man at one of the tables who was winning heavily. His calmness and indifference to his luck surprised me. He was there, physically, yet his mind and thoughts were elsewhere. At once I recognized him as Savinkoff. He was older and almost bald.

For many minutes I stood nearby, watching his game and unnoticed by him. His stakes were very high, and he played carelessly as if wishing to lose. Luck was with him. He won again and again, on red and black, on zero, against the most peculiar odds. And then he stopped. He collected the chips, turned, and his eyes met mine. He smiled. But his smile was sad, almost desperate.

"Not a chance; I came here to lose my winnings from yesterday. But I couldn't do it. . . . Too bad." I didn't understand what lay behind his words. He invited me to the terrace bar and, as we drank sherry, he began to talk.

"All my life I've been blessed by fortune. I come out of the most harebrained adventures unscratched. For some time now I've been considering a trip to Soviet Russia, incognito of course, to resume revolutionary activity against the Soviet regime. I can't live the inactive life of an exile. The strength of the Soviet regime is in their do-nothing adversaries. All my plans are made. I'm going to cross the border into Russia, where I have devoted friends still faithful to democracy."

He stopped and sat in silence for several minutes. I did not break in on his thoughts.

"It's not a hopeless task. No. I fought against the Czarist government under similar conditions. . . ."

"Not quite," I objected.

"No, not quite," he agreed. "Their Cheka is more active,

their power is farther reaching. Yes, the odds are greater. But you have to take the chance . . . and yet . . ."

"You hesitate?"

"Not exactly. But I have a strange premonition that my mission will be a failure. A trip to Soviet Russia will destroy me. Still, I cannot accept the premonition. I reject it. It's a sign of weakness, I tell myself. But it persists, it affects my self-confidence. For days I've been undecided, and this is foreign to my nature. I've almost been sick. Mentally exhausted. I've even made a test."

"A test of what?"

"A test of my luck. I decided to gamble for three days at roulette. For three days, two hours a day. I decided to play without any system, carelessly, throwing money on red and black, on zero, on any other number. If I lose the money I start out with, I said to myself, I shall not go to Russia. It would mean that Fate is against me, that luck isn't with me anymore."

"Have you played three days?"

"Yes," he answered gravely. "I've played three days. Each day I've won a fortune. I'm not happy about it. My premonition is stronger than ever. But I'm going to go ahead with my plans."

"Do you think you should?"

"I must. It's my destiny, or whatever it is we call by this name."

He shook my hand. "Adieu, my friend. It *is* an adieu."

With any other man, this scene would have seemed melodramatic. But this was Savinkoff, a man of iron nerves and unlimited will power. I was impressed.

Ten months later, the Moscow newspapers reported that a suspicious-looking man was arrested trying to enter the Russian border near Czechoslovakia. He was soon identified as the "archenemy of the Soviet government," Boris Savinkoff. He was brought to Moscow. The Communist newspapers were jubilant. "The dirty dog, the spy of Wall Street is captured," they said.

Several weeks passed without any news of his fate. Then the Soviet newspapers published Savinkoff's confession. According to this confession, the authenticity of which was never proved, he acknowledged his guilt, his regret, his admiration for the Soviet regime. A few more weeks passed without any news, then a brief bulletin from Moscow informed the world that Savinkoff had taken his own life by falling from the seventh floor of the Moscow prison where he was confined. Was he killed? Or was it suicide? Did he confess, or was this a lie? Was he betrayed by friends when he crossed the Russian border, or was this an accident? It all remains a mystery still, many years after his death. Perhaps it was predestined that he should go to Russia and die there under the most cruel and humiliating circumstances.

Colonel Polkovnikov, a youngish-looking man in his late thirties, received me amiably. I showed him Lenin's letter. He was not impressed. "Perhaps," he said, "it's a forgery." I patiently explained to him the circumstances under which I had got hold of the letter. His thoughts wavered for a few minutes. At last he made up his mind what to do.

"Leave this letter with me and I shall bring it to the attention of Kerensky."

I flatly refused.

"This document is of prime importance and I don't want it to be lost in your files, Colonel."

"It is safe with me. . . . But, anyhow, our policy is that of a true democracy. We fight our enemies by democratic means and not by police measures."

"Do you mean," I inquired, "that you fight a conspiracy against the government with conciliatory gestures and discussion?"

"Yes," he admitted. "We cannot arrest Lenin and his followers. . . ."

"Why not?"

"My good fellow, they are our brothers in the democratic revolution."

"Are they?" I almost shouted. "If they overthrow the present government by armed force, what will you do? Talk with them? Try to convince them that they act undemocratically?"

"They will never do such a foolish thing. . . . This is all imagination on the part of the scared bourgeoisie. . . ."

"Thank you, Colonel, for the enlightening conversation." I left him without saying good-bye.

In his anteroom, I collided with Kamkoff, a handsome man whom I knew from the university. He was a left-wing Socialist, and he and his faction had joined the Communist attacks against Kerensky's government.

"What are you doing here, Kamkoff?" I asked him. "You should be in Smolnii."

Taken by surprise, he murmured, "I'm visiting my friend Polkovnikov."

Two weeks later, at 3:00 o'clock on the afternoon of October 25, Colonel Polkovnikov, the military governor of Petrograd, was dismissed for inefficiency and appeasing behavior toward the Communists. It was on the day of the fall of Kerensky's government.[2]

I was in Alexandrovsky Square again, undecided on my

2. "Kishkin, enraged by his inertia, fired Polkovnikov." *The History of the Second Russian Revolution*, Paul Miliukoff, v. 1(3), Russko-Bolgarskoye Isd., Sophia, 1922, p. 227.

next step. So far, I had accomplished nothing. Lenin's letter was still burning my inside pocket, and my promise to Nicholas Pyatakoff was still unfulfilled. In despair and perplexity, I went to visit my old friend and professor Islomin, who lived a few blocks from where I stood.[3]

It is often said that the teaching in public high schools everywhere is too formalistic, if not pedantic. The schools are accused of teaching youth nothing but bare facts. They teach but do not educate. It is claimed that the word "educator" is misused when applied to public-school teachers. Perhaps there is a good deal of truth in this. It was certainly true of the public-school teachers in the Russia of the past. Yet there were many striking exceptions to this general rule. One was George Islomin, our teacher in ancient history. He was much more educator than teacher. He cared little, if at all, if we learned chronological data, the year of this or that event, the names of emperors or kings, the wars and the battles. Actually, he taught us the history of civilization, the story of man as such.

He told us that there is a psychic evolution of the human race, through which man is gradually liberated from his atavistic and primitive inheritance. The primitive forces inbred in the human race are as old as the animal world itself. They were born of violence, fear, and ignorance, and are simply a composite of all the primitive instincts of our animal ancestors. They have been the prime source of human misery through mankind's history. Islomin taught us that modern humanitarian civilization was trying to control our atavistic drives through moral education. It was idealistic in that it

3. The names of my friends Islomin, Demidoff, and Serk are fictitious. Their true names are not given because their relatives are behind the Iron Curtain.

believed in humanity, in man, in human nature, as guided by the psychic evolution.

Again and again he pointed out to us that the basic attribute of living matter is an extensively progressive individuation. On every side of life, one witnesses the manifestation of individualistic trends—in our reflexes and reactions, in our thoughts and ideas, and most of all in our creative activity. These individualistic tendencies of the living world, and of man in particular, reflect the manifestations of the freedom instinct. Both individuality and freedom serve as a fertile substratum for creative evolution. Without these fundamental attributes, evolution of the human race would be improbable, if not impossible.

The democratic doctrine is a product of these basic, positive attributes of the human race. It reflects the fundamental drivings of man to develop and express individuality and freedom. For thousands of years, the human race has been fighting for the realization of its dream, instinctively and almost blindly nursing the image of Free Man. But again and again, through the centuries of human civilization, the atavistic forces inbred in man's nature have tried to suppress, and have suppressed, this trend. Despots and tyrants, dictators and fanatics have annihilated the feeble attempts of man to create a democratic state.

It is fallacy, Islomin declared, to believe that an ideal democratic society can be built if it is not composed of truly democratic members. It is based on faith in the human race and its future, in the goodness of man. Without such belief, democracy cannot exist, it must fall under the attacks of the aggressive, atavistic-minded elements of mankind.

Vividly, Islomin painted pictures of the past, pictures of man's unsuccessful attempts to live according to democratic principles. And yet, in spite of all the dark lessons of the past,

Islomin believed and he called on us to believe in the future of democratic doctrine, as the sanest and highest concept ever created by man's imagination.

Islomin was a strange man. Soft-spoken, generous, and kind, he appeared to be detached emotionally from everyday existence. His tolerance and open-mindedness were unlimited. He was ready to forgive and find an excuse for every wrong inflicted upon him by friends and acquaintances. "I live, emotionally, over the span of a thousand years," he would say, smiling when some injustice was done to him. "I measure man's behavior from the viewpoint of eternity." He called himself a pragmatist in his emotions. "Not in my ideas," he would add. "There I am a Platonist." He lived very moderately, paying very little, if any, attention to his personal material comfort.

A man of independent income, he spent most of his money on poor students, contributing to their tuition fees at the university. His friends were many. We were all devoted to him and went to him for consolation and help in any difficulties we might have.

His personal life was a paradox of emotions. While an instructor in history at the University of St. Petersburg, he met a girl named Catherine Volchovsky, who was a student at the Neurological Institute. From a well-to-do Southern family, Katia chose psychiatry for her profession, against the wishes of her parents. Brilliant and studious, she was self-willed to an obsessive degree. She developed a friendship with Islomin on a purely intellectual basis. They discussed new books and magazine articles, went to the theater and concert together, and taught at the same school for orphan children.

"We were good friends. Nothing else," insisted Islomin.

"There was never a hint of love between us." Was she pretty?
I would not say so. She was small, with a fine face, and she
usually dressed in black. She was a moralist in a peculiar
sense of this word. She believed that man must be honest,
free of vices, and should have a strong sense of responsibility.
At the university, she lived a spartan existence, in an un-
heated room, on bread and milk, working very hard and
denying herself all pleasures, with the exception of spending
an evening out, now and then, with Islomin. Her parents
offered her all the money she might have needed for a more
comfortable existence, but she refused their help and earned
her livelihood by giving lessons in French and English.

One summer, while on vacation in her native town, Katia
met a young man of bad reputation named Victor Perlin. He
was very handsome, indeed, a lazy, easy-going, good-for-
nothing man, slightly older than she. She fell in love with
him and, to the horror of her family, announced her intention
of marrying him.

"She never *really* loved this man," Islomin insisted. "I
haven't any doubt about this."

She soon learned, however, the worst about Victor: he was
a local gigolo, supported by a rich old woman. To Katia, an
ardent moralist, it was a terrific shock. Yet she still was sure
she loved him, and she was unable to control her own emotions. But now she decided to reform him. He promised
more than once to change his behavior. For several months,
she tried by every means to convert him to the morality of a
"true man," but he was always evasive, pleasantly conciliatory, attentive. Victor was an experienced seducer, and this
daughter of a rich landlord and army colonel was so deeply
involved with him that he considered her reforming attitude
a tremendous joke. He soon found that he had misjudged her.

She was unable to stand any longer the inner conflict of

overwhelming love and intellectual conviction. She decided to try a solution, a cruel and incredible solution.

"Katia told me this morbid story in detail," Islomin said to me. "One morning, she invited Victor for a walk along the prairie road. He was very pleased indeed. But he did not know that she had taken her father's army revolver along. It was in her purse, with a pen and a sheet of paper. When they had walked far into the prairie, she confronted him with a demand to give an immediate answer: would he live as an honest man? would he work hard? 'I might,' he answered laughing, 'if you promise to marry me.' Such an amazing little girl, he thought. She was not satisfied with his answer and persisted in her questioning. 'I love you,' he said, trying to appease her. 'Isn't that enough for you?'

"Of course, it was not. She drew the revolver from her purse and ordered him to write a suicide note. He still did not believe in the seriousness of her threat, and so, jokingly, he wrote that he was taking his own life because he was tired of living a senseless existence.

" 'And now,' he said, 'come here and kiss me, my little darling.' Instead, she shot him in the chest. Half-mad, in a daze, she returned to her home, leaving him and the revolver on the road.

"A traveling salesman found him and brought him to the hospital. He was gravely wounded, but survived. The strange thing was that he never said a word to the police about her. He simply said he had tried to kill himself. Katia hurried away to Petrograd. And here she was, unhappy, miserable, her spirit broken, without the will to live. I asked her to marry me. She consented. And that's the story of my marriage."

But this was not the end of the story. For two years they lived together uneventfully, a contented if not exactly a happy couple. One night she did not return for dinner. She did not come home for five days and nights. The only news he had from her during that time was a brief postcard informing him that she had had to go away for a few days. On the sixth day, while he was eating his cold supper alone, she arrived. He had guessed what had happened. He offered her supper and they ate in silence. After they had eaten, he lit his pipe and casually asked her, "Was Victor in town?"

"Yes, he was," she admitted. "I was with him, I slept with him."

He continued to smoke his pipe.

"Do you want me to leave you?"

"To leave me?" He was astonished. "Why?"

"I was unfaithful to you."

"What if you were? Let me ask you a question: why did you leave *him*?"

"It was all a mistake. I found out I didn't love him. I think I love you. . . ."

He changed the subject and never again returned to it. Their married life went on as before, without any apparent deviation in his attitude toward Katia. The only change was in her. She became extremely jealous of Islomin and objected if any woman was attentive to him.

One day, shortly before I left for the front, I met Katia's brother, Stephan Volohovsky, at the Islomins' home. He was the handsomest man I had ever seen. Fresh from the front in his Imperial Dragoon uniform, glittering with military decorations, he was a striking contrast to his intellectual sister. But I quickly found that my first impression was all wrong. Like his sister, he was a moralist, but on another psychological level. He was obsessed with religion.

He was in a talkative mood and told me that the war was unbearable to him. The sense of guilt for participating in "killing my brothers" was so strong in him that "I am losing my mind," he frankly admitted. "I can't leave the army . . . and I can't participate in this butchery any longer." He had taken sick leave from the army and was spending his time in churches and reading the Old and New Testaments. "I did everything possible to be killed. But I wasn't. . . . God wants me to bear this heavy task. . . . But I'm on the verge of going to pieces. . . ."

I liked him very much. There was almost a saintliness in his personality and a sincerity bordering on greatness of spirit.

A few days after our meeting, I read a terrible story in the Petrograd newspapers. It told how, on Good Friday, a well-dressed man came to a private hospital on the Isle of Vassilii. He requested a room for several days for a check-up. He assured the chief physician that there was nothing wrong with him but exhaustion and bad spells. He gave his name as Stephan Volchovsky and paid in advance for three days. He was very calm and polite, and nothing in his attitude indicated mental disorder. He went to his room and took a bath, but refused his supper.

An hour later, suppressed moans were heard in his room. A nurse and a doctor rushed in and found the patient lying unconscious on the bed. A heavy stream of blood was flowing from his left eye socket, and in his right hand he clutched the bloody eye. On a little table beside a New Testament was a piece of paper with a few words written in large, firm letters.

"If thine eye offend thee, pluck it out. . . . Lord be merciful to your poor servant who was too weak to overcome his vanity." It was not signed.

I had had no opportunity to see the Islomins before my departure for the front, and for the first time since the tragic death of Katia's brother I ascended to their fourth-floor apartment on Millionaia Street.

Both were home, and they warmly welcomed me. "I expected you, my friend," remarked Islomin. "In fact, I was sure you would come tonight. . . . No, no . . . no trace of premonition. Much simpler . . . it was Flekkel who called me. And there is a surprise for you. We invited your friends Serk and Demidoff for dinner. They're quite excited by your coming."

"You might help us to calm Serk down," Katia hurriedly remarked. "Oh, nothing serious, except that he became a leftist Socialist and is all for the Bolsheviks."

"Serk? But what has he got to do with politics?" I asked, perplexed.

"Let's not argue right now about Serk and his mental aberrations. . . . When he comes you'll have plenty of time to find out what's wrong with him. But first tell us about your problems. . . . Flekkel mentioned a mysterious letter you brought with you. . . ."

I told them about my visit to Pyatakoff. Showing them Lenin's letter, I bitterly complained about the appeasement of Bolsheviks that was going on in government circles. Islomin chuckled.

"I knew it. . . . Didn't I say, Katia, that I knew he had forgotten my lessons in history? You think in terms of years or decades, instead of having a vision of the whole course of time through which civilization is slowly moving. You're anxious and upset that the Bolsheviks should be taking the upper hand in their fight with the democratic government. You're afraid they'll overthrow Kerensky's regime. Aren't you?"

"Of course I am," I acknowledged.

"Calm yourself, my friend. Be prepared for the worst. The

Bolsheviks will overthrow Kerensky and take power into their hands. . . . And it may be soon. I could have told you that six months ago. . . ."

"It's incredible," I protested.

"Incredible? A more proper word would be 'unavoidable.' Let's analyze the situation as an impartial historian should do. The February revolution brought the democratic intelligentsia to power. You agree? All right. Who are they? Who are the people that surround our Prime Minister? Who in fact is he? An idealistic humanitarian with a moderate, vague Socialistic concept. As such, Kerensky, along with his followers, is a believer in man and the goodness of man. In a sense, they are like the ancient Christians. Not unlike their brothers, the first Christians, they have no other weapon to fight with than their beliefs, their Faith. As the foxy Polkovnikov told you, they are using nothing but democratic measures and democratic weapons. Meaning no effective weapons at all in this bloody civil-war epoch. Of course, he only repeated what every one of Kerensky's fellows would say. To them, the Bolsheviks are brothers. To use police measures, to arrest Lenin, to shoot this whole crew of aggressors and unscrupulous adventurers would be a violation of their fundamental principles. Democracy . . . Democracy, to them, means a fraternity of true human beings. Democracy signifies love and confidence in a fellowman. The power of the first Christians was that they left politics aside. They didn't crave political power, power on this earth. They called for a heaven after death. Christianity was an escape from life. But our modern neo-Christian friends have taken power into their own hands, they call for a heaven on earth. A very laudable attempt, but you can't fight for power unless you're ready to use all possible weapons and to fight hard and cruelly. Thus there is a contradiction between reality and ideology. No, my poor friend, Kerensky must go down. It's a historical axiom!"

"It's a terrible prognosis," I murmured.

"Console yourself. . . . Look at the history of mankind. . . . When we view history as a steady advance toward freedom, we have to regard exploitation and slavery of all possible kinds as the normal state of man—and the brief epochs of liberty as tremendous achievements. My goodness! For eight full months our long-suffering mother-Russia has been free; she's had complete liberty, she's been living a truly democratic life. My friend, this is an enormous achievement from the historical viewpoint. And we must thank the Lord and the Kerensky regime for this admirable experiment in freedom. Yes, we must be grateful to them and not attack them for appeasing the dark forces which assault them."

"But the Bolsheviks? What do you expect from them?" I inquired, appalled by my friend's logic.

"The Bolsheviks? What do I expect from them? Here we can be realistic. Bolshevism, or Lenin's communism, is nothing but a continuation of Czarist despotism and absolutism. They use new words, new slogans. They use them very cleverly, I admit; they dress themselves in clothing that's attractive to the simple folk, but their real goal is as old as the world itself: they want power. They will bring a despotic rule more cruel than any that Russia has suffered for centuries. They disregard humanitarianism, they despise it. They will enslave the Russian people for decades to come. They will turn Russian civilization back to feudal days, and this is the price we shall pay for the eight or nine months of democratic honeymoon. You and many others would say this is too high a price. I, a historian, say it is an insignificant price when measured in terms of centuries. For we know that the time will come again when the Russian people will be free and live in a democratic state. It shall come. . . . It must come. . . ."

Katia was crying. "It's awful. . . ."

"Does this mean that nothing can be done to stop Lenin?" I asked.

"Nothing," stated Islomin, almost gloomily. "Nothing. Unless the Kerensky group becomes realistic overnight and, while retaining its democratic ideology, starts fighting like a mad dog against the Bolsheviks, using all possible means. But this is an impossibility. It would be a historical paradox. Now, let's not talk any more about this painful subject. Let's have some hors d'oeuvres before our dinner is ready."

Islomin's dispassionate analysis of Russia's situation came to my mind three months later. It was January 5, 1918, the opening day of the All Russian Constituent Assembly. One hundred thousand people thronged the streets around the Tauride Palace, where the Assembly was to convene. They were demonstrating against the Bolsheviks, who threatened to dissolve the Assembly.

I threaded my way through the crowd on Liteinyi Prospect, trying to reach the cordon of Red soldiers who encircled the Palace. I was in a melancholy state of mind, and I thought about William Fitz-Osbert, one of the first Englishmen to lose his life for democratic principles. What a nuisance, I thought, that after seven hundred years one must still fight for liberty and democracy.

At this precise moment, a large group of workmen from the Poutilovsky factory tried to penetrate the military cordon. At the head of it, I saw Islomin. He held in his hands a banner reading, "Long Live Democracy!" When the distance between the Red soldiers and the slowly moving throng became less than fifty feet, the Reds opened fire. They aimed directly into the crowd, singling out the men who carried the banners.

Islomin was shot and fell in the snow. I rushed to his side and with the help of some other men succeeded in bringing him to a nearby house. Fortunately, it was the office of a surgeon, who readily gave him first aid. Islomin was gravely but not fatally wounded. The bullet had gone through his upper left lung. "I know, I know," he said to me, smiling, "you are ready to reproach me for contradictory behavior. I apologize. . . . But we historians are logical only when we're discussing academic postulates."

They arrived shortly before dinner. All three were in uniform. Demidoff, his sister Olga, whom I had met only once before, and Serk. Olga and Serk were engaged. I was quite excited to meet two of my old friends. I learned that Demidoff, an army captain, was assigned as instructor to the Pavlovsky officer's school and Serk was still in training there.

Olga Demidova was a striking girl, with very blond hair and a fine figure. She wore the insignia of a first lieutenant. When I asked what military service she was in, her brother proudly explained that she was a battalion commander in the First Women's Regiment.

"The Women's Regiment?" I was perplexed.

"Koronoky's now idoa . . ." Serk angrily remarked. "Since his reactionary government can't depend on men to defend it, he's been calling on woman volunteers for active service. He, a capitalistic . . ."

"Stop, Nicholas." Olga's voice was icily severe. "I will not tolerate any more of your erratic accusations against Kerensky."

"I'm sorry," Serk replied meekly. "I promise . . ."

Islomin smilingly intervened: "Let Serk give us his views on the present situation in Russia. We're all interested."

Serk gladly responded to this invitation.

"I know that you are all against the Bolsheviks. To me, it's the narrow-mindedness of a shrew-mole. Lenin is opening new horizons to mankind. He's carrying into practice the dreams of Bakunin and other true Communists.[4] He's bringing liberation to the Russian people, after the imperialism of the governing classes and their economic despotism. He will create a heaven on earth and will succeed where Tolstoy failed. The land and factories will belong to the peasants and workers, who will govern the country. We, the writers, poets, musicians, and artists, will help him in this audacious enterprise. You hate the Bolsheviks because you are steeped in bourgeois prejudices. With Lenin we shall introduce eternal peace on earth and liquidate international capitalism. . . ."

"My goodness, what naïveté," Demidoff groaned.

"Who are 'we,' Serk?" asked Islomin.

"We . . . the left Socialists, Kamkoff, Steinberg, and many others, including me, who are tired to death of your bourgeois trampling, your coddling of the dying class. . . . We're not afraid of blood and killing, for this is the greatest of all social revolutions, inspired by our greatest leader, Lenin. . . ."

"Outrageous!" cried Olga.

"He's a baby in politics."

"A baby!" shouted the enraged Serk. "I am not a baby. . . . But I have a vision, the wisdom of a clairvoyant. . . . I foresee the wonderful time when there will be no poor, no suppressed, when there will be complete equality, political and

---

4. Bakunin was, of course, an anarchist, but the Russian Communists considered him to be their predecessor.

economic, in this world, and the Bolsheviks will bring it to us. . . ."

"I refuse to listen to this idiot any more!" shouted Olga. "It's all over between us. . . . I won't marry you. . . . I can't marry a man who talks like an infant, who has no common sense, who's as blind as a dozen moles!" And she abruptly left the room.

As if awaking from a deep sleep, Serk cried: "Olga . . . Olga . . . stop. . . ." and ran after her.

"He's in love with her," Demidoff murmured to me, as if to excuse them both. "But now that the children have left us, we may talk business. . . . I'm glad you came. We need more men in our little group. . . . Islomin doesn't belong to our group, but he's with us. We have decided to liquidate Lenin and some of the other leaders of this reactionary movement. They threaten the very existence of democratic civilization in our country. We feel sure that once Lenin is destroyed, the Bolshevik movement will lose its impetus and will easily be brought under control by our government."

And he told me that an active group of men who were disgusted with the wavering attitude of Kerensky's followers had decided to take the initiative into their own hands. Their plans were already elaborated.

"We shall use automatics," Demidoff gloomily concluded. "And we need an extra man to help, a man we can depend upon completely."

I agreed.

As I left that hospitable home, I was very distressed by the emotional conduct of my friend Serk. From my early youth I had had a sort of protective feeling for him. For he was a dreamer, a poet at heart, endowed with a sincere and naïve soul, a man of another world. And as I walked that night along the banks of the Neva, my thoughts went back to my early encounter with Nicholas Serk, who never had been able to accept the realities of life and lived in a world of fantasy and imagination.

Chapter 7

MY FRIEND SERK

D₀ you believe in God?"
The speaker was a small, eleven-year-old boy with curly hair
and large, blue, questioning eyes.

"What?" I asked, astounded.

We had just got acquainted, during noon recess in the
school garden. I was a class above him and inclined to feel a
bit contemptuous toward this strange little boy. But he repeated the question, very seriously and calmly.

"Do you believe in God?"

"But, of course."

"That's good. If you didn't believe you would not be able
to live." And he asked in a whisper: "I realized that yesterday
in church." Then he sighed. "I felt very unhappy yesterday—
so full of doubt. And so I went into the church. Don't you
see, my mind was just full of questions, and it almost seemed
that life wasn't worth living. But in church I prayed and

119

prayed, kneeling there for a long time; and everything became clear. Do you understand me?"

"Of course I do." I grew a little impatient. His questions, his reasoning, seemed peculiar and obscure. In those days I was not given to meditating about life. I was enthusiastic about sports and read nothing but tales of adventure. It was a shock to encounter such solemn thoughts in a boy even younger than I, thoughts far beyond his years and mine.

He continued, more seriously still: "Let's be friends. It's very hard to live when you're as lonely as I am." He gave another deep sigh. "I'm frightfully lonely. . . . Imagine, yesterday my mother scolded me terribly. I wanted to cry, but I didn't. It happened at dinner. I asked her: 'Mama, why live? Why do we live?' And she got cross. 'Don't bother me with your stupid questions,' she said. 'You don't realize what you're talking about.'"

He shrugged his shoulders and looked hurt. "The old people are so funny. Believe me, they hurt us very much. I knew what I was asking about, didn't I?"

He became excited as he talked. He gave me a quick smile and continued. "But in the mornings, when everyone is still asleep in the house, I lie awake and think. . . . I'm always thinking. I look out of the window at the blue sky. Why should it be blue, and not green? And what is beyond the sky? The stars. And beyond the stars? More stars? But there must be an end somewhere. . . . You see, I never cry, but there are times when I want to cry, thinking about the sky, the endless sky. My sister—her name is Lida—always makes fun of me, but she's rather stupid, even if she is four years older than I am. She never thinks about anything. She likes to sleep and eat and dance. . . .

"Do you know, I can go without eating. Last summer,

when mother went away, I didn't eat anything for two days. I thought I was going to die. Our nurse always used to tell me: 'If you don't eat, you'll die.' But I didn't die."

All of a sudden he jumped up—we had been sitting on a bench—and asked mysteriously: "Do you want me to show you? . . ." He took my hand and pulled me after him. "Come on, quick. You'll see. . . ."

He led me to a deserted corner of the garden, a corner no one ever visited. With his hands, he separated some branches. "Look . . ." But his words lost themselves, unspoken. I looked, puzzled. Between the lilac bushes, a few geraniums had been planted. He had planted them in great secrecy. But some mischievous hand had found those flowers and had broken them all, brutally and senselessly. He didn't say a word. He just stood there, speechless and dazed. Then he turned away and covered his face with his hands, crying bitterly.

This was the beginning of my friendship with Nicholas Serk.

From that time onward, on endless occasions, we spent the noon recesses at school together, eating our luncheon and talking. In fact, it was he who did all the talking while I, now and then, inserted a few words. He read extensively. He knew Dostoevsky and Tolstoy by heart and analyzed them with amazing clarity for a boy so young. He had no friends but me. In a sense, he was antisocial and always engrossed in his own thoughts and dreams. Nothing interested him or moved him except the various "ideas" which he absorbed from books and music. He was a good pianist. "I'm happy," he said, "only when I play or hear music." But even in music he preferred Grieg and Scriabin, as if he enjoyed the personal drama of the composers.

He was the son of very wealthy parents. His father, of Norwegian extraction, was in the silk-manufacturing business, while his socially prominent mother belonged to an old aristocratic Russian family. They lived on the Quay of Palaces, the most exclusive district in the capital. The windows of his room opened directly on the Neva, in all its splendor and immensity.

In spite of his family's social prominence, he was sent to a public school. Serk confessed to me that it was his democratic-minded father who so decided, against his mother's opposition. "He did it, I suspect, to irritate my mother. She wanted to enroll me in the Pravoved School."

Although we were close friends, I rarely visited his home while we were in high school. We were not what one would call socially acquainted. Our parents never met one another. And only after graduation, when he was a student at the university, studying literature and philosophy, did I become a frequent visitor at his place. By that time, his mother was dead. He lived in a palacelike mansion built at the time of Catherine the Great and remodeled by his father. The rooms were large, with high ceilings, and richly furnished in the style of Louis XIV. Numerous servants, butlers, maids, and whatnot were at his service. His father adored him and was ready to give him anything he wanted.

Our meetings differed but little from the ones we had held in the school garden. He talked and I listened. I remember one of my visits to his home. It was in the afternoon. The butler brought me to his rooms, which were in semidarkness. Nicholas was sitting in a deep armchair. His eyes were wide open, staring fixedly into space. He was silent, as if he were not willing to see me. "What's the matter with you?" I asked him.

"You've interrupted my . . . dying!"

"Please, Nicholas, don't die," I joked.

"You're always mocking," he gently rebuked me. "But really there is no basis for your irony. I've been reading Johan Reinke's marvelous book *Die Welt als Tod*. I advise you to read it. It has given me a curious, out-of-the-ordinary idea. Of course, you'll think it's queer, but let me tell you about it. . . . My idea is about death. . . . In reality, there is no death, only continuity. Life and death are interchangeable phenomena. There is great truth in this concept. For death is an infringement on harmony; but then harmony is at every moment being disturbed in the organism. And a man, every man as he grows older, is partially dead, for he lacks complete harmony in his organism. So that it's impossible to draw a line between life and death. Do you agree?"

"Certainly not. You talk like a writer, not a biologist. . . ."

Dismissing my objection, he continued: "And, having understood this, I made up my mind to experiment on myself, to try to die. . . . I feel that one must seek and find the harmony of death. There should be no forcing life out of existence. One should be able to die when one wishes, by sheer force of will power. One must desire to die with such concentration of will power that death must come as a victory of the mind over the body. So, today, as soon as it began to get dark, I sat down in this armchair, and by enormous force of concentration I began to feel death creeping slowly nearer and nearer. And then . . . you disturbed me."

"I'm not sorry that I interrupted your experiment in death."

"But what do you think about my idea?"

"A fantasy in controversial and unsound ideas." I was almost rude. But he apparently had not heard me. He was engrossed in his thoughts.

Serk was a writer of promise, having published several forceful short stories and a novel. He once came very near to a complete breakdown. How well I remember that night, a white night in St. Petersburg in June.

During the white nights, I often wished to be slightly in toxicated with dreams. I wanted to believe that the line of demarcation between the existing and nonexistent was effaced, obliterated. All sense of time was lost forever. Clocks were stopped—hadn't the fog engulfed them? And the sense of space, this eternal handicap of man's existence, was dissolved, had disappeared in miraculous fashion.

When St. Petersburg was under the spell of those white nights, houses seemed alive and the white streets, grotesque in the fog, hummed with whispering inhuman voices that sounded like the pealing of church bells.

Somewhere were footsteps, light and airy, the laughter and soft murmuring of trees, the voices of slumbering sphinxes guarding the Neva, the river serene in her loftiness.

In the white nights, living things seemed like phantoms, illusive as ghosts. And the ghosts themselves—realities, living things. During such nights one might see a fast-moving, emaciated man with red beard and shabby clothes looking for unforgettable heroines who were trying to escape from him in the thick fog of the air. It was Dostoevsky, perhaps— always in a hurry, always searching for someone who wanted to suffer, whose suffering was the goal of life.

Now and then, the stony bank of the river was bared and the fog, that dream of old St. Petersburg before sunrise, would float, rising and falling, and at once the illusions of the white nights would fade away, and reality with all its colorfulness and despair bring us back to earth.

Serk led me to the open window.

"Now, I almost feel at home," he murmured. "I've been

losing hold of myself lately. Sometimes I sit reading or thinking. And all of a sudden I see quite clearly that *I* am no longer
within my own body, which is lounging in the armchair. My
body is a stranger to me. And *I*, my real self, am outside of
this body. I seem quite distinctly to see my own face, this
disgusting face with its baby mouth and large, expressionless
eyes. I try to smile, and immediately, as in a mirror, I per-
ceive this smile. . . . It's a painful experience, a sort of split
personality and yet it's not split."

Suddenly he stopped. He opened the door to the balcony.
"Let's go out. Tonight I feel in a solemn mood. I think I've
settled once and for all the problem that's been troubling me
so much all these years. I and society. I versus the human
race. To live alone is a difficult task. For there is a tremendous need in me for human contact, for love, for the expression of my hidden emotions. Yet there's an impenetrable
barrier between me and mankind. I've tried hard to break
through it, to destroy it. But this wall is in me. It's a part of
my ego."

"You're too absorbed in yourself," I said.

"I am. But why? I'm searching for the truth in life, in my
life. I'm not satisfied with placidly living like the man in the
street, like my neighbors and even like you. I'm tormented
by the problems of existence. I can't find any answer to them
either in books or in other men's lives. To me, man's existence
is nothing but a vanity of vanities. He lives, he works, he
struggles, he suffers, or he exerts himself in petty pleasures.
At thirty-five, or even before, his hidden worry is about
death: in ten or fifteen years, sooner or later, he must die. No
other solution is offered to him. The middle-aged man, my
father, my aunt, my uncle, your father, everybody's father is
doomed to a not-too-distant death. Is there a Supreme Power
which directs our fate? Or is there a gigantic nonentity of

senseless and purposeless accidents that governs our planet? There is no answer to this question, no sensible and convincing proof. Yet the human race accepts this situation as normal. Men live like ants. But I can't do this. I rebel against this insoluble problem of human existence. . . . I'm very tired. I'm exhausted. But I've recently begun to arrive at a partial solution of my own existence. . . ."

And, smiling, he began loudly, with great pathos, as if mocking himself, "I vow by old St. Petersburg," and he raised his hand in the direction of the faintly glittering spire of the Admiralty in the distance, "I vow by the gray mist, by the granite quay of the Neva, by the memory of the Great Peter, who created this magnificent city of seekers of the *truth*, I vow in the name of my city, which itself is laughing at the whole world, at all humanity, and which is living its own life, a life of mist, of snowstorms, of never-ending drama, I vow that I will find the answer to man's existence. And now, let's have champagne, let's be drunk on champagne."

Two months later, Serk tried to kill himself. I was in Sevastopol at that time, doing research at the Marine biological station there, when the news reached me. I returned to St. Petersburg to find that he had almost recovered from his serious head wound and was resting comfortably at home.

I went to see him.

"Still alive?" I asked him, not very gently.

"Apparently I am." He was calm and smiling.

On each side of his forehead I noticed a tiny blue spot. One was a trifle larger and more oval, the other quite round.

"What was the purpose of this experiment of yours?"

"Don't be angry," he gently reproached me. "I was only trying to find out if I was afraid of death. What's wrong with this perfectly natural desire to face the eternal problem of every man?"

"It was quite a dangerous experiment?" I persisted.

"What if it was? Every man's life is full of danger from the time he is born. The shadow of death follows him everywhere . . . disease, accidents, heart failures, whatnot. . . . One night I felt very lonely and restless and unhappy. I decided that I needed some strong stimulus to arouse my desire to live. So I shot myself. . . ."

"Very simple, indeed." I was still irritated.

"No, I wouldn't say so," he said gravely. "It wasn't. It might easily seem so. The facts are simple . . . by themselves. I took my father's gun, stood before a mirror, raised it to my right temple, and fired. . . . That's all. The bullet came out here. . . ." With his finger, he touched the blue spot on the left temple. "They told my father that I had one chance in a thousand of surviving. They were afraid I might lose my eyesight. . . . Well, I'm still here and quite well, except for occasional headaches."

"What foolishness, my God!" I exclaimed.

"It was not foolishness," he said severely. "A man has a right to solve his own problems, his own conflicts. Hasn't he?"

"Weren't you afraid you might kill yourself?"

"I don't know. . . . Perhaps not. I remember those few minutes very clearly. I stood before the mirror with the gun in my hand. A few minutes . . . perhaps hours. It seemed hours. The decision was made, and I knew that I would kill myself. I stood before the mirror and carefully inspected the face I saw there. It was the face of a stranger. He was calm, yet a certain pallor revealed his inner tension. I thought: here is a man who will die soon. Yet there was a sort of apathy, of fatalistic acceptance of the unavoidable end in this face. I tried to think about death and life and immortality. But, instead, the silliest things came to my mind. I remembered that I had borrowed books and that they ought to be returned. But I decided it was too late and it wasn't really worth worrying about. Some gay melody I had heard a few days before suddenly sounded in my ears. Some verses I learned in school. My morning talk with the butler. And I realized at once that my experiment would be a failure, that my subconscious mind or whatever there was in me was trying to escape being confronted with imminent death. My ego refused to meet death face to face. I was on the verge of giving up the experiment, but decided to go ahead anyhow. I fired. My hand was steady. And my face was immobile, masklike. My mind was blank, completely blank when I lost consciousness. . . . And that's all there was to this experiment in death. . . ."

Soon after his complete recovery, Serk left St. Petersburg and for more than a year I never heard from him. One day he called me and asked me to come see him. I found him in a gloomy mood.

"I've been bitten. . . ." he abruptly announced. I learned that he had wandered from one monastery to another. He visited the anchorites in the Solovetsky monastery in the far north and remained with them for many months, fasting for days and craving peace of mind. He was very thin and pale and on the verge of desolation. "Their lives are an escape," he said. "They can't face the tragedy of life. . . . There's no solution for me except insanity."

And then a miracle occurred. A small and apparently insignificant incident broke his isolation from life wide open. It was a cold afternoon in March. The streets of the capital were covered with icy snow and were very slippery. Here and there, horses drawing trucks and carriages would fall down and were unable to get up. Serk was on the Alexandrovsky Bridge, idly watching the people, "who move like ants." An emaciated old horse dragging a heavy truck slipped and fell. The driver, angered by her fall, began to lash the helpless animal. As if awakened by lightning from a long sleep, Serk lost all his normal calmness and indifference. He jumped on the driver like a madman and knocked him down. He rushed to the poor horse and clasped her neck in his arms. And then darkness wrapped his mind. He lost consciousness and awoke two hours later in a hospital.

When I saw him the same evening, back at his home, I found him smiling and happy. "It's a miracle," he said. "Something in me which kept me a prisoner of my ego was destroyed. I lost my inhibitions, my fear, my sadness. Unlike Nietzsche, who experienced the same shock and ended in a mental institution, I was cured. A miracle."

And it was indeed a miracle of psychological paradox. Serk returned to his literary activity and was more eager to mix with people. His antisocial attitude was less pronounced. And now, two years later, I found him in love with a girl and hopelessly involved in pro-Communistic activity. This man whom I loved dearly but had always considered an incurable neurotic, if not a psychotic, a spoiled son of rich parents, ignorant in political matters, had become a leader of the left Socialistic party, an ardent promotor and defender of communism, and an enemy of the democratic government. I decided to see him the next day and try to persuade him to change his strange political ideology.

He was pleased to see me, and we spent an evening talking about old times, our school and our teachers. He was in a gay and even exuberant mood, freely confessing his love for

Olga and his overwhelming absorption with this emotion. He was reluctant to discuss the political quarrel he had had with her or even his political beliefs in general. When I persisted and questioned the rationality of his pro-Communistic inclinations, he became irritable, almost angry.

"I would prefer not to discuss this. I want to remain good friends with you. . . . But, if you wish . . . I can only repeat what I said yesterday. I believe in Lenin's doctrine. I believe that he brings a new world to the suffering human race. I follow him with an open mind yet I haven't joined the Bolshevik party. . . . I will give him my full support, enthusiastically and sincerely. . . ."

"Do you realize," I said, trying to convince him, "that his slogans and doctrines are nothing but cleverly disguised demagoguery?"

But he refused to listen; he was unwilling to be drawn into polemics in a field about which he had but little knowledge. "Why do you want to deprive me of my illusions, even if they are nothing but illusions?" he cried.

I shrugged my shoulders. "All right. . . . Let's not discuss politics anymore. But I warn you, you will pay dearly for your illusions. . . ." And I turned our conversation to more neutral topics.

I had no opportunity to see him again during the next three months but I heard of his fiery speeches at various meetings. Together with Kamkoff and Steinberg, he contributed greatly to the victory of communism in Russia. His sincerity, his enthusiasm, his unlimited belief in Lenin appealed to those who still were ready to give support to the democratic government. Without fellow travelers like Serk, the triumph of communism in Russia would hardly have been possible.

Two years went by. The honeymoon of the Communists with the left Socialists had long since ended. Kamkoff and many others perished in Soviet prisons. Some, more clever or lucky, escaped from the cruel police state created by Lenin and his adepts. A few fellow travelers remained, hiding under assumed names and dreaming and hoping against hope to find their lost freedom outside their native country. Among them was Serk. His father had died and his entire fortune was confiscated. He was an embittered man, working as a farmhand near Petrograd. But his bitterness toward communism, which was mounting each day, was not incited by the loss of his fortune. He had never cared about material comfort. Even the shock which he had experienced from the treachery of the Soviet leaders and their betrayal of friends who had helped them to overthrow the Kerensky government was not the actual cause of his hatred for communism. This was all in the past, as far as he was concerned. His bitterness, which was acute and often unbearable, was caused by the absence of Olga. He had lost trace of her in the early days of the October *coup d'état*. As month after month passed without news, his love for her became a growing obsession. He could think of nothing else. He tried to find her, but in vain. Her brother was in the Crimea, but she was not with him. It was not until the end of the second year that he learned from Islomin that she had escaped to Archangel and was working as a nurse in one of the Red Cross hospitals.

They were separated by one thousand miles and by the civil war that was raging everywhere. But Serk's Norwegian inheritance suddenly revealed itself in a superhuman tenacity. He left the farm without a moment's hesitation, penniless but warmly clothed, and set out for the north.

He took the train to Vologda. The winter was severe. Trains moved at a snail's pace for lack of fuel. Hunger hovered over the cities. Prisons were overflowing. In White Russian prisons were the Reds; in Soviet prisons, the Whites. Graves were everywhere: crosses were hastily joined together and badly painted. At times, in the darkness of night, timid figures would steal into the cemeteries, saw off these crosses, and hurry home with them. There, the flames in the brightly burning stoves would lick off the Ivanoffs, Petroffs, and names of other Russian unknowns.

Serk arrived in Vologda after an exhausting trip, and now was confronted with the more difficult task of making his way across the front lines to Archangel. A narrow strip of railroad tracks stretched from one city to the other, and on both sides of it were impassable forests covered with deep snow; villages lay scores of miles apart. On this stretch of tracks, halfway between the two cities, protected at their flanks by forests, two armies stood facing each other—Whites and Reds.

The Whites despised the Reds, and vice versa. On the slightest suspicion, often through some misunderstanding, captured foes were shot on the spot. Ivanoffs killed Ivanoffs in merciless fashion.

Serk, making his way on skis through the dense forest, was discovered by a patrol as he was cutting a wire fence. The patrol became tangled in the wire, and only two soldiers succeeded in finding his tracks. But Serk, with the aid of the moonless, starry night, got off to a fast start and continued on in his flight.

The two soldiers were trailing him, step by step; apparently they were northerners, accustomed to the impassable snowy forests. Several times Serk changed his course, going farther and farther from the railroad line. Yet the pursuers kept closing in. He did not doubt for a moment that he would reach the other side of the front. He fell into a bear's den.

The pursuers were now dangerously close. Several shots were followed by a sharp pain in his arm. Far from stopping, he accelerated his pace and came to a small meadow. This bright meadow impressed itself upon his mind for many months to come. In his delirium, many days after his rovings in the woods, he would shout: "Again the meadow! Cursed! Smooth! Endless!"

Again came shots. They grazed his fur coat. The impenetrable forest now hid him from his pursuers. But he had lost his way.

He did not count the days. He ate his last lump of bread. He devoured the snow, avidly, almost feverishly. Yet he did not feel tired. He was in a state of exaltation, of enchantment. All his thoughts were with Olga. As if propelled by a force stronger than himself, he continued through the forests. With each passing day, it seemed to him that his strength doubled, tripled, that he was skiing ever faster and faster, racing at almost incredible speed.

On the sixth day of his wanderings in the woods, he met a large brown bear, to all appearance replete and half asleep. Man and beast faced each other: the man lean, with unkempt beard, his eyes like those of a madman; the beast cunning and sleepy. The bear mumbled indistinctly and slowly turned away into the depths of the forest. The man stood motionless for a long while and then, forgetting the encounter, went on.

He was in the ten-mile-wide no man's land between the two front lines. He kept on to the northwest, more by instinct than by logic. On the seventh day, he broke one of his skis. It was useless, and he was forced, to his great regret, to throw it away. He now used his snowshoes. During the tenth day, he barely managed to advance a hundred paces. He did not walk—he crawled, falling down every few minutes. But it seemed to him as if he were walking very fast; that the trees, the valleys, the snowdrifts were rushing past. Nothing mattered but to find Olga.

He reached the limit of his physical strength, unable any more to move, and lay down in a snow pit. He was feverish from his infected wound, from utter stress. He had a dream, or advanced delirium. He was sighing, calling her; it even seemed to him that she was near.

At nightfall, he regained his strength and with the same feverish anxiety crawled along the forest floor. The weather was mild, and this saved him from freezing to death. Now he thought that Olga was hiding in the woods nearby, beside an old pine tree. It was a hallucination. Completely losing his mind, he shouted wildly: "Olga! Olga!"

The echo mocked him. But also there was the voice of a stranger close by, calm and at the same time very rough: "What are you shouting about? What Olga are you looking for? Are you drunk, or what?" He had been discovered by White soldiers patrolling the forest near the railroad. But by an even more incredible coincidence, they brought him to our hospital unit, a mile away.

For two weeks he remained in a state of delirium, with a fever of up to 105°, a skeletonlike creature emaciated beyond imagination. His recovery began to progress with miraculous speed as soon as Olga arrived from Archangel, in answer to my summons. They were married in a modest ceremony in the hospital by an old village priest. Serk had very little time to talk with me; in fact he ignored my presence. Enchanted, he chatted incessantly with Olga, who had forgiven him his past infatuation with communism.

"He paid dearly for his mistakes," she said to me, trying to justify Serk's conduct.

They left North Russia soon after on an English boat, and I heard from them for the last time several years later. They had bought a chicken farm in France, somewhere in the Var Valley, and had three small children. He was taking care of baby chicks and the children while she worked as a nurse in a local hospital. They were very happy, I was told.

Chapter 8

THE LANGUOR OF AUDACITY

OLD ST. PETERSBURG was in my bones. To the man born there, this unique city is enchanting. It was created on a whim of Peter the Great, the drunkard, the dreamer, the violent-tempered fighter, the visionary of unhindered audacity. To the newcomer, the coldness, the demureness, the abstractedness, the emotionlessness of the city was oppressive, if not hostile. It was a city of introversion, of split personalities, and only a native could love it with tender passion and enjoy the silent, gloomy nights, the muddy autumns, the dirty canals and rivers, the snow and savage ice of winters, the icebreaker of the Neva in the spring, the unsmiling passers-by, the small, poorly lighted bars where endless talk about the futility of life went on night after night. The majestic churches, the *sobors* where numbers of men and women prayed before the image of Christ. The city of ideas, exuberant and vibrant, fermenting in an extreme individuation, conflicting, inspiring, utterly foreign to the realities of men's lives.

And, walking slowly along the banks of the Neva after my unsuccessful visit with Serk, I was once more enchanted, as I had been in my youth, by the unbroken and unbreakable soul of my city. What can bolshevism, this crude and elementary materialism of an immature and unimaginative mind, do to this city? Conquer it? Nonsense, I said to myself. Bolshevism might conquer it politically, might suppress it superficially, but the soul of my city will live forever, long after bolshevism has joined the past. I became calmer, as if convinced of the city's spiritual invincibility.

The evening was still young and my meeting with Demidoff was scheduled for a later hour. As I walked the streets, muddy from thawing snow and poorly illuminated by gas lights, the noisy streetcars rushing, bars and beer halls overcrowded, the basement windows revealing peaceful family gatherings around the boiling samovars, I lost for a moment the acute sensation of forthcoming tragedy. It cannot be, I said to myself, that the freedom so dearly gained by the Russian people will be taken away by political adventurers.

I entered the famous bar, "The Cave of the Wandering Dog," the meeting place of writers, musicians, and artists. The enormous basement hall was full of drinking, shouting, and singing. All the tables were occupied. As I elbowed my way through the crowd, someone called me by name. It was the celebrated poetess Anna Akhmatova, whom I knew from early youth. At the other end of her table, Alexander Blok, a famous poet, was whispering a story to Chaliapin, the singer.

"Take a seat," invited Akhmatova. As I sat down, she introduced me to a balding, toothless, youngish man sitting near her: "This is Ilya Ehrenburg," she said.

The future Communist writer was drunk and in a very ex-

pansive and talkative mood. He immediately confided to me
that Kerensky was the greatest man who had ever lived.
I silently agreed with him. Blok got up, unsteady from champagne, and started to recite one of his poems:

> *Aye! Long ago your race has ceased to love*
> *As we of Russian blood love evermore,*
> *You have forgotten that there is a love*
> *That burns and kills, and shrivels to the core. . . .*

The crowd suddenly fell silent, listening as if hypnotized to
his really masterful performance. Blok had scarcely finished
when Chaliapin began to sing "The Volga Boatman."

Three years later, I was again in my beloved city. It was
summer and, unable to sleep because of the whiteness of the
night, I wandered along the banks of the Neva. St. Petersburg was dying, conquered by the Communists. And men
still were searching ceaselessly for a solution to their problems, for a semblance of eternal truth, indifferent and hostile
to triumphant communism. But the eternal truth kept slip-
ping away from them as relentlessly as the white nights.

It was almost morning when I entered "The Cave of the
Wandering Dog." The bar was open but almost empty. A
woman was sitting at a table, sipping black coffee and smoking a thin cigarette. Very slender, tall and pale; pale cheeks,
pale lips, cold eyes impassive and unseeing. She had changed
—Anna Akhmatova. She recognized me and smiled timidly. I
joined her, and we sat in silence for many minutes. She suddenly came to life and quoted in a low voice:

> *All is plundered, all is sold and betrayed—*
> *And the wing of Black Death is widespread,*
> *All is gnawed by a hungry anguish—*
> *Why then does light show suddenly ahead?*

There's a miracle drawing close
To drab houses that want repairs,
It is something that no one knows,
But we've hoped for it for years.

And she added, quite unexpectedly: "Everything is dying, but real love is immortal. . . .

"The soul of our city too is immortal," she assured me when I left her a few minutes later.

We met at Islomin's apartment: Demidoff, Flekkel, Philonenko, Sourgoutscheff, and two other men unknown to me. Demidoff briefly outlined his plan. The situation of the democratic government was critical, if not altogether hopeless. The appeasing attitude in government circles toward communism paralyzed any action against it. Softness, inertness, and impotence there made the victory of the Communists an easy task.

Something drastic had to be done. His group, Demidoff said, had decided that the "liquidation" of "Comrade" Lenin would bring the government out of its "appeasing hibernation" and force it to suppress the rising Communist movement swiftly and effectively. The plans were set. In fact, the day of "liquidation" was scheduled for the coming Friday. The present meeting, he added, was called to have a friendly exchange of opinions on this drastic measure. "The opinion of our host, of course, is of particular value to all of us," remarked Demidoff.

Islomin responded immediately. "You might be surprised to hear that I approve of this plan. I believe in direct action when there is a grave crisis. But I must warn you that by destroying the great leader of bolshevism in this fashion, you will betray the basic principles of democracy. You will be resorting to the same tactics that the Bolsheviks are using. 'The end justifies the means'—that is the essence of their political activity. But does the end justify the means? Democracy answered no, long ago. Yet, as I said the other day, this is the tragedy of democracy. For the democrats have been fighting for power against an unscrupulous enemy with Christian methods, which are utterly ineffective in political struggles.

"Let me refresh your memory about the first Communist in Russia. It is a very instructive story, for in the teaching and behavior of Sergei Netchayev you can find all the essential elements of the present Communist movement."

And Islomin told the story with which we were all somewhat familiar.

It was 1869, and autumn was late in coming. Although it was the end of November, the brook that flowed near the Moscow Agricultural Academy had not frozen over. The watchman was making his usual inspection early one morning, when he noticed part of a man's overcoat protruding from the north side of the brook. After much tugging, he pulled out a man's body with a bullet hole through the head. A red scarf was tied tightly around the throat, and attached to the ends of the scarf were two heavy stones.

The police were inclined at first to regard it as a simple case of murder, committed in the course of a robbery. However, it was soon established that the dead man, Ivan Ivanov, a student at the Agricultural Academy, had been a member of a revolutionary movement. Thereupon the murder assumed a different character. It was found that he had often been seen in the company of a bookstore employee named Ouspensky. Ouspensky was immediately arrested, and without hesitation he named four other accomplices. The murder, he said, had been committed in the interest of a Communist group.

Five men had participated, but only four were arrested and brought to trial. The head of this revolutionary gang had escaped across the border several days after the murder. There seemed to be no doubt that he had planned the crime. The captured men agreed in every detail of his physical description, his character, and the circumstances surrounding the crime.

Slowly the picture of this strange man, Sergei Netchayev, took shape before the court and the general public. He was a ruthless, immovable, narrow-minded fanatic. Despotic by nature, he was easily aroused and could tolerate no opposition. He was stubborn, strong-willed, suspicious, distrustful, totally devoid of scruples.

The son of a house painter from a textile town, Ivanovo-Vosnesensk, he himself had been a house painter in early youth. By dint of superhuman patience and hard work, he passed the teacher's examination and was made the principal of a St. Petersburg trade school. At twenty-one, he entered the University of St. Petersburg and was soon taking active part in the student revolutionary movement. Within a year, he was the leader of an independent revolutionary organization.

He soon founded a number of small revolutionary "nuclei," not only in Ivanovo-Vosnesensk but also in Moscow and St. Petersburg. Each of these groups was composed of five members, "the revolutionary quintet." The majority of his followers were entirely ignorant of Netchayev's purpose or political doctrine, but they were all impressed by his personality, his enthusiasm, his belief in an immediate revolution. They were practically hypnotized by his intense, aggressive propaganda. Among his followers were students, workmen, clerks, noblemen, retired army officers, and even society girls.

In addition to the four directly involved in the crime, the court indicted seventy-six more of Netchayev's followers. The testimony brought out that he had posed as a commissar of the Internationale, a Communist organization headed at the time by Bakunin, with headquarters at Geneva. Yet, it was later established that he had never been delegated by any revolutionary faction and that his organization had been initiated by himself under his personal leadership, or dictatorship.[1]

Netchayev demanded absolute and unconditional obedience from every member of his organization, and to keep his followers under control, he introduced a system of spying. Each member of a quintet was obliged to spy on the other four and make regular reports to Netchayev.

He applied a peculiar code of ethics to his revolutionary activities. "Anything goes as long as it assures the success of our enterprise!" he would repeat to his followers. And he meant it.

Why was Ivanov murdered? This was the question that interested the court and the public most of all.

One of the defendants, Kuznetzov, a student at the Agricultural Academy and a member of the same quintet as Ivanov, gave a graphic description of the murder.

"It was a brutal, savage crime," he confessed. "Ivanov was my friend. . . . I loved him dearly. He was a goodhearted, generous fellow but somewhat stubborn and utterly independent in his opinions. Soon friction arose between Ivanov

---

1. The testimony was reviewed in a St. Petersburg court session which lasted two and a third months, July 1 to September 11, 1871. The presiding judge was Prince Troubetzkoyi, a progressive jurist who manifested a strict impartiality, giving the defendants every opportunity to defend themselves. The trial was open to press and public.

and Netchayev. My friend objected to the despotic rule of our leader. As a matter of fact, he objected to some unethical actions of Netchayev's and he disliked some of his ideas." The conflict was soon noticed by other members of the organization.

It was then that Netchayev made up his mind to kill Ivanov. "Whoever is not with us is against us!" he told Kuznetzov. He called the other members of the quintet and told them that Ivanov would have to be liquidated—"as he is dangerous to our organization once he leaves it." It was in vain that we all tried to dissuade him.

Kuznetzov was visibly moved. "I," he said, "who had nothing but love and regard for Ivanov, protested against it especially. But Netchayev was adamant. 'He must die,' he kept repeating. He simply ordered us to induce Ivanov to come with us to the grotto near the pond. Ivanov, suspecting nothing, readily agreed; we told him we were picking up a printing press.

"As soon as we entered the shaded grotto, Netchayev threw himself at Ivanov and grabbed him by the throat. Ivanov tried to fight back. He bit Netchayev's hands until they bled. Gasping for breath, he tried to shout. Then Netchayev drew out a revolver and shot him in the temple. Ivanov was silenced.

"The rest of us were too stupefied to move. . . . All but Netchayev. He calmly proceeded to search Ivanov's pockets and remove anything that might be incriminating. Then he barked at us to find two large stones. We found them in the grotto. Netchayev knotted Ivanov's scarf around his neck and tied the stones to the ends of the scarf."

Several days after Ivanov's body was found, Netchayev escaped across the border with the aid of a false passport. He settled in Geneva.

However, he did not renounce his creed nor deny the killing. He did not even bother to apologize for the misery and punishment he had brought upon the four who were sentenced for his crime. He proudly admitted that he had done the killing "in the interest of the revolution" and that he had been right in doing so. He stated frankly that he did not respect any codes, that he hated "the morals of the civilized world." He believed in a new morality, according to which anything was permissible if done for the revolution. "Friendship, love, gratitude, honor itself must be sacrificed to the cold passion of the revolutionary cause," he said, "and the foulest means are fair. Whatever advances the cause of the revolution is moral; whatever hinders it is immoral and criminal." Thus he denounced all human aims and branded them as "bourgeois frivolities."

In an article, "He Who Is Not With Us Is Against Us," Netchayev presented Ivanov's case. He explained that "membership with us is eternal, invincible, and inseparable. Any deviation from, or any question as to, the policy established by us, necessitates that the individual in question be cast out of our midst like a rotten limb." And he made it very clear just what he meant.

"Expulsion from the group," he explained, "is at the same time expulsion from the numbers of the living. Death for anyone who would desert the revolutionary cause or show any sign of disobedience!"

A man who enters the Communist organization must limit his attachment to party members. In Netchayev's "Catechism of the Revolution," which was found after the arrest of his followers, he makes clear the proper relationship among the members of his organization.

"A Communist," he wrote, "may feel friendship or attachment *only* to those who have proved themselves by their activity to be Communists like himself. The measure of friendship, devotion, and other obligations toward such a comrade is determined solely by the degree of his usefulness to the cause of the all-destructive Communist revolution." [2]

Netchayev developed his viewpoint still further in a magazine, *La Commune*, which appeared in London in 1871.

"The people are stupid," he maintained, "and, as such, must be guided and ruled by the revolutionary faction of mankind. This Communist party must exert a benevolent but unlimited despotic power over the people. But, in its turn, the Communist party itself must be under the dictatorial power of a small committee or of one man who is the head of this central committee." [3]

---

2. An open letter written in 1873 by Engels, leader of the German Social-Democratic party, was widely publicized in the newspapers of that time. In it, Engels denounced Netchayev's moral code, calling him "that unscrupulous and dangerous mountebank, who is a disgrace to the revolutionary movement." Yet, fifty years later, Netchayev won recognition as "the first Communist" and a "true revolutionary" in the minds of Russian Communists. A lengthy biography of Netchayev by a leading Communist writer, Alexander Gambaroff, was published in 1926. "He [Netchayev] was the first Russian Communist, the only one who understood the essence of class war and who visualized its practical application. The Russian intelligentsia could not accept Netchayev because of their small, bourgeois mentality. He was a true Communist." *Netchayev*, A. Gambaroff, Moscovsky Rabotchyi, Moscow, 1926.

3. On August 14, 1872, Netchayev was arrested by Russian detectives in a restaurant in Geneva. He had been fighting extradition for several months, but the Swiss government finally decided that he was a common criminal. He was brought to Moscow on January 20, 1873, charged with murder in the first degree, and sentenced to twenty years' imprisonment. He died nine years later in cell No. 5 of the Petropavlovskaya Fortress. There was no capital punishment in Russia at that time.

"Thus," Islomin said, concluding his story, "there is no doubt that Netchayev favored a party dictatorship, in fact a sort of military communism under his own dictatorship. All the elements of today's bolshevism were well defined in Netchayev's teaching."

"What is the moral of this sad story?" Islomin continued. "When a political party numbering many thousands of members resorts to the philosophy that 'the end justifies the means,' as in the case of the Bolshevik party, what should the democratic government do? Common sense would say, 'liquidate them mercilessly.' But democracy lives and acts according to its ideology. Democracy would say, and as a matter of fact does say: 'The Bolsheviks are bad, misled boys. Let's try to persuade them to reform and to become good boys. Are they not our brothers in humanity?' And while democracy tries to persuade and appease the Bolsheviks, they are engaged feverishly in armed conspiracy to overthrow our government."

"Of course," Islomin smiled, "the truth of the situation is that it is democracy which is misled and not the Bolsheviks. Very cleverly misled by Lenin. He is a genius in strategy. His slogan is that everyone who disagrees with him is a reactionary, an imperialist, a lackey of capitalism.

"A very clever slogan," he continued; "a very effective one. For our liberals and radicals—not all, mind you, but many of them—have a soft spot in their mentality. They are deathly afraid of being accused or even suspected of political conservatism. And Lenin, by this simple slogan, puts them on the defensive and forces upon them a sort of psychological premise to an appeasing course of action. But most of the confusion comes from the inability of our left-wingers to make a clear distinction between the doctrine and the tactics of bolshevism. Again Lenin and his friends adroitly mislead our soft-hearted intellectuals. The doctrine of the Russian breed of bolshevism is nothing but window dressing. They change it, they modify it, they reverse it as the needs of to-day's strategy demand. The essence of the Bolshevik move-ment is the drive for power. Power, complete, unlimited, uncontested, dictatorial power. That is their goal, their dream. And, in pursuit of this goal, all methods are allowed, for their end justifies their means.

"This fact is completely overlooked by our left-wingers. Bolshevism calls for the nationalization of industry and land, a slogan that appeals to many idealists. Actually, it means that the Bolsheviks want not only complete, un-challenged, political power but economic power as well. Very clever indeed. And our liberals are eager to discuss and analyze their doctrine instead of examining the danger. It's a sad picture. . . .

"But, returning to our urgent problem," Islomin con-cluded, "may I say that I give my blessing to any undemo-cratic act against the Bolsheviks. If only you are bold enough to do it. . . ."

And we began to discuss plans for the forthcoming Friday.

It was freezing cold that Friday night. The streets and sidewalks were covered with a thin, icy shell. Our car moved slowly and painfully along the Viborgsky Highway, now and then fighting desperately to remain on the road and not to skid into the ravine. Impatient and tense, I was unable to restrain myself: "We'll never get there," I exclaimed.

Demidoff smiled. "We can't fail to miss this day of reckon-ing," he murmured.

We did arrive. It was almost 11 o'clock. House number 14 was almost dark, silent in its winter sleep. The windows were closed and only a few dim lights glimmered through them.

We drove four blocks past the house and stopped. "Here," whispered Demidoff, "is where Lenin meets a comrade. Lenin has just returned from Finland and now lives in Fofanova's apartment, not very far from here.[4] But his place is well guarded: we tried to get to him there, without success. But he comes here to meet his friend in apartment 23, where Nicholas Kokko, a Bolshevik employee of the Aivas Plant, lives. There aren't any cars near the house, so I assume that Lenin sent his chauffeur home. Stepan Til is his name."

Demidoff checked our automatics. While he was doing so, two silent figures in sheepskin army coats appeared from nowhere and came toward our car.

"Who are they?" I asked my friend.

"Don't worry," he replied. "Our men."

One of them whispered to Demidoff, "They're both there. Arrived 30 minutes ago. Lenin and another man."

"And their bodyguard?"

"He left in a car, and Lenin told him to come back about midnight."

"Splendid," remarked my friend.

"The front door is locked, but here are the keys," said the man, giving two keys to Demidoff. One was to the front door and the other to Kokko's apartment. "The porter is in his lodge, sound asleep," continued the man. "We had beer with him and gave him a sedative. He was glad to have company."

"You may go home now," ordered Demidoff. "I will see

---

4. On October 20, 1917, Lenin returned to Petrograd from Finland, where he had been in hiding. For four days, October 20-24, he stayed at the apartment of his friend M. V. Fofanova, Viborgsky District, 41 Serdobolskaya Street. The apartment had two bedrooms and was very small.

you tomorrow at our usual meeting place." The men left in their car, which was parked on a side street.

We were alone, facing the four-story building. There, behind locked doors, were two men who intended to destroy democracy and change the destiny of the world. It was up to us to prevent it. The price was the murder of two unarmed men.

For several minutes we stood silent and immobile, watching the light in Kokko's third-floor apartment. "Well," said Demidoff, "we must go." He unlocked the front door and we entered a small, dark hall. "You stay here," he whispered to me. "I'm going up." He ascended slowly, step by step. He reached the second floor. He was ascending again. He was on the third floor.

My heart was beating fast. The tension was unbearable. "He is opening the door of the apartment," I said to myself. "Now . . . there must be shots anytime now. . . . How many? . . ."

But there were no shots, no screams, no fight. Time was dragging. How long had I stood there? Had time stopped? Then I heard steps. Descending steps. Unsteady steps. As if the person were very sick and walking with enormous pain and effort. They were close to the bottom now. And I saw, or rather sensed, Demidoff. He was close to me now. Not a single word from him. He opened the front door and we went out on the street. In an oppressive silence, we reached the car and entered it. Only then did Demidoff speak. His voice was low and came with difficulty, as if he were suffocating.

"It was stronger than myself," he said. "I entered the vestibule of his apartment. The door to the living room was open and I saw them sitting in armchairs, drinking tea and talking.

I was only fifteen feet away. I leveled my automatic on Lenin. I was ready to fire. And something held my finger when I ordered it to move and press the trigger. You can't kill an unarmed man, a voice in me protested. I stood there several minutes with the leveled revolver in my hand. I couldn't overcome my feelings and shoot him. It was justified murder, I knew. . . . But all my upbringing revolted against it. If only he had been armed . . ."

I remained silent, too shocked by his failure.

"Why don't you scold me?" he shouted angrily. "Why don't you tell me I'm a soft-hearted intellectual, an impotent imbecile, a good-for-nothing fellow? Why don't you go in there and do what I couldn't do? . . . We still have plenty of time. . . ."

But I shook my head. "I'm no better than you when it comes to that. I could never shoot an unarmed man, no matter how much I hated him. I couldn't. . . ."

And suddenly Demidoff began to cry like a child. "But I'm an army man! I killed dozens of Germans in the war. . . . And here's a scoundrel who deserves to be shot . . . and I failed. . . . I failed completely. . . ."

The night was clear and moonlit. The air was sharp and cold. We drove in silence and stopped before my house.

"Islomin knew that nothing would come of it," murmured Demidoff. "He knew. . . . Well, we must admit our defeat. It was inbred in us, in me, in every one of us. . . . The intelligentsia . . ." Bitterly, he added, "What are we good for? . . . For sacrifice . . . for peace, for creation. . . . But we're not fighters, not fighters enough to take care of the Bolsheviks."

I didn't say a word. I left the car and he drove away.

Demidoff did not give up his plan. It was not in his nature to accept defeat meekly. He slowly recovered from the shocking realization of his "humanitarian" trait. He had been sure he was free from any of the weaknesses characteristic of the Russian intelligentsia. And after he witnessed the fall of the democratic government, he returned with new energy to his original plan of destroying the Communist leaders.

On January 1, 1918, he organized a new assault on Lenin's life. This time I took no part, for I was deeply involved in the affairs of the forthcoming convention of the All Russian Constituent Assembly. But Demidoff kept me well informed about his attempt—which also ended in failure.

On the evening of January 1, a large crowd gathered in the famous Tschinizeli Circus, a building almost as large as Madison Square Garden. Soldiers and workers were coming to hear Lenin. It was a meeting of prime political importance. The Communist party leader was expected to denounce the Constituent Assembly for its "bourgeois tendencies."

Lenin arrived at 8:00 o'clock in a limousine driven by his faithful chauffeur and bodyguard, Stepan Kasimirovitch Til, a Lithuanian Communist. Lenin brought with him as guest of honor Fritz Platten, a Swiss Social Democrat. This foreigner was to play an unexpected role as the savior of Lenin's life.[5]

"I planned this attack carefully," Demidoff recounted to

---

5. Fritz Platten was the Swiss Socialist internationalist who arranged the passage of Lenin and other Bolsheviks through Germany in March 1917. General Ludendorf writes in his memoirs: "Our government, in sending Lenin to Russia, took upon itself a tremendous responsibility. From a military point of view his journey was justified, for it was imperative that Russia should fall." *Meine Kriegserinerungen,* Erich Ludendorf, Berlin, 1919, p. 407. Platten became a member of the Communist party later. See also *Three Attempts on Lenin's Life,* Gosizdat, Moscow, 1925.

me later. "I knew well in advance the tag number of Lenin's car. It was 4547. I could repeat this number in my sleep. I had decided that only three persons should take part: Anton Spiridonov, a private from my former regiment, a former university student and a courageous soldier, an ardent anti-Communist who hated their guts; Safronov, a steel worker, and I. A special role was assigned to each of us. Spiridonov was supplied with a powerful bomb, and Safronov and I, with excellent Belgian revolvers.

"At first I was inclined to attack Lenin on his way back to the car. The situation was ideal for this. But after careful consideration, I abandoned this plan; too many innocent bystanders might have been killed by the bomb. So we selected a small bridge across the Moika River, over which Lenin was to pass on his return from the meeting."

It was a dark night. No moon. The meeting had started. The three men approached the car, examined the license number, and, satisfied that Lenin was at the meeting, took their posts near the bridge.

"As soon as the car comes near the bridge, throw the bomb," Demidoff ordered the young man.

"I will," was the firm answer.

Demidoff and Safronov guarded the far side of the bridge, ready to shoot after the explosion.

Time went slowly. But at last the lights of the coming car illuminated the bridge. It was moving slowly, because of the deep snow.

"Now!" cried Demidoff. And he saw Spiridonov raise his hand, hesitate, and, instead of throwing the bomb, disappear into the darkness beyond. The car was already crossing the bridge when Demidoff and Safronov both opened fire.

"I saw Lenin's face clearly through the open window. I

wasn't more than ten feet away when I leveled my revolver and fired. . . . I was sure I had killed him."

But he had not. Platten, the Swiss, who was sitting beside Lenin, was faster. He saw the gun and with a lightning movement pushed Lenin's head down. The bullet scratched Platten's hand, wounding his finger slightly.

The chauffeur increased his speed and the car disappeared down a side street.

From under the bridge appeared Spiridonov, a very unhappy young man. He still held the bomb in his right hand.

"I lost my nerve," he muttered. "There was an innocent man in Lenin's car. I couldn't throw the bomb. . . . An innocent man . . ."

Demidoff, in a rage, threw the bomb into the Moika River. There was a splash and a detonation.

Demidoff still refused to admit defeat. It took him eight months to prepare his next assault on Lenin. By that time, I was already in Samara, where the Czechoslovakian army, formed from prisoners of war, was fighting the Communists. Lenin and the Politburo were in Moscow, the new capital of Red Russia.

On August 30, 1918, a large meeting was called unexpectedly at the Michelson Plant in Serpouchovo, a Moscow suburb. Only a few persons knew in advance that Lenin would appear there. Demidoff was one of them, and he decided to strike at once. This time, however, his accomplice was a girl. A former student at the University of Moscow, Fanny Kaplan impressed him as a person of strong character and unusual courage. She was a calm, reserved girl in her late twenties, a firm believer in democracy, and convinced that communism was bringing destruction to her country.

Lenin arrived at the plant in his limousine. The chauffeur

again was Til. Lenin was met by officials of the plant, who conducted him to the meeting. A few minutes later, a black-haired young girl in a dark overcoat, hatless, approached the chauffeur.

"Has Lenin arrived?" she asked.

Til, an agent of the Soviet secret police, became suspicious. He answered curtly: "I don't know."

The girl smiled. "I'm sure he's here," she said, and walked off toward the hall. Til saw a tall man, blond and clean-shaven, stop her, exchange a few words, and disappear into the crowd surrounding the entrance.

An hour later, Lenin came out of the building, accompanied by several persons. Among them was the dark-haired girl. Lenin was engaged in heated discussion, in which the girl apparently was taking part. As they approached the car, they all stopped and Lenin was just about to enter when suddenly five shots were fired, one after the other. Lenin stumbled and would have fallen if Til had not held him. In the confusion, the girl ran away but was captured when she tried to cross Serpouchovsky Street to a car parked on a side street. The car, driven by the blond man, escaped and was never found. The girl was seized and beaten by the crowd and taken to the local Cheka, where she admitted that she, Fanny Kaplan, had shot Lenin, "the enemy of Russian democracy." She was executed after a thorough interrogation by the Moscow secret police.

Four bullets had entered Lenin's body. One went through his lung, one passed dangerously close to the arteries in his neck, one bullet broke his collarbone, and the fourth scratched his shoulder. He was taken home in a semiconscious state and immediately operated on by Dr. Minz, a noted surgeon. For ten days he hung between life and death, but gradually he recovered from his wounds. One bullet remained in his body.[6]

I met Demidoff in Samara, where he told me about the failure of this last attack. He admitted that the "liquidation of the leaders of communism" was no real solution to the problem. He soon left for the south, where he joined General Wrangel's army. I heard that he was gravely wounded, evacuated to Constantinople, and from there emigrated to Brazil. The last news I had of him was that he had become a prosperous businessman, was married to a Spanish girl, and lived on a plantation somewhere in western Brazil.

---

6. This attempt on Lenin's life is described in detail in *The Life and Work of V. I. Lenin*, E. Jaroslavsky, Gosizdat, Moscow, 1924, pp. 76-83.

Chapter 9

THE FALL OF THE
WINTER PALACE

To a foreigner visiting Petrograd in October 1917, the city gave the appearance of living a normal, full, animated existence. The bars, the restaurants, the night clubs and theaters were crowded with well-dressed people, gay, nonchalant, and apparently indifferent to the political turmoil in the government. The ballet premières in the Mariinsky Theater attracted the élite of the capital as they had done for decades. And on such occasions, one would have seen the Communists Trotsky and Lounatcharsky sitting in the boxes almost side by side with Nabokoff, Kishkin, or Miliukoff, representatives of the liberal parties.

The throngs of servicemen on the streets and in public gatherings were a logical consequence of the war which was raging several hundred miles away. The cost of food and other items was not excessive, although much higher than in peacetime. There was some inflation, yet an army physician's salary of 300 roubles, equivalent to 200 of today's dollars, was still sufficient to meet daily expenses on a modest scale during a sojourn in Petrograd.

But the calm was deceptive. A grave political crisis was menacing the very existence of the newly born democratic state. The situation was so confused that even an experienced observer was somewhat at a loss to evaluate the forces fighting for power or to make any sound prognosis of those turbulent days before the overthrow of Kerensky's government by Lenin's party. I can offer here only a brief outline of what was going on.

The Romanoff dynasty fell on February 27, 1917. The February revolution was a spontaneous movement fomented by the war. It was a protest against the Romanoff government. No political party organized the revolution. No one incited or even directed it.

The first provisional government was formed on March 2. Prince G. E. Lvov, a man of progressive and liberal traditions, was elected Prime Minister, with Paul Miliukoff as Secretary of State and A. I. Goutchkoff as Secretary of War. A considerable, if not exclusive, role in the organization of the first provisional government was assigned to the members of the Russian Duma, or Parliament, which operated during, approximately, the last ten years of the Romanoff regime. Politically, almost all the members of the government were moderate liberals, some of whom belonged to the Constitutional-Democratic party and were known as "Cadets."

In this government, the only Socialistic representative was Alexander Kerensky, a member of the Duma and the leader of the Labor party there. He was appointed Vice President and Secretary of the Department of Justice.

The life span of this government was short, only two

months, lasting from March 2 to May 2. For it was under ever-increasing pressure from the Socialistic parties. The story of the democratic governments in Russia—there were, altogether, four consecutive governments from the time of the February revolution to October 25, 1917—was essentially that of an unsuccessful attempt to find a common language, a *modus operandi,* between the non-Socialistic liberal elements and the right-wing Socialists, while the Bolsheviks (Communists) and left-wing Socialists were ardently preparing the ground for an armed *coup d'état.*

The political situation of each of these four governments was complicated and handicapped by the existence of the Soviet of Workers, Peasants, and Soldiers, organized soon after the February revolution. In the beginning, the executive committee of the All Russian Soviet was composed mostly of moderate or right-wing Socialists. Thus, Kerensky, while Secretary of the Justice Department, was also vice chairman of the Soviet executive committee. After Lenin's arrival in Petrograd, however, the political picture was changed drastically. Lenin demanded action. He called upon his party members to put up an energetic fight against the "bourgeoisie," meaning the non-Socialistic liberals and moderate Socialists. By hook or by crook the Bolsheviks infiltrated the various soviets, particularly the soviet of Petrograd, steadily increasing their influence in these organizations. Directed by Lenin and Trotsky, they were aggressive, able propagandists and demagogues.

The second of the four governments was formed on May 2. This time, it was a coalition of liberals and moderate Socialists. Prince Lvov remained Prime Minister. Kerensky was Secretary of War; Victor Tchernoff, Secretary of Agriculture, and Tzeretelli, a Social-Democrat, Postmaster General. This government also lasted two months only, being confronted with the growing menace of Lenin's party. While the Communists still remained a small minority and were not yet dangerous to the existence of the democratic government, there was unfortunately no unity of plan, with regard to them, in the ranks of the Socialist parties supporting the coalition government, which was composed of very able men. There was a strong, underlying trend of appeasement, and this soon was to become the source of tragedy for Russian democracy.

One must realize the difficulties with which the democratic government was confronted. The whole apparatus of government had been destroyed by the February revolution; this had been an unexpected explosion, and was followed by severe shortages of food and transportation. Political sympathies were numerous and conflicting, even though most people recognized the need for unity. These factors, added to the threat from Lenin's party and from the German army, made the task of governing Russia an extraordinarily difficult one.

The largest political party was the Social-Revolutionary party of Kerensky. Its role in the past revolutionary movement, the support it received from working class and peasants during the first months after the February revolution, and the fact that it was composed mostly of "intelligentsia" gave this party a leading role during the ten-months' life of the democratic governments. Regrettably, the party was far from being uniform in its political concepts. Its right wing, with Savinkoff, Maslov, and others, was aggressively and uncompromisingly anti-Communist. The liquidation of communism became the most urgent if not the only problem for the right wing. The center, with Kerensky, Zenzinov, and Avksentiev, was sincerely anti-Communist and would have been ready for any action against Lenin and his followers except for the strong pressure exerted by the party's left wing. Victor Tchernoff, one of the most influential figures of the Social-Revolutionary party and its acknowledged leader, advocated an appeasing attitude toward the Communists. The party also had an extreme left wing, with Kamkoff, Steinberg, and others who were definitely and openly pro-Communist.

The left wing, in fact, soon formed a separate party known as the Left-Social-Revolutionary party. It was partly due to its support that the Communists were able to overthrow the democratic government.

The other major Socialist party was the Social-Democratic party, also known as the Mensheviks. Its position toward the Communists was uncertain and vacillated from day to day. The right wing, with Plekhanoff, was violently anti-Communistic, the left wing, with Martov, was appeasing.

On July 3 the Communists commenced armed demonstrations against the government. Lenin, from his headquarters in the mansion of the famous ballerina Mrs. Kshesinsky, called for the overthrow of the government and for the assumption of power by the Soviets. The streets were filled with armed workers and soldiers, who stopped cars, smashed shop windows, and gradually encircled the Tauride Palace, where the conference of ministers was taking place.

The Bolsheviks renewed their demonstrations with even greater vigor the next day. "All power to the Soviets!" was the cry of the crowd around the Tauride Palace. Kerensky was absent, since, as Secretary of the Army and Navy, he had been ordered by the Provisional government to restore discipline at the front and to help develop military operations against the Germans. The Semenovsky and Ismailovsky regiments, however, remained faithful to the government, and by the night of July 4 the revolt was liquidated. The Kshesinsky mansion, the Dournovo villa, and the Petropavlovskaya Fortress, all of which had been occupied by the Communists, were cleared. The crowning sensation of the day was the publication of documents relating to the financial support of Lenin's activities by the German government.

Some of the government ministers—Liberals—resigned, and the crisis continued for about three weeks, until July 24, when a full coalition government was formed. Kerensky was nominated Prime Minister and Secretary of the Army and Navy. Boris Savinkoff received the post of Deputy Secretary of the Army, Tchernoff remained Secretary of Agriculture, and M. I. Teretschenko, Secretary of State. This government was composed of Liberal Socialists and non-Socialistic Liberals and Democrats. All in all, it was politically moderate, except for Tchernoff.

The none-too-stable situation of the government was aggravated by the unsuccessful military operations on the southwestern front. In July, Kerensky appointed General Laurus Kornilov as Supreme Commander of the Army. But relations between the two men soon deteriorated and a grave conflict ensued between them, culminating in an uprising led by Kornilov and his subsequent arrest by the government. Kerensky, continuing as Prime Minister, was appointed Commander-in-Chief of the Army, and on September 1 he proclaimed Russia a republic.

Kornilov's revolt inflicted great damage upon the cause of democracy, for Kerensky, in being compelled to remove him, alienated the army leaders, willy-nilly, and lost considerable support on the part of Russia's non-Socialistic elements.

After a crisis lasting several days, the fourth and last democratic government was formed early in September. It was at first composed exclusively of moderate Socialists, except for Teretschenko, but by September 26 a few non-Socialists were added to the cabinet. Among them were A. I. Konovalov, H. M. Kishkin, M. B. Bernadsky, and S. N. Tretyakoff.[1]

One of the first acts of this fourth democratic government was the convocation of the All Russian Supreme Council, consisting of representatives of all political parties, cooperatives, labor unions, soviets of workers and peasants, municipalities, and various other organizations. The purpose was to create an institution which would support the government until an All Russian Constituent Assembly should be elected. The convocation was fixed for October 7. The principal goal was declared to be to speed the elections to the Constituent Assembly, which would, in turn, elect a new government.

I was at the front while all this turmoil was going on, and I had but a vague and confused picture of the painful events which were taking place from February to September. Such information as I had was culled from newspapers and rare letters from friends. When I arrived in Petrograd on October 7, carrying the letter which Lenin had written to Gregory Pyatakoff, I realized at once that Kerensky's new government stood almost alone, sandwiched between the two opposing political forces of right and left. The non-Socialistic elements were manifesting a hostile, though passive, attitude toward the Prime Minister, while the Communists and left-wing Socialists were actively conspiring to overthrow his government and seize power.

Kerensky apparently did not realize the gravity of his situation, and he still had faith in the power of his personal prestige with the Russian population. True, a large part of the people were behind Kerensky and still had confidence in him

1. See Paul Miliukoff, *op. cit.,* pp. 32 and 75.

as the leader of the democratic revolution, but their support was of little practical significance. It was essentially an emotional condition and was not grounded on a strong political apparatus. Even the Social-Revolutionary and Menshevik parties were in a state of disorganization and inertia.[2]

By October, the soviets in Petrograd and Moscow were completely dominated by the Communists. This did not mean that the working class was with them. Far from it, as one could judge by the labor unions' attitude at that time. Once they were firmly entrenched in the organization which claimed to represent the working class of Petrograd and Moscow, the Communists opened a cold war against the government, accusing them again and again of being "the lackeys of imperialists and bourgeois." They demanded an immediate convocation of the All Russian Constituent Assembly, the elections for which were already in preparation.

But, intensive and ferocious as the Communists' cold war might have appeared, it was only one manifestation of their subversive strategy. Actually, all their efforts were directed toward the same goal: to overthrow the government by conspiracy and armed force and to take power into their own hands. Bands of Communists were brought to Petrograd from many cities and armed without much difficulty. The Latvian, Estonian, Lithuanian, Ukrainian, and Georgian Communists had all gathered in Petrograd by October. It was estimated

---

2. The municipal elections in Petrograd demonstrate this quite clearly. In June 1917 Kerensky's party received 374,585 votes, or 58 percent of all votes. In the September elections, the votes for this party dropped to 54,374, or 14 percent, a strong indication that the Social-Revolutionary party was giving little, if any, attention to its own organizational problems. On the other hand, the non-Socialist Liberals (the "Cadets") increased their votes from 17 percent in June to 26 percent in September. See *ibid.*, p. 80.

that by the middle of that month, the Communists had at their disposal about 15,000 armed men, hidden in various parts of the city.

What was the democratic government doing to stop this aggressive Communist movement? Preoccupied with reorganizing the coalition and with working out a platform acceptable to the political parties which were only halfheartedly supporting it, the government took lightly the resolution made by the Petrograd soviet of workers and soldiers on September 25, under Communist pressure. The resolution stated that "the All Russian Congress of the Soviets should take power into its own hands." It was an open and direct call for the overthrow of the democratic government.

And when, on the same day, the question of the Communist menace was discussed at the conference of the democratic parties in the Winter Palace, the leader of the moderate Social-Democrats, Tzeretelli, announced that "democracy will fight the Bolsheviks only with political measures, considering any other drastic measures unacceptable." (On September 23, the newspaper *New Life*, organ of Maxim Gorky and Soukhanov, ridiculed the suggestion that the Communists might try to take power in their hands "as absurd and senseless.")

The members of the new cabinet complained bitterly about the erratic conduct of Prime Minister Kerensky. Nabokoff, in his memoirs (*Archives of the Russian Revolution*, Vol. 1), sadly remarks that he was daily in despair because of Kerensky's instability. "Almost every day," Nabokoff writes, "some decision would be accepted by the cabinet in the presence of Kerensky and with his approval. In the next few hours, one learned that this decision was reversed by Kerensky, and an opposite measure was taken by him."

It has often been said that the Communists were in the majority at the time of their uprising against the coalition government, and that the country was behind them. It is true that they were quite numerous in the large cities of Russia, like Petrograd and Moscow. But the municipal elections which took place in September, seven weeks before the *coup d'état,* gave them only about three percent of the votes.[3] Thus, in spite of their aggressive activity and the ineptness of the democratic parties, they were a very small minority, indeed.

On October 7, the All Russian Supreme Council was convened. All political parties but the monarchists were represented. The best men, the "cream" of the nation, had gathered together in the hall of Mariinsky Palace; they numbered 550. Kerensky opened the meeting, Avksentiev presiding, and called for the continued support of the Allied armies and for the active maintenance of the western front.

Trotsky, speaking for the Communist group, declared that they were making a complete break with the Supreme Council and were quitting the conference. "The present government is a government of treachery and betrayal of the Russian people," he proclaimed. "Bourgeois capitalism has decided to strangle the All Russian Constituent Assembly. . . . " He called for an immediate peace with Germany, disregarding the interests of "the capitalist Allies." With this declaration, the Communists pulled out of any further parliamentary ac-

---

3. On September 2, 1917, municipal elections took place throughout Russia, and 16,935 town councillors were elected. The Communists received seven percent in the district cities and two percent in other towns. The Socialists received 58 percent of the votes in the district cities and 34 percent in other towns. The rest of the votes were received by non-Socialistic parties and were as follows: 35 percent in the district cities and 64 percent in other towns. B. Veselovsky in *Russkoye Slovo,* October 8, 1917. Also Miliukoff, *op. cit.,* pp. 84, 85.

tion and carried the conflict between them and the democratic parties into the streets.

Shortly after I arrived in Petrograd I had an opportunity to talk with Dr. Kishkin, a member of Kerensky's cabinet. "Why is the government so inefficient in its fight against the Communists?" I asked.

"The root of all evil in our government," he answered, "is the complete absence of daring, of political audacity. Besides, there are too many words flying back and forth, and they cover up the inactivity. Our decisions, no matter how definite and drastic they might be, are never realized, never transformed into action. Passivity and indecision are the symptoms of our government's mental illness. . . . Our Prime Minister should be blamed for the whole distressing situation."

During the next two weeks, the questions of peace and war and foreign policy in general were debated at the conference. Should an immediate separate peace be signed with Germany? Or was Russia under moral obligation to continue the war, which still was tying up large German armies on the eastern front? Here again a sharp difference of opinions between the right and left factions of the conference was evidenced. While the "Cadets" and the right wing of the Social-Revolutionary party called for continuing the war, in spite of its heavy burden upon Russian resources, the left-wingers demanded peace with Germany at any price. The striking fact was that Verchovsky, the Secretary of War and Kerensky's protégé, came out with a statement which perplexed the cabinet. He announced that Russia was not in a position to continue the war, that peace with Germany must be signed immediately, and that any delay would be catastrophic for the democratic republic. Only a few days earlier,

Secretary of State Teretschenko had stated his strong opposition to a separate peace with Germany and had stressed the
obligations of the Russian republic to her allies. Apparently, Verchovsky's opinion was not approved by Kerensky's
cabinet, for he was obliged to resign on October 23, two days
before the downfall of the government.

While the conference debates went on, rumors that the
Communist uprising was imminent became more and more
persistent. Army Intelligence reported that plans were made
by the Communists for the night of October 16. However,
they were canceled. On October 17, Trotsky, the black sheep
of the Communists whom they expelled from Russia a few
years later, and who was killed by their agent in Mexico, announced the formation of a military-revolutionary committee.
Its goal was clear. Trotsky made no secret of it: to replace
the army general staff in the Petrograd district. Representatives of various regiments, all Communists or fellow travelers,
were elected to this committee. Tirelessly, Trotsky visited
regiments and factories, calling upon servicemen and workers
to join the Communists in their forthcoming armed attack on
the government. His appeal was warmly received in some
regiments and enthusiastically in many factories.

The government was still inactive.[4] Kerensky was away

---

4. Konovalov, a member of Kerensky's cabinet and a man of action,
   repeatedly requested the Prime Minister to take drastic measures to
   crush the Communist conspiracy. Kerensky assured him that all precautions were being taken. But when Konovalov on October 14
   discussed this question with General Bagratouni, chief of staff of the
   military district of Petrograd, it was disclosed that nothing had been
   done in this respect and that the government had no specific plans
   for preventing the Communist uprising. See Miliukoff, *op. cit.*,
   pp. 193, 194.

and did not return to Petrograd until October 17. Colonel Polkovnikov, Commander in Chief of the Petrograd Military District, a man without military experience and with an appeasing attitude toward communism, was in charge of the capital's defense. His action was limited to issuing a declaration forbidding any meeting against the government. Nobody listened to him. Nobody obeyed him. The situation in Petrograd was well described in the October 20 issue of the Petrograd newspaper *Russkyi Vedomosti:*

"Bolshevik agitation for an attack against the government is in full swing, unopposed, in many large plants. . . . For the last few days there has been an unbelievable influx of army deserters into Petrograd. The Warsaw railroad station is full of strange-looking, agitated servicemen. The suburbs all give a terrible impression in this respect. Along the Obvodnyi Canal, masses of drunken sailors walk purposelessly."

The Police Chief of the Narva District reported that a large band of sailors had appeared there, agitating for communism.

On October 23, the military-revolutionary committee organized by Trotsky and located at the Smolnii Institute sent out a telegram to all regiments of the Petrograd District, requesting that they obey the committee's orders and not those of the army general staff.

This act by the Communists awoke the government from its somnolence. On the same day, a cabinet meeting took place at the request of Konovalov, the Vice Prime Minister. Kerensky was present also. All members agreed that the actions of the Communists were criminal and lawless. Colonel Polkovnikov's conduct was severely criticized and it was suggested that he be replaced by a man of action and experience.

Colonel Polkovnikov was requested to attend the night meeting of the cabinet. His report was not optimistic; he painted quite a dark picture of the progress of the conspiracy, announcing that the Communists had taken over the arsenal. Konovalov suggested that the members of the military-revolutionary committee be arrested immediately. Kerensky advised, instead, that the government wait "a little longer," and he instructed Maliantovitch, the Attorney General, to prepare the case against the Communists for legal action.

On October 24, the Petrograd soviet of workers and soldiers published a proclamation. It was a call for open revolt against the government. The servicemen and the populace at large were requested to obey only the orders of the military-revolutionary committee headed by Trotsky. Thus was civil war declared by the Communists.

On the same day, Kerensky made his speech before the Supreme Council. It was his last. "In spite of all our discussions with the representatives of the military-revolutionary committee," he declared, "we have not received a definite answer from them that they have canceled their orders of disobedience to the government. Thus, they are criminals."

Sitting in the gallery of Mariinsky Palace, I was stupefied by his declaration. His mind, the mind of a legal man, was concerned primarily with the legality of the situation. He was pleased to be able to announce that the lawless and criminal activity of the Communists was proved beyond any doubt. No wonder that the response of the audience to his speech was ironic. "Naïve. . . ." "How absurd!" were the replies from the members of the conference.

"I have ordered that legal steps be taken and that arrests be made accordingly," Kerensky said. And, with emotion, he continued: "Our government can be accused of weakness and enormous patience, but no one has the right to say that our government, during the whole time I was its head, ever resorted to any active measures unless there was a threat to the very existence of our Republic. . . . And I address those members of the Supreme Council who accuse our government of inactivity and ineptness. . . ."

Cries came from the seats: "Complete slackness. . . ." "Inaction."

". . . I remind them," Kerensky persisted, "that our democratic regime, the regime of freedom, must be completely redeemed from any possible reproaches for repressive and cruel measures." [5]

While Kerensky was delivering his speech, his secretary, Flekkel, hurried into the hall and gave him a printed leaflet. Kerensky stopped. He glanced through the paper. In a slightly shaking voice he read it aloud: "The Petrograd Soviet of Workers and Soldiers is in great danger. I order your regiment to prepare for action and to await further instructions. Any delay or refusal to obey this order will be considered as a betrayal of the revolution." It was signed by Podvoisky, vice chairman of the Communists' military-revolutionary committee, and had been sent out to all regiments in the Petrograd district.

Instead of calling for immediate action against the Communists, Kerensky continued his speech for another twenty minutes. He appealed to the common sense of the aggressors, he justified his own conduct, he promised to give the Russian people everything that the Communists were claiming to be able to give. The speech was pathetic in its unreality. And yet, there was great sincerity in it, unquestionable belief in democratic principles. There was no doubt that, in spite of his instability and indecisiveness, Kerensky was always an enemy of the Communists and their totalitarian ideology. He never was, himself, an appeaser.

---

5. See Miliukoff, *op. cit.,* pp. 203-205.

Kerensky ended his speech with a call to all political parties which believed in democracy and were opposed to dictatorship to give full support to the government, menaced by the Communists. This, they did not do. Instead, the left-wingers of the democratic parties decided to have a "peace talk" with the Communist leaders. This was only too agreeable to Lenin and his followers, for it gave them additional time to organize their military forces.

The "peace talk" continued from the evening of October 24, through the night, and up to noon of the next day, October 25. The left-wingers were hopeful, as they always have continued to be in Europe and elsewhere. They believed, as still some men believe, that cooperation with the Communists is possible and that the best way to deal with them is to appease them. The "peace talk" ended without result, as all appeasement talks with the Communists have ended since their victory in Petrograd.

Late on the night of October 24, Kerensky held a conference with the leaders of the moderate wings of the Socialist parties: Avksentiev and Gotz of his own party, Dan and Skobelev of the Social-Democrat party. He accused them of not giving their full support to the government at this critical moment. Dan replied that they were much better informed than he and that "the reactionary army staff" exaggerated the gravity of the situation. He assured Kerensky that the Bolsheviks were ready to subside from their efforts at an uprising.[6]

Two hours later, at 1:30 A.M. on the 25th, Kerensky received the representatives of the Cossack regiments, which still were untouched by Communist propaganda and repre-

---

6. "Gatchina," Alexander Kerensky, Sovremenyi Zapisky, v. X, Paris, 1922, pp. 137-180.

sented a substantial military force which could save the situation. The Cossacks demanded, as a condition of their participation in the civil war, the immediate arrest of Trotsky, Lenin, and other Communist leaders. Actually, they were not very enthusiastic about giving support to Kerensky's government, and in the end they did not do so, save for their token defense of the Winter Palace.[7]

On October 25, at 10 A.M., the military-revolutionary committee issued a proclamation, obviously premature, that the government was overthrown. The Communist patrols began to move into the center of the city from the suburbs. By noon, they occupied the central telephone station and state bank. Kerensky, informed of the hopelessness of the situation, decided to leave for Gatchina, twenty-five miles from Petrograd, where several cavalry regiments faithful to the government were located. The rumors that Kerensky had left Petrograd, that he had "run away," spread rapidly through the city and produced a depressing effect on all who were trying to resist the Communists. But the fact was that he believed, in all sincerity, that he would be able to bring in reinforcements.

I was still asleep, after having listened to the all-night conference, when the telephone rang. It was Demidoff, calling me to come without delay to the Winter Palace. "Watch us die for democracy," he said. It was 11:30 on the morning of October 25.

One afternoon, returning from the hospital where I had served my internship, I was passing the magnificent *sobor* of Isaakyi. The streets were covered with a white shroud of fresh snow, two feet deep. I stopped hesitatingly on the cor-

---

7. Miliukoff, *op. cit.*, pp. 216, 217.

ner before trying to cross the snowy square. "Here he is," a by-stander murmured to me. I looked up and saw the most fantastic sight. A luxurious sledge of eighteenth-century design, drawn by six white Arabian horses, was passing before my astonished eyes. A coachman, an enormous man with a big black beard and dressed in a red caftan, was driving the sledge with his master, a handsome young man with whiskers and a high top hat, who sat comfortably behind.

"Who is this imbecile?" I asked the by-stander.

"Count K.," he answered, with a feeling of respect. "He is the great-great-grandson of Count K., the favorite of Empress Catherine the Great."

"Is he crazy, this young man?"

"Not at all. I was told that he is a brilliant man, well educated, and an expert in the fine arts. He converted a part of his famous K. Palace, the Empress's present to her lover, into an art museum."

"But why does he dress so strangely?" I persisted.

"I believe," continued the talkative by-stander, "that he's hostile to present-day civilization and prefers to remain in old Catherine's glorious time. He refuses to buy a car and drives the phaetons his ancestors used. He dresses like the young gentlemen of that time, and his many servants all have to follow his pattern."

"An inferiority complex?"

"Whatever complex he has, he's got all the money he might need to satisfy his whims. He's a multimillionaire. The K.'s were money-saving boys. . . ."

Intrigued by this paradoxical man, I asked my uncle to make an appointment for me with Count K. The Count accepted my intrusion when I explained my interest in human nature and the out-of-the-ordinary. He offered me century-old champagne and fresh caviar—it was four in the afternoon—remarking that he despised tea and coffee and was accustomed to champagne, the only beverage which "makes me see life in its true colors."

He showed me his gallery of excellent paintings and talked expansively about art. His knowledge and erudition in this field were exceptional. He had received his education at Cambridge and spent several years in Paris studying art while still in his twenties.

His studio was enormous. The windows were ceiling-high and the walls were covered with portraits of his male ancestors; all were magnificent specimens of masculinity, very tall and broad-shouldered, blond and handsome, like the Slav knights of the past.

"You wonder," K. remarked, "don't you, why I'm small and dark and so unlike them? What an irony! To be a descendant of these glamorous men, to be a K., with my insignificant appearance. . . . Well, it's a heavy heritage. At nights, when I'm working in this studio, I hear their loud voices, the laughter and the jokes. I know the life of every one of these glamorous scoundrels by heart. I live through their lives with them, again and again. . . . They are in my blood, in my mind, in my soul. I envy their dashing, buccaneering spirit, their ability to translate emotion into immediate action. They lived in the present, and they took from life what they could. They died as easily as they lived, unconcerned about death, sins, morals. Yes, they are in my blood, they make it hot and restless. This inheritance has poisoned me. I've wanted to be like my ancestors. . . ."

He walked nervously back and forth across the studio.

"I am, of course, a transcendentalist . . . not so much from logic as from personal experience. Heredity to me is much more than the transmission of physical or mental properties. I believe in God and in man's soul, and I am sure

that the 'soul' of one of my ancestors was transmitted to me.
But here I am, with my daring soul and without their courage. I can't fight, I can't even make a decision without
painful hesitation and long thought. Instead of being a buc-
caneer as they were and as I dreamed to be, I am an esthete,
an esthetic dilettante, a sybarite, a sensualist *par excellence*.
I live in the world of unreality, in the past of my ancestors. . . .

"I know it's childish to dress the way I do and pretend to
myself and the world that I belong to the past. Yet it's
stronger than myself, a sort of psychosis, whatever that
means. The masquerading brings me a little closer to reality
—or complete unreality. I consulted a psychiatrist. He said
something about a schizophrenic personality. . . . But he
added that as long as I'm harmless and not antisocial, and
perfectly normal in all other respects, he preferred to use a
milder term—eccentric."

Twelve years later, I met K. in Nice, dressed in twentieth-
century clothes. He had lost his fortune and looked like any
other man. He was an art dealer, struggling to make ends
meet.

K. and his fantastic dreams came to my mind as I hurried to the Winter Palace, the majestic building that had witnessed the glory of Catherine the Great and her dramatic
romances with the brothers K.

I walked rapidly along the Palace quay, avoiding the Red
patrols. They still were not too numerous and were uncertain
of the ultimate success of the Communist uprising.

A small band of Communists stopped me near Alexandrovsky Square. "Where are you going, citizen?" they asked.

"I'm going to a hospital," I answered curtly.

"Let him go . . . he's a doctor," one of them said.

I crossed Nevsky Prospect and reached the Square of the Palace, which was free of Communists. Patrols of cadets from the military schools formed a cordon around the Winter Palace. Here and there were a few guns manned by artillery cadets. They made no objection to my entering the building.

There, chaos reigned. The hall was filled with soldiers, officers, and civilians. They were walking aimlessly back and forth, talking, and no one seemed to be in charge.

I went at once to see Flekkel, Kerensky's secretary. "It's a bedlam . . . no one knows what to do. . . ." he complained bitterly.

"Where is Demidoff?" I asked.

"He and Paltchinsky are the only ones who are doing anything. I believe he's patrolling the right wing of the Palace adjoining the Hermitage. . . . How can anyone defend the Palace when there are so many entrances on all sides? Let's go upstairs."

He brought me to an enormous room of unbelievable luxury. It was the former studio of Emperor Nicholas II, which had been occupied for the past months by Kerensky.

"Meet our government, minus Kerensky," remarked Flekkel ironically. In armchairs, on desks, on window sills sat the ministers and other government officials. There was no general discussion, nothing but small talk, and this would stop abruptly when someone entered with news of the latest developments in Petrograd. A tall, mustached man, in a state of agitation, tried to convince a group of men, who listened without enthusiasm.

"We must, we must," he said again and again. "We must defend the Palace at any price! In forty-eight hours, not later, I assure you, we shall receive reinforcements. The Cossack regiments are coming from Pskov and other places. . . . I beg you, I beg you, let's fight hard, at any price."

It was Teretschenko, Secretary of State, trying to inject enthusiasm into his colleagues.

"Kerensky betrayed us by leaving Petrograd," Tretyakoff remarked bitterly.

A heavy man, blond and youngish, hastily put in, "Of course, we must defend the Palace. It's the seat of our government. Once it's captured by the Bolsheviks, the battle is over. But how? How can this monstrosity of a building be defended? Three hundred ceiling-high windows and twenty-two entrances. You gentlemen have talked too much the last two months. Now we are harvesting the crop sowed by our esteemed friend Kerensky, who left this mess in our hands." This was Sergei Maslov, Secretary of Agriculture and one of the most ardent enemies of communism.

It was 2:00 P.M. when Dr. Kishkin hurried in. He was met by an outburst of questions: "What's new?" "Where are the Cossacks?" "How is the General Staff Headquarters?"

Kishkin was in an angry mood. "The General Staff is doing nothing. . . . They're sitting and waiting . . . for what? God only knows. . . . I fired Colonel Polkovnikov, the scoundrel, the appeaser. I took charge of defending Petrograd myself. . . . But I'm afraid it's too late. . . . The democratic parties are in complete confusion. . . . Nevsky Prospect is occupied by the Bolsheviks. They have armored cars. They're moving toward the Palace. They're also coming in from Millionaia Street. . . ." He was interrupted by an officer who had just entered.

"The cruiser *Aurora* has been seen in the Neva delta, moving up the river," he reported to Kishkin.

"My God!" exclaimed Maslov. "This is the end. The *Aurora* is in the hands of the Bolsheviks. They'll bombard the Palace. . . ."

"Let's not lose courage," cried Kishkin. "We shall fight . . .

and fight," and he left the room. He was the most courageous of the lot, a man of action and firm decisions.

The other ministers remained in the room, discussing the chances of survival.

An elegantly dressed, middle-aged man, clean-shaven and distinguished looking, who was sitting in an armchair yawned loudly and stood up. "I believe I shall go. There's nothing for me to do. I see no action so far." And without saying good-bye to anyone he made his exit. Nabokoff was a prominent leader of the Constitutional Democratic party and a wealthy landlord.

Together with Flekkel, we left the Emperor's former studio and began to circulate among the numerous suites of the Palace. With the arrival of Dr. Kishkin, a certain order was established and the Palace defense was better organized. We found Demidoff with his cadets in the right wing. He was barricading the entrances from the Hermitage, the State Museum of Arts. On Alexandrovsky Square, the cadets were busily erecting barricades around the building.

"A pitiful defense," murmured Demidoff angrily. "We are defeated . . . we are . . . We deserve this. . . . The soft-hearted intellectuals . . . We must take our punishment right up to the end. . . . Our destiny is to be defeated in glory, like the first Christians."

Darkness descended on the unhappy city. The spirit of the defenders faded as the hours went by without any encouraging news from the outside. Here and there, suspicious-looking men in uniform were agitating for the Palace's surrender. In the chaotic hours of morning, when everyone was admitted freely and welcomed as a potential defender of democracy, many an agitator succeeded in penetrating the

Palace. Demidoff and Paltchinsky rounded up such men and put them under arrest in one of the rooms.

Tension became so strong that the cadets from the military schools of Oranienbaum and Peterhoff, composing the bulk of the defense forces, decided to call a meeting and debate the advisability of further fighting. They were almost all former university students drafted by the army and sent to officer training schools. Yes, they said, they were ready to fight and defend the government, but they wanted a strong leadership. They wanted action, not a passive, depressing anticipation of the forthcoming attack by the Communists. "They'll kill us like sheep in this undefendable building," they complained. It took Dr. Kishkin more than half an hour to persuade them to carry on their duties for democracy.

Reinforcements came. There they were, a few hundred men altogether. Cossacks, army veterans decorated with the Cross of Saint George. They were followed by a woman shock battalion.

Demidoff, standing with me in the lobby, exclaimed: "My lord! Olga brought them here!" The battalion commander was his sister, very military looking in her army captain's uniform. All the girls were tall and athletic looking. They carried their rifles smartly and marched in military formation. On their shoulders they bore a black skull on white, a symbol that they were ready to die for their cause. They marched through the gloomy Palace hall full of courage, smiling and cheering the defenders.

Hopes raised high by the arrival of reinforcements were short-lived. By seven in the evening, the situation became desperate. The Palace was surrounded on all sides. A strong group of Communists entered the basement on the side of the Palace Canal and penetrated deep into the building. Some cadets were killed, a few captured by the invaders.

New barricades were built to prevent their further advance. At precisely this moment, two soldier delegates of the Communists requested admittance to the Palace. They demanded immediate surrender in the name of the military-revolutionary committee.

Generals Malinovsky and Verderevsky advised the government to submit to the enemy's demand. The government refused. They still hoped that something might occur to change the situation.

I was in the front of the Palace, facing the Neva River, when the *Aurora* opened fire. Windows were broken and fragments of glass flew in all directions. Bullets smacked into the walls. Fortunately, it was only machine-gun fire. One bullet made a hole in the portrait of Catherine the Great, hanging on the wall. By a peculiarly ironic coincidence, it penetrated her heart.

The defenders remained silent. There was no sense in answering the fire of the enemy, protected by the armor of the battleship.

There was a commotion in the lobby. Flekkel ran toward me, shouting, "The girls are crazy. . . . Stop them! Stop them!" The woman shock battalion, he said, had decided to leave the Palace and attack the Bolsheviks. "It's madness . . . they'll all be killed." But neither Demidoff nor I was able to convince them that their act would be suicidal.

"We must save General Alexieff," Olga firmly replied to her brother.

The Square was in semidarkness. A few gas lamps threw a dim yellow light on the men who formed a gigantic circle around the Palace. Like an octopus, the Communist troops moved slowly, pushing tentacles here and there. Somewhere in the distance, behind the Imperial monument, there was animation, the constant movement of men coming and going . . . Communist staff headquarters.

The woman shock battalion advanced in battle formation, rifles in hands. The women crossed the barricades which were defended by the cadets. A female voice shouted an order: "Shoulder rifles. . . . Fire!" They fired and ran on, advancing faster and faster. They charged the left flank of the Communist forces. Surprised by the suddenness of the attack, the Communists retreated, some slowly, some quickly. A few fell, killed or wounded.

"They're in trouble," cried Demidoff, who stood with me, watching the battle anxiously. "Look, the scoundrels are encircling them. . . . The Bolsheviks are attacking their right flank." A large group of Communists was moving swiftly from the river against the battalion's rear.

Shots and inhuman wails abruptly dispersed the deceptive tranquility of the blue, starry night; the attacking Communists were beginning to shoot the girl soldiers. Some of the girls were killed, some taken prisoners.[8]

Seeing the attackers' incredible savagery, Demidoff immediately called the cadets guarding the barricades. "After me!" he shouted. "All of you . . ." They ran as if possessed by the devil. They did not shoot. They charged with bayonets into the massed Communist troops. With mad ferocity, they attacked the superior forces of the enemy, killing whom they

---

8. "The only attempt to break through the Bolshevik line was made by the woman shock battalion. . . . This attempt merely shows that any sally through the barricades constructed by the cadets was fatal. Those of the shock women who . . . were taken prisoners were subjected that same night to dreadful molestation by the soldiers, to rape and execution." Miliukoff, *op. cit.*, p. 230. See also "The Defense of the Winter Palace," Alexander Sinegoub, *Archives of the Russian Revolution*, v. 4, Berlin, 1922, pp. 121-197.

could. The Communists retreated, terrorized by the unexpected outburst. The cadets succeeded in freeing a group of girl soldiers and retreated, bringing them back to the Palace. A few of the girls were seriously wounded, but the majority had escaped with only slight wounds. Their commander, Demidoff's sister, was among the rescued. Her uniform was torn, she was covered with mud and blood. Her shoulder was bleeding profusely from a bullet wound.

We took them to one of the Empress's bedrooms. They lay on bed and floor, exhausted, frightened, yet full of spirit. "We shall have revenge," murmured Olga, grim and angry, while I was attending her, cleaning her wound.

Tranquility again descended upon Alexandrovsky Square after this unsuccessful adventure on the part of Kerensky's woman shock battalion.

The situation in the Palace was deteriorating fast. By midnight, it became evident that no further help would arrive. With gloomy faces, silent, utterly tired, the members of the cabinet realized their defeat. Dr. Kishkin alone was trying frantically to get help. He called Khroutschoff, executive secretary of the Social-Revolutionary party, and begged him to send a few hundred men. "What is your political party worth if you can't mobilize in an emergency?" he demanded. Khroutschoff's refusal was the last communication of the Palace's defenders with the outside world.

In the Empress's bedroom, Demidoff held a conference with his few officers and the girls. "We must find some way to escape from the Palace before it is taken by the Bolsheviks. We cannot allow the girls to be taken prisoners by those beasts." We all agreed. But the building was surrounded and all exits blocked by the Communists.

"I have a plan. It might work," he said, and left the room

with two of his aides. In thirty minutes he was back, almost joyful. "We have a chance. A slim chance, but it might work." And he explained that in the attic there was a door to the roof. He had found it and broken the padlock.

"Then what?" asked Flekkel, skeptically. "Where do we go from the Palace roof?"

"There's a back stairway in the east side of the Palace leading to an underground passage. From there we can reach the Hermitage," said Demidoff.

"What good would it do us to reach an underground passage? There are sure to be Bolsheviks there," persisted Flekkel.

"Let's try and see. Anything is better than waiting here."

One by one, the girls left the room, followed by a few cadets of the Pavlovsky officers' school. Flekkel and I were last. We quickly reached the roof and, slowly and silently, stumbling now and then, moved to the east side of the Palace. We reached the far end and descended, in complete darkness, to the underground passage, a relic from the time of Catherine the Great. We made our way into the Hermitage, with Demidoff in the lead. I later learned that he was a frequent visitor to this state gallery of the arts.

"We'll be safe here," he whispered. "This is the Egyptian room. Very few people ever visit it." He locked the door and with relief in his voice added, "We'll be here for many hours to come. Relax and be patient."

We lay down on the floor, close to the immobile figures of Egyptian princesses. We tried to sleep. Someone yawned loudly and murmured, "What glory to fight for democracy!"

"At least we're in distinguished company tonight," a girl's voice answered.

"Silence," ordered Demidoff.

Soon I was asleep, and a disturbing dream came to me. I

was present at a conference, which was seated around a large table. Kerensky was presiding, with an Egyptian princess at his right hand. The speaker was Potemkin, the minister of Catherine the Great. He angrily accused the Prime Minister of killing his beloved Empress. Kerensky in his turn declared his forthcoming marriage to the Egyptian princess. And then the ceiling came down with a crash and I awoke. Someone's heavy shoe was pressing hard against my face. It was morning, bright and sunny.

The rest were still asleep, snoring and moaning. Only Demidoff was up, sitting in a comfortable armchair. He was reading a book on Egyptian art which he had taken from the bookcase. "An exciting treatise," he said. But I was in no mood to discuss the symbolism of Egyptian design.

He soon left the room, locking us in. Two hours later he returned, bringing sandwiches and coffee. "Everything is under control," he announced. "The Hermitage is free of unfriendly elements. All Bolsheviks have left it. They are occupying the Winter Palace." And he advised us we would have to remain in the room for another ten hours, when darkness would facilitate our escape to freedom. He offered to give us a lecture on Egyptian art. His offer met with a coldness not surprising in the exhausted girls.

Time went by with distressing slowness, small talk wavering through the hours. When twilight came, our room was again plunged in darkness. I stood with Demidoff by the window opening on the Neva. We were silent, both experiencing the same premonition. Our Russia, the Russia of idealism, of searching and tormented soul, of passionate love and craving for sacrifice, this Russia was lost forever.

At seven in the evening, two women entered our room, bringing civilian clothes for the girls. They told us that the Winter Palace had surrendered early in the morning and that nineteen members of the government and other high officials had been arrested by Antonov, the commissar of the military-revolutionary committee, and sent to the Petropavlovskaya Fortress. A new government of Communists and left-wingers had been formed.

We left the room and, guided by one of the women, descended to the Hermitage basement, through which we reached the Summer Garden and freedom. Freedom from what? In two short days, Petrograd, the citadel of democracy, had been transformed into the center of victorious, militant totalitarianism.

Chapter 10

LIFE AS USUAL

I was awakened early by the doorbell. The postman handed me my mail. Astonished, I asked him, "Is the post office functioning today?" It was October 26.

The postman, whom I knew from student days, smiled broadly. "Of course. Why not?"

"But isn't there a civil war going on in the city?"

"Oh, that. . . . Yes, indeed."

"I've heard there's a new government. . . ."

"Yes, they say Kerensky ran away," he whispered, as if this were a secret.

"And who took over?" I persisted.

"Lenin and his comrades."

"What do you think about the change?"

He scratched his head and with a sly smile replied, "For better or worse . . . who knows?" And he departed.

There was a letter from my friend Dr. Alex L., resident at the Saint Helen hospital. It was an urgent call for me to come to his clinic. There were two cases of cancer, he wrote, and my opinion was requested. In the turmoil of political events, I had completely forgotten that man might suffer disease, that there was such a thing as cancer, that my duties were with my profession.

There was no sign of civil war. Street cars were running with the same regularity as two days before, but with fewer passengers. Bakeries and grocery stores were open and newspapers were on the stands. The big news of the day was the new government, which declared itself the Government of the People. No news of Kerensky or his whereabouts. The cabinet ministers had been placed under arrest.

Nevsky Prospect was empty. No sign of the leisurely crowd that usually walked along its splendid sidewalks. Instead, groups of Red sailors patrolled the capital's main street.

I found the hospital engrossed in its daily activity. Nurses and physicians attended their patients, surgical rooms were ready for operating, the maternity ward was filled with cries of newborn babies.

I found Dr. L. in the doctors' room. He was discussing a case of acute nephrosis with two interns.

"I'm glad you've come," he said, shaking my hand. "Let's go."

"What happened yesterday . . ." I began.

"Yes, yes," he impatiently interrupted, "a terrible thing . . . The Bolsheviks seized power . . . but let's hurry. Dr. K. is dying and wants to see you. He asked for you several times yesterday. I couldn't reach you by telephone. . . ."

"What's he dying from?"

"Cancer of the lung."

Dr. K. was certainly dying. The end was near for this

brilliant man. Physician and philosopher, he had been my professor of pathology. We had spent many hours together discussing problems of science and medicine. We always disagreed. His sharp, analytical, dialectical mind had led him to a materialistic philosophy and made him an adept of extreme mechanism in the field of biological science. He was an atheist, uncompromising and astute. He knew Bacon and Democritus by heart and often cited them to me. He found no fault with the theories of Roux and Weismann, the protagonists of materialistic biology. I never was sure I liked him, in spite of my great respect for his mind and scientific activity.

And here he was dying. What does he want from me, I wondered, following Dr. L.

Emaciated, very pale, he was lying in bed reading a book.

"I'm glad to see you," he said, with difficulty. "Very happy," he added, with an emotion unusual for him. "Of all men, I needed you most. Only to say a few words before I leave for the other world."

I noticed he was reading C. I. Lewis's *Mind and the World Order*.

"An interesting book," he remarked, "an enlightening book. The American philosopher Dewey tends to agree with him. But I see very little in common between Lewis's thinking and Dewey's. He's much more Kantian, or, if you prefer, neo-Kantian. But," he said, smiling, "I didn't call you to talk about books. I must make a confession to you. . . . It's very strange how the human mind can be obsessed by an idea. There were many nights when I was alone with my thoughts —and badly needed to see you and tell you about myself. I know we never were friends, and I always suspected that you disliked me—not personally, perhaps, but everything I believed in and taught. Now the day of retribution has arrived."

I looked into his large, gray eyes, tender and friendly, calm and penetrating.

"I know I'm dying; I've known it for three months. Even when I had no symptom but a cough, I was certain that I had cancer of the left lung. There was no clinical evidence of this condition, and none of my colleagues who examined me could find any trace of malignant growth. Yet I was sure. And I have cancer.

"I'm ready to go. I admit that it took some effort to accept the fact that my time has come. A very painful fact. Man is never able to reconcile himself, as long as he's alive, to the thought of his own death. And so much work is left behind unfinished. It never will be finished.

"From the moment I became certain, three months ago, of having an incurable disease, something went wrong with the acceptance I had of my approaching death, *my* death. I reasoned that after my death nothing would survive. Complete disintegration of my poor, exhausted body. Nothing but a combination of chemical substances. And yet, gradually, step by step, something in me began to protest violently against this fact, which I have believed all my adult life. No, no," he said, as if to prevent my interrupting him, "I'm not afraid of death. I'm too sick to be afraid of death. Life is too painful. Death will be a salvation. It has been a salvation in many similar cases of crucifyingly painful disease." He was silent for a few minutes.

"As my physical body began to lose its vitality, and my strength dropped to its lowest possible level, I experienced a strange sensation. It grew stronger every day as my disease progressed faster. It became overpowering, almost independent of my chain of thoughts. It was foreign to my mind and logic. It started as a vague sensation, and I dismissed it. Then it developed into a belief, irrational, illogical, and yet stronger than my intellectual convictions. . . . It is a belief in the immortality of my soul.

"As a biologist, I've been trying to analyze this new belief of mine. My body is dead, almost dead. My mind is clear, still skeptical, and analytical. Logically, I do not admit any possibility of my soul, any man's soul, being immortal. . . . I do not. . . . But intuitively I know that my soul is immortal. I have argued with you violently about the existence of intuition, yet I feel its presence in me as if I were seeing a cell under a miscroscope. It's a very strange phenomenon. . . . I'm trying to grasp its scientific meaning. Perhaps, when the power of our physical body over our soul is close to nothing, when it goes down to a negligible quantity, only then, perhaps, does a man experience this powerful belief in his own immortality."

He was breathing hard and speaking with great difficulty.

"And that's all I wanted to tell you . . . to make friends with . . . I'm exhausted . . . but very happy to tell you about my last hours on this earth. . . . Good-bye . . ."

I bent down and kissed his forehead. I was unable to utter a word. When I left the room he was asleep.

Dr. L. met me in the corridor.

"How is he?"

"I didn't examine him. But he can't last long."

"What did he want to see you about?" Dr. L. was very curious about my visit with Dr. K.

I was evasive. "About his work, mostly."

"I want your opinion about the other case," he said. "We diagnosed it as sarcoma of the mediastinum. However, I'm not so very sure about it."

"Who is the patient?"

"Oh, a youngish man. A fine fellow by the name of Kharitonov."

"Kharitonov?" I asked anxiously. "Not Ivan Kharitonov?"

"Yes, I believe his first name is Ivan."

"This is impossible!" I cried. "He was so healthy looking when I saw him not more than a year ago!" But there was no doubt of it. It was my dear friend Ivan Kharitonov, affected with an incurable disease.

As a high-school student I had spent two summers working as a lithographic apprentice. It was fun. It was exciting to study the precise art of lithography—and earn a little money besides.

I was assigned as a helper at a lithographic press. From the moment I entered the plant, I liked the atmosphere—the smell of paint and turpentine, the artistic attitude of the workers. I was fascinated by the multitude of colors and their bizarre combinations, all taken from an impression on stone. My master was Ivan Kharitonov, master lithographer. He loved his art. Some of the pictures were beautiful lithographs of old Dutch masters. Often the effect was achieved by the use of ten or more colors.

Kharitonov regarded me with some suspicion at first. "Your hands aren't a working boy's hands," he said dryly. "Why do you want to become a lithographer?"

I left his question unanswered. What could I say? But I tried hard to please him, and the next morning he was more friendly. He showed me the delicate intricacies of lithographic art.

He was a remarkable man in many respects. In his late twenties, he was very handsome, with a kindly face and a generous and friendly smile. The son of a typographical worker, he was widely educated and read, although he had not had a chance to finish high school. He had married early and was obliged to earn money to support a family. But he never regretted remaining in the ranks of the working class. With his ability for learning quickly and his extraordinary memory, he could easily have become a physician or a lawyer. But he had no personal ambition and was indifferent to material comfort. He lived with his wife and two small children in a three-room apartment in an old brick house. His room was filled with books and magazines and looked like an old bookshop. At the time of our acquaintance, he was organizing the international lithographer's union. He was elected president and soon made the union one of the best labor organizations in Russia.

Kharitonov liked to talk with me. While we were working together on some complicated print, he would tell me in his deep, musical voice about his ideas and dreams and plans. "Some people think," he used to say, "that there are bad men and good men. That, *droujok* [my little friend], is a great mistake. There are no good or bad men, but all can be bad and good. In every one of us there is the seed of good. The problem of our civilized society is to bring forth these good seeds and make them grow. And that's quite a problem.

"It is very easy to say: I believe in a democratic doctrine. But there is a long, extremely long, road from there to the state in which one feels and acts like a democrat. Democracy is a heavy responsibility for those who say that they believe in this doctrine. It means the sacrifice of personal desires and ambitions. It means the love of one's neighbor, good will, the restriction of all, or almost all, egoistic drivings."

He returned again to the real meaning of democracy. "It's very easy," he said, "to say that I believe in democratic principles, because the majority of us understand democracy as a full realization of human rights. Nobody ever gives the slightest consideration to the responsibility that is imposed on the members of a democratic society. Their responsibilities and obligations are incomparably heavier than for the citizen of an absolute monarchy or a dictatorship. Yes, *droujok,* one must grow into being a proper citizen of a democratic republic."

Kharitonov was strongly opposed to Marxism, which was beginning to be quite popular with the working classes of Russia. "Marxism is foreign to the Russian people, to their mentality, but it unfortunately has a popular slogan: the class war."

From time to time, Kharitonov would take me to political meetings. Usually these took place in the hall of a cultural society, "Nauka," which means "Science." There was nothing scientific about the discussions there. As a rule, the debates were bitter and noisy and revolved mostly about the relative values of two ideologies, Marxism and idealistic socialism.

At one such gathering, Kharitonov murmured to me: "There's an extraordinary man. Migounoff. Over there. He was very rich and he gave his whole fortune to building night schools for the workers, here and in his native town. Now he is poor. He has nothing. He works as a mechanic in a Franco-Russian plant."

After the meeting was over, he introduced me to Migounoff, a man about forty, very tall, clean-shaven, with dark, deep-set eyes. His graying hair was cut very short.

Migounoff looked at me and said to Kharitonov, "This boy is too young, Ivan Mikhailovitch, to come to these silly meetings."

"He's a regular workman, earning his own living," answered Kharitonov. "He's eager to learn."

"Come here, my son," Migounoff said to me. "I want to talk with you about yourself."

We found two chairs outside the hall and sat down. He looked at me for several minutes without saying a word. "Yes," he said, "you belong to our family of wanderers. I doubt whether you will ever be happy unless you find your point of application. And that's not easy. Not easy at all. We Russians are a strange race of people. Our brain belongs to the Occident, our heart to the Orient. That is what makes us what we are. We are sitting between two stools. We do not know what we want. We live in daydreams, and these daydreams are of such strength that often they become reality with us. This is the tragedy of our people. And it is my tragedy too. God bless you, my son." And he went away. I did not understand him, but somehow he made a very strong impression on me.

I told Kharitonov about our talk. "He is a very good man," my friend explained. "A self-made man. He was born in Siberia, of poor folk, graduated from a mining college, and soon made a fortune somewhere in the Urals. Yet, he couldn't bear to live a life of leisure as a wealthy man while his people, the Russian people, were poor. He is a Christian, I believe. However, he interprets his duty as a member of the Church in the way that the early Christians understood it. He gave up his fortune. Every rouble he had, he gave to charity."

While I was at the university and in medical school, I rarely saw Kharitonov. Once a month, I would stop at his home and chat with him for an hour or so. I remember with delight the summers I worked with him in the lithographic plant. Not only did I learn the art of lithography there, but I received my proper education in democracy.

And here he was at the hospital, gravely ill.

When he saw me, Kharitonov jumped out of bed and shook my hand. "The last person I expected to see here," he said, excitedly.

He didn't want to talk about his illness. "To hell with me!" he exclaimed. "Of course, I'm going to die. But who cares! Everyone dies sooner or later, so why all this fuss about nothing? These medicos!" he pointed his finger at my friend. "He and his colleagues visit me every day with morbid expressions on their faces. They tap my chest, listen to my heart, and shake their heads grimly. What nonsense! Tell them I live life from day to day and don't care if I live tomorrow or not." And he laughed.

He was terribly upset by the victory of the Communists.

"It's a devilish thing. The poor Russian people. It turns Russian civilization back a hundred years. I know these scoundrels; all they want is power. They don't care about the little man, the poor man, about any human being. I was furious when my illness kept me here the last four weeks. I begged the doctor to let me go and have a chance to fight them. . . . But they took my clothes. . . . These doctors, what do they know about a man's psychology?" And he started to ask me about my experiences of the last few days.

Dr. L., who had been present from the beginning, hurried out of the room, asking me to meet him in the intern's room as soon as I had finished the political discussion. "I have too many patients on my hands to take part in politics," he said.

I told Kharitonov about my adventures in the capital. "I'm sorry," he said, when I had told him everything, "that I wasn't with you and Demidoff on your expedition to Lenin's home. I wouldn't have failed, believe me." And I believed him.

At last, I turned the talk on his illness. He refused to discuss it. "How dare I think about myself when my people, my country, are in mortal danger? I don't want to stay alive under the Bolsheviks. . . ."

As I left, he repeated the farewell words which I had heard from him long before: "Democracy is a great word if it's properly understood. But many of us don't understand its true humane meaning."

Dr. L. asked my opinion of Kharitonov's condition.

"He refused to let me examine him," was my answer.

"Here's his case history." Dr. L. took out the hospital's record from the file case.

"About seven months ago, in April, acute tonsillitis, with sore throat and high fever. Apparently streptococcus hemolyticus. No bacteriological examination. Tonsillectomy, uneventful recovery. Six weeks later, sore throat and fever, enlargement of lymph nodes. The condition subsided gradually and the lymph nodes reverted to normal size. During the following two months, repeated attacks of throat infections. Two months ago, in August, chill, high fever of 103°, and considerable enlargement of lymph nodes on the neck. Diagnosis was made by Dr. Ludmiloff, his physician, as that of mononucleosis. This diagnosis was apparently not correct, no blood examination was made. Six weeks ago, on September 14, he was sent to our clinic by his physician. Complained of short breath, slight pain in the chest, weakness and cough. Examination: enlargement of the submandibular glands. Moderate anemia. Leukocytes: 22,000. Palpable tumor in mediastinum. Tentative diagnosis: Lymphosarcoma of the mediastinum."

I told Dr. L. and the interns my impressions of the diagnosis they had made. High fever, an enlargement of the lymph nodes, a moderate leukocytosis would rather have indicated Hodgkin's disease. I asked if the spleen was enlarged. Apparently it was. After we had discussed at length the history of this disease, first described by Thomas Hodgkin, an English physician, they agreed with my diagnosis. And the treatment? they asked. The recent work of Dr. Blumenthal, a German cancerologist, suggested the use of organic arsenic compounds. It might not cure him, yet it might prolong his life.

"And we have another case of cancer—I beg your pardon, 'psychosis of cancer,'" said Dr. L., as he led me up to the third floor. "This patient, a woman in her late thirties, had a growth on her shoulder," he explained. "She was sure it was cancer. We removed the growth and diagnosed it as a fibroid. We told her this. We said it was an innocent, harmless growth, such as often affects persons in middle age. She didn't believe us. A few months later, another fibroid appeared, on her neck. We removed it, and again it proved to be a benign growth. Since then, she's been obsessed with the idea that she has cancer. She has complained of pain in her stomach or chest and claimed that she felt that cancer was traveling around her body. Every month, she returns to our hospital for a check-up and treatment. Perhaps you can cure her, I mean, her mind."

We came to her room. She was a handsome woman, with large brown eyes and dark hair. When she saw me, she declared at once that she had cancer. "I know I have," she said. She was tense, on the verge of hysterics. "But they don't believe me. They're hiding the truth from me. But I want to know the worst and not be in the dark about my condition."

She seemed to be an intelligent person, and I went to some pains to give her a lecture about cancer. "The tumors which were removed from your shoulder and neck didn't grow fast, did they?" I asked.

She admitted they had remained stationary for several weeks. "Now," I said, "cancer as a rule grows fast. But even if the tumors were malignant or cancerous, they were taken out while they were still very small, or, as we say, incipient. There is no reason to be afraid that a cancer of that kind will spread or come back. In fact, it did not come back, did it?"

She agreed that there was no trace of new growth where the tumor was removed.

"But the fact is," I persisted, "that the microscopic investigation demonstrated on both occasions that your tumors were nonmalignant, that they were nothing but fibroids. Thousands of persons have fibroids and live for decades with them. So believe us, please, when we tell you that you have no cancer. Go home and forget your morbid thoughts about this disease. Will you?"

She smiled shyly. "I will try to believe you," she murmured.

Dr. L. and I left and walked to the lobby. Shaking my hand, he said laughingly, "Your visit was very fruitful. . . . I hope you 'cured' Mrs. S. of her cancer. I enjoyed listening to your talk with her. Good-bye, old man, and stick to your profession. It's much safer than politics!"

I left the hospital greatly perturbed. I was thinking about the life of the individual, with his personal emotions, preoccupations, worries, and diseases, facing his own death; and about the life of the community, the nation, the world at large. This, I thought, was a much more impersonal affair, abstract, remote, while the medical profession was closely interlocked with the sufferings of the individual man. My visit to the hospital had brought me abruptly back to earth, with its germs and diseases, and to man, who urgently needs medical help, whether he lives in a free democratic state or under a Communist dictatorship.

Dr. Pavlov's laboratory was not far away. In my desire to escape the memories of the night before, I decided to drop in and see what was going on.

Research was in full swing. There were no signs of confusion or slackening. Dogs were barking and howling as usual, and the experiments with conditioned reflexes were going on uninterruptedly in many rooms. Here and there a heated discussion among the assistants would attract my attention, but it was never of a political nature.

"Can an unconditioned reflex be transformed into a conditioned reflex?" asked a young medical student.

"Of course it can," insisted Dr. Zelenyi, whom I had known for several years.

I interrupted. "Did you hear about what happened last night?" I asked Dr. Zelenyi.

"What was that?" he asked in surprise.

"In the Winter Palace." Seeing the perplexity on his face, I added, "Have you read today's papers?"

"I hardly ever read them. Today, I've been very busy operating on a dog, fixing a hepatic fistula. What things are you speaking about?"

"Nothing that would concern a dog's fistula," I remarked with some bitterness. "Only that the Bolsheviks have overthrown Kerensky's government."

"What if they did?" Zelenyi was sincerely astonished. "I was under the impression he was no good. . . ." And, changing the subject, he invited me to his laboratory and showed me three dogs, each in a separate cage.

"This dog was operated on today. He still isn't feeling very well. A ligature was made on the hepatic vein, and by tying this blood vessel, a hepatic fistula was created. That, of course, is the idea of Ivan Petrovitch [Pavlov]. He feels that such an operation will make it possible to prove the predominant influence of the central nervous system on the liver. . . . But look here at the other two dogs."

They were ferocious-looking creatures. They snarled menacingly at Zelenyi and me.

"Only three months ago," said Zelenyi, "these two dogs were the quietest and most docile animals. Now, since this operation, their personalities have changed completely. . . ."

"How do you explain this?" I asked.

"Frankly, I don't know. Neither does Pavlov. Possibly it is due to an increase in bile in their blood. We shall check soon. But that isn't what I really wanted to show you. . . . Come into the next room."

Here we found five or six emaciated dogs of various breeds, small and large, in cages. They were all in a state of extreme agitation. They howled, they whined, they moaned. They were in perpetual movement, restless, upset.

"What is wrong with these poor creatures?" I asked. "What have you given them to make them so nervous?"

Zelenyi laughed. "This is our prize project. Ivan Petrovitch attributes great importance to it. As you know, he has proved that the central nervous system directs and controls all functions of the body, in man and animals alike. But now he wants us to establish, through a series of experiments, that such diseases as cancer are also influenced by the central nervous system. Or that neurotic persons, whose nervous system is overstrained, are much more predisposed to cancer than persons with a well-balanced, normal nervous system.

"An ambitious project," I remarked.

"Quite. . . . But we hope to prove that the etiology of cancer is in the alterations of the central nervous system. . . . Well, this is the first step in that direction. I rendered these dogs neurotic."

"How?" I was fascinated.

"By using the technique of conditioned reflexes. First, by forming them with a bell or light, and then inhibiting them. This technique can induce a state of extreme neurosis in normal dogs. You can see yourself that they are neurotic."

And they were, indeed.

"Now," Zelenyi continued, "we shall see if a malignant tumor develops in these dogs. We might know in a year or two."

It was to take more than twenty years, however, to complete the investigation. Not until after the death of Pavlov and Zelenyi were the results published by Dr. Maria Petrova and other Pavlov students, partially confirming their master's theory.

I left for the front the same day, taking the evening train. I found an upper berth in a half-empty car and slept the whole night. I wired my hospital from Kiev, requesting Ilya, my orderly, to meet me in Rovno. He was there with a car, smiling and happy to see me again. But he was indignant about the Communists' daring to attack Kerensky's government.

"The fight isn't over yet," he proclaimed as we drove along. "We army shock troops will restore the democratic government to power." And he told me that the shock brigades of the XIII Army were all for Kerensky and against the Communists. "Why hasn't he called on us to fight the scoundrels?" It was beyond Ilya's understanding. "Something was wrong there," he argued. "Some traitors betrayed him, I'm sure." Then, turning to the subject of hospital life, he proudly informed me that our laboratory car was completely repainted and ready for me to work in.

We arrived at Rojitsche in the evening. "We've missed dinner, Doctor," Ilya said regretfully.

"I'm not a bit hungry," was my reply.

I found the hospital personnel playing bridge in the living room. They welcomed me, and after shaking hands with each of them, I told them to go on with their game.

"What news from the capital?" asked Lochvitzky. "Heart," he announced, without waiting for my answer.

"The government was overthrown."

"A terrible thing to happen," remarked the chief surgeon. "Three spades."

"Four hearts," replied Lochvitzky. "Where's Kerensky?"

"Slam in spades," the head nurse declared.

I silently left the room and went outside. It was a cold, calm night, and the first snow had covered the earth. I took my usual path along the banks of the Malta and entered the old church. I sat on a bench. Through the hole in the church roof, which had been destroyed by a German bomb, the stars were glimmering from their distant immobility. The quiet of the night, undisturbed by any sound, brought me to a state of detached solitude. I was far away from mankind, its worries and despairs, its search for happiness, its victories and defeats. I tried to recollect my thoughts and systematize the experiences of the last three weeks. There were the Communists, aggressive, brutal, without scruples, in a mad pursuit after power. There was democracy, soft, good-hearted, seeking peace, dreaming about freedom, unable to resist the force of the aggressor. And there was the multitude of men and women, engrossed in daily activity, full of complacency, indifferent to everything except their own small world of happiness and contentment, misery and suffering.

I tried to detach myself from actuality and to see present-day political events in the light of centuries, as a small part of the road over which the human race was moving . . . moving whither?

In this light, the history of mankind became a struggle, filled with dramatic moments, between two civilizations. One—as old as the world itself, produced in the depths of the wild forests, born of the rapacious instincts of primitive men, our prehistoric ancestors, full of violence, wrath, hatred, bloodthirsty hostility instigated and supported by an insignificant minority—is the civilization of conflicts and wars and is the greatest source of human misery. The other civilization is new, grown from the study of the laws by which man lives and feels, and prompted by faith in man and the desire to see him happy. This civilization, the product of "real" humanity, insists upon man's right to freedom, to equality, to remaining himself. It denies the right of the minority to impose its will upon the majority—for it is the civilization of goodness, of love. It is born of the love of life and of humanity, of democratic principles, and of Christianity.

As I reviewed the tragic events which I had recently witnessed, I realized acutely that democracy was much more than a political system, that it was an ideology inbred in human nature, nursed by man in the depths of his heart, almost a religion. For it reflects the basic drivings of man, his unconscious belief in a free, happy, and unoppressed future for humanity. I realized that this belief was not blind or unfounded, for it was based on our intuitive knowledge of human nature, of the creative evolutionary development of the race to a final end.

As I sat in the darkness of the church, it became clear to me that the force which directed evolution was actually more than final. It transcended finality—if we understand by finality the fulfillment of an idea conceived in advance—since finality is too narrow a category for human evolution in its entirety. And a new concept began to crystallize in my mind, the concept that democratic ideas reflected and were intimately associated with the positive drives inbred in the human species; they were an essential part of man's psychic evolution. Democratic ideas can never be abolished or annihilated by the dark forces surviving from prehistoric civilization; they might be suppressed, their realization might be delayed, but in the end they will emerge victorious over the obsolete, atavistic, truly reactionary forces of the human race. Let the Communists enjoy their temporary victory over democracy. Their victory is a painful, yet perhaps unavoidable, setback in man's evolution, the goal of which is an ideal democratic state, a church on earth, where there will be no war, no bloody conflicts, and where man will be able to attain happiness to the full extent of his creative capacity.

"*Sie buddi . . . sie buddi*" ("This will come . . . this will come"), I said aloud, and my words were echoed in the vastness of the church.

Chapter 11

THE ALL RUSSIAN
CONSTITUENT ASSEMBLY

THE end of November 1917, and I was again on my way to Petrograd.[1] Against my wishes and expectations, I had been elected a member of the All Russian Constituent Assembly from the southwestern front. The armies had given me about three hundred thousand votes, on the strength of my uncompromising stand against communism. It was a clear-cut vote of confidence. But I was leaving behind me a front demoralized and in a state of anarchy. Servicemen were deserting by the thousands.

In a train already overcrowded with soldiers, thirty-two faithful men of the shock brigade accompanied me. They were fully armed with rifles and guns and were going to the

---

1. The events I describe in chapters 11 and 12 were reported by me in the article "The Defense of the All Russian Constituent Assembly," published in the *Archives of the Russian Revolution,* v. 13, Berlin, 1924, pp. 5-70.

capital to defend the Assembly, which was scheduled to convene on January 5.

In spite of the fact that the Communists were in power and had directed and supervised the elections, they had received a minority of votes: 175 seats out of a total of 701. About eighteen million votes were cast for Kerensky's political party, or a little more than 55 percent of all votes. Together with those of other democratic parties, Kerensky's total votes were 22,690,202, against 9,562,358 received by the Communists.[2] It was a disappointment to the Communists, for they had felt sure of controlling the election in their favor. Had they not succeeded in overthrowing Kerensky's coalition government on the pretext that the democratic parties were purposely delaying the elections? In October, they had called for "an immediate convocation of the Constituent Assembly," and now they had one. It was hostile to them, yet it had been conducted with unprecedented freedom, for it was the result of the first all-Russian political campaign based on the voting equality of all citizens.

What would the Communists do now? Would they prevent the convention from taking place? Would they dare to dissolve the Constituent Assembly and thus disregard the

---

2. According to Mark Vishnyak (*The All Russian Constituent Assembly*, Sovremenyi Zapisky, Paris, 1932, pp. 91, 92), the Communists and left-wing Socialists received 30.4 percent of the seats in the Assembly, and the democratic parties 69.6 percent. These figures differ slightly, but not significantly, from those given by the Soviet writer I. S. Maltchevsky in his book *The All Russian Constituent Assembly*, published in the *Archives of the October Revolution*, 1930, p. 115. His figures indicate that the Communists received 178 seats, as against the 175 credited to them by Vishnyak. The fact remains that the Communists and left-wing Socialists, who seized power, were in a minority in the Constituent Assembly.

people's vote? These questions were on the tip of every tongue in the smoky train that moved us slowly to the capital.

The moment I arrived in Petrograd, I contacted my friend Demidoff and asked him to come to the station. He came at once, and I was glad to see that he was his old self again, energetic and full of plans. He was assigned as a battalion commander to the Semenovsky Regiment, and he took charge of the servicemen I had brought with me. "They will be a valuable addition to our regiment," he said. "We shall house them in our barracks."

He came to my house that night and told me at length about the political situation in Petrograd.

The Communists were disturbed by the results of the election and were starting a campaign against the Constituent Assembly. Demidoff told me about a conversation which Lenin had had with Nathanson, one of the leaders of the left-wing Socialist party. Nathanson himself had admitted to Demidoff that he had been called by the head of the Communist party.

"How about dispersing the Constituent Assembly by force?" Lenin had asked Nathanson.

"Well," the other answered, "it might be necessary to disperse it."

"Bravo!" cried Lenin. "What is right is right, but how about your workers? Will they consent to this?"

"Some of them are hesitant, but I think that in the end they will agree." [3]

---

3. This conversation between Lenin and Nathanson was reported in *Pravda*, No. 91, April 20, 1924. As late as October 7, 1917, Trotsky declared in the name of the Communist party that "the bourgeois classes, who direct the policy of the provisional government, made it their goal to break up the Constituent Assembly. This is the fundamental purpose of the capitalistic elements." (*Facts and Documents*,

Pravda, the Communist paper, opened the attack on the Assembly. Then came a decree by the Soviet government outlawing the leaders of the Constitutional-Democratic party. "As enemies of the people, they must be arrested," read the decree. Three newly elected members of the Constituent Assembly, Paul Dolgoroukoff, Dr. A. Schingareff, and F. Kokoschkin, all highly esteemed liberals, were arrested and sent to prison. No trial was ever held. As a result of the arrests, these moderate progressive and liberal assemblymen were actually deprived of their seats. This act of the Communists was only the beginning of a savage campaign. Soon four leaders of the right wing of the Social-Revolutionary party were sent to jail: Avksentiev, Argounoff, Goukovsky, and Pitirim Sorokin. (Sorokin at present is a professor of sociology at Harvard University.)

Lenin was feverishly preparing the "ideological" ground for the forceful dispersion of the Constituent Assembly, and discussions were going on at the closed meetings of the Communist leaders. Demidoff learned that Lenin was exerting great pressure upon his right-wing leaders, who still were hesitant to act against the people's will, and soon the dispersion of the Assembly had been firmly decided upon.

The next day, when I went in search of my colleagues of the Constituent Assembly, I was informed that they were lodged in a house formerly occupied by the Red Cross hospital, somewhere on Bolotnaia ("Muddy") Street.

Moscow, 1918, pp. 147-190.) On October 26, a day after the *coup d'état, Pravda* wrote: "Comrades! With your own blood you have secured the convocation, without delay, of the master of the Russian land, the All Russian Assembly." But when the results of the election became evident, the Communists and left-wing Socialists sharply changed their attitude toward the Assembly.

"Of course," Demidoff informed me, "the Communist Assemblymen are not there. They've taken over the best hotels."

Our building was oppressive looking indeed. Dirty, long unpainted, gloomy. I entered the small vestibule, which apparently had been a hospital reception room. Twenty or more men were crowded into it.

"What are you waiting for?" I asked a bearded old man.

"For our meals, of course." And he explained that the dining room, located on the ground floor, was very small. Not more than twenty could be seated at a time. The rest stood for hours, waiting patiently for their scanty meals.

"The Soviet government is not very generous," I remarked to the man with the beard.

"I wouldn't accuse them of generosity," he replied. His name was Lazareff, a fine type of man, and he was a deputy from the Volga region. I liked his sense of humor.

He brought me to his room, which he occupied with three other deputies. It was small and had only one window. There were four army bunks, two night tables, and one chair. No closets.

"Where do you keep your belongings?" I asked, perplexed. "Where do you sit?"

Lazareff laughed. "On the bed . . . Sit down. And our clothes, we keep in wicker baskets under the beds. The true democracy . . ."

I told him about the situation in Petrograd and the plans of the Communists.

"I suspected we were in a jam," he gravely remarked.

"How are we going to defend the Constituent Assembly against the Communist attack?" I was eager to have his reaction.

"Defend the Constituent Assembly? Defend ourselves? What a ridiculous idea, my dear man." There was sarcasm in his voice. "Do you realize what you are saying? Do you realize that we are the people's representatives, that we have received the high honor of being elected by the people to write the laws of a new democratic republic? We are here as lawmakers, the builders of a great new democracy. But to defend the Constituent Assembly, to defend us, its members . . . that is the duty of the people. Is it not so? They must defend us. That's the idea most of us have. Of course, I am more realistic, but my voice carries little weight."

I was astonished. I had expected everything, but no such situation as this. I hoped he was wrong, but during the next few days I talked with many assemblymen and came to realize that the majority of them thought as Lazareff had said they did. They considered themselves exclusively lawmakers, parliamentarians, elected to write the fundamental laws of their country. To fight with laws and democratic principles within the walls of the Tauride Palace, where the convention was to take place . . . yes, that they were ready to do in a most effective manner. To fight with words in an open plenum with the Communist leaders, to argue with them, to vote according to democratic rule—for all this they were prepared. Many commissions and subcommissions had been elected. There was an agricultural commission, a commission of foreign affairs, of education, of budget, and many others. Among them, a prominent place was given to the commission of rules, which was to direct the program for the opening day. The deputies worked hard in their commissions. They discussed every detail of the proposed bills, as if the future of Russia depended upon making them perfect. They were sincere. There was no doubt of their deep conviction that they were doing the right thing and fulfilling their obligation before the people who had elected them to the Constituent Assembly.

Except for the gloomy appearance of the building and the miserable conditions in which the assemblymen lived, one might have gained the impression that this feverish pre-parliamentary activity was taking place in a democratic country like England or America, that there was no danger to the convention's very existence. The assemblymen's idealism and absence of all sense of realism were appalling. They were almost hypnotized by the "sanctity," even the "holiness" of the great All Russian Constituent Assembly. Further, many assemblymen refused to do anything which in the smallest degree could be considered undemocratic. They wanted to avoid any act which the Soviet government could interpret as hostile. But in this "perfection" of democratic ideology, they forgot that they were dealing with an utterly antidemocratic government that cared nothing for the ethics of a democratic state. Their position was, in one sense, an extreme form of loyalty to democratic principles: *they believed what they wanted to believe.* They refused to believe that Communists acted and lived by other rules of conduct. They evaluated them by their own standards of political morality.

"Appeasement" was strongly in favor among the leftist assemblymen. Tchernoff and his numerous followers believed, as, years later, Bevan and his followers in the British Labor party were still to believe, that collaboration and friendly political coexistence between democracy and communism were not only possible but desirable. As a consequence, the majority party of the Constituent Assembly took almost a neutral, and certainly a passive, attitude toward the dramatic events taking place beyond the confines of Bolotnaia Street.

Our small group of army assemblymen was the only group that persistently demanded action. The anabiotic state in which the democratic factions of the Constituent Assembly

remained at this critical period seemed to us the consequence of grave and inexcusable misjudgment, the serious
results of which could easily be foreseen.

In vain, we pointed out to them that the Communists were
very active, that they were preparing a conspiracy against
the Constituent Assembly, that the entire press was in their
hands and all opposition newspapers closed, that they had
all the facilities for poisoning the people's minds. The democratic parties, we insisted, were engrossed in endless discussions of laws and bills which might never even reach the
Constituent Assembly.

In vain did the delegations from various civic and professional organizations demand coordination between themselves and the assemblymen, so that the Communists might
be hindered from their expected armed attack on the Assembly. Their calls met with cold reservation on the part of
the Assembly's bureau of the majority party. In vain did the
delegation of the Russian cooperatives, a powerful organization with more than forty thousand active members, call for
action. Headed by Nicholas Tchaikovsky and Birkenkheim,
both men of excellent and progressive reputation, the delegation offered to proclaim a general strike.

"We could paralyze the country almost overnight," announced Birkenkheim to the bureau. "Such a strike would
make a strong impression on the Bolsheviks. It would dis-
rupt or even stop their plans for the attack. But we must have
your full endorsement of our action."

The endorsement was never given.

But our army group was very persistent. Again and again
we demanded action or, at the very least, permission to act
on our own. After long discussion, it was finally decided by
the Assembly's bureau to organize a military commission and

authorize it "to secure and prepare means of defending the Constituent Assembly."

It became the defense commission's task to organize the democratic elements, military as well as civilian, in such a manner as to prevent and counteract any possible physical assault upon the sovereignty of the Assembly.

I was elected chairman of this commission, and my task was a heavy one. Only four weeks were left before the convention was to meet, and our commission was very small. There were only ten members, all assemblymen from the army. Against us was a strong organization of Communists already in full operation. They were the government party, protected by the police and armed forces. We had on our side no more than a sincere and unbreakable belief in the rightness of our ideas and principles.

The situation in Petrograd was not very favorable from our point of view. Yet, when viewed realistically, it was not altogether hopeless. At that time, many thousands of servicemen were overcrowding barracks and streets and private houses in Petrograd. True, the majority of these soldiers and seamen had never been under fire. They had never even reached the front. Poorly trained, the young soldiers could hardly be called an army. On the other hand, there were military units composed almost exclusively of war veterans. These servicemen retained a sense of responsibility and were largely immune to Communist propaganda. They were better educated and more political-minded than the masses of newly enlisted men. With them, we were able to talk the same language and find grounds for cooperation. From this large group of war veterans, we formed the nucleus of our defense organization.

In general, the Petrograd garrison was in a deplorable state of demoralization. Nevertheless, a few regiments maintained the appearance of military discipline and kept their chain of command unbroken. It was on these regiments that our activity was concentrated. Among them, the Preobragensky and Semenovsky regiments were in best shape. The regimental committees had many educated servicemen on their board, and these exercised a good deal of influence upon the soldiers. In a matter of days we established close contact with the two regiments, as well as with the armored division, in which democratic tendencies were strongly pronounced. My colleagues and I were fortunate enough to obtain assurances that these military units would give full support to our plan for the active defense of the Assembly.

The Red army was not actually in existence at that time. The only real force at Lenin's disposal consisted of the military bands of Communists which had played such a predominant role during the October days. All the evidence that has become available since that period indicates that their military strength was inadequate for meeting any serious attack by the population. Trotsky, for example, in his reminiscences written when he was still in Russia, reported: "Lenin was worried about the day of the convention. Lenin insisted on ordering a Latvian regiment to Petrograd. He did not trust the Russians. 'Russian men might hesitate in a case of urgency,' Lenin said, 'and there we need determination.'" [4]

And Maxim Gorky's newspaper *Novaya Gisn* ("New Life"), which had full information on popular sentiment in the Soviet of People's Commissars during the last days before the convention, said: "Sovnarkom passed these days in great worry. News arrived that the Preobragensky and Semenovsky regiments had decided to support the majority party of the Assembly and would participate in a demonstration under

---

4. *Pravda*, April 20, 1924.

the slogan 'All Power to the Constituent Assembly.' The same tendencies were reported in the Second Baltic Regiment. Alarm extended from the Smolnii to all Soviet institutions. . . ."

Commissar Kuzmin, in charge of the Petrograd garrison, confirmed the actual weakness of the military forces at his disposal.

And what were the feelings of the Petrograd population? They were whole-heartedly behind the Constituent Assembly. Although the Russian people were confused and apathetic in the days of the October civil war, disappointed in Kerensky's government, and irritated by its ineptness and indecisiveness, they were strongly behind the new, properly elected Constituent Assembly. The working class, industry and commerce, and the liberal professions all were ready to support it. And the Communists knew this. In spite of their intensified propaganda and the fact that they had closed down all the democratic newspapers, their achievement was slight. There is no question but that the population was angered by their attitude and their tactics.

There was no publication in existence which was free to raise its voice against Soviet propaganda.

"We must have a daily independent newspaper," I announced. "But how?"

Any attempt to publish an opposition paper would have been stopped at once by the Communists, and the publisher and printer thrown in jail.

Demidoff made an excellent suggestion. "The paper should be published by the Semenovsky and Preobragensky regiments, which are sympathetic to democracy. And the editor in chief should be a member of the regimental committee."

Thus was born the famous newspaper *The Soldier's*

Capote, which for three weeks mercilessly and relentlessly attacked the Communists. It was the only free newspaper in those preconvention days.

The publishers were announced as the committees of the Preobragensky and Semenovsky regiments. The editor in chief was Boris Petroff, a private in the Semenovsky regiment. I acted as managing editor. My knowledge of printing helped me considerably in this extraordinary venture.

Our paper was violently anti-Communist. We attacked the strategy and the hypocrisy of the Soviet leaders. We boldly stated that they intended to dissolve the convention because they had received a minority of votes. We emphasized again and again the importance of this convention, and the role it would play in the democratic progress of our country. Unhesitatingly, we declared that the Communist movement was reactionary and its only goal was power.

The success of the paper was fantastic. All ten thousand copies were sold in a few minutes, and the price of a single copy rose to several roubles. Of the second issue, we published twenty thousand copies.

Pravda attacked us at once, denouncing us as "capitalistic servants." But we had decided on a policy of boldness which we believed was the only justifiable course, under the circumstances. We knew that, were it not for the patronage of the two regiments, we would never have been tolerated for a day. But the military might of the regiments was a reality which the Soviet leaders had to take into consideration. On the third night, however, they sent a detachment of Red sailors and confiscated our third issue.

We did not capitulate. We found a new printing shop and began the publication of the *Bullet-torn Soldier's Capote.* We attacked the Soviet government even more aggressively than before. We accused them of suppressing a free press and of using dictatorial methods. But this time we took careful precautions. A detachment from the two regiments protected our little printing shop on Tchernischeff Square.

These days, or nights, we were in a state of feverish activity. Petroff, Demidoff, and I, together with three soldiers who formerly were newspapermen, wrote the editorials, articles, and news stories. One of our group was a good cartoonist, and we carried cartoons of Lenin and his fellow Bolsheviks. In one cartoon, Lenin, with a crown on his head, was sitting on the Czar's throne and saying: "Comrades, I am the dictatorship of the proletariat." A private who had lost a leg in the war was asking him, "But where is the proletariat?" "I don't know," Lenin replied. "And I don't care. The important thing is that the sign is already painted."

We couldn't meet the ever-increasing demand for the paper. It was sold by the soldiers of the two regiments, and for some reason there were only a few attempts on the part of the Communists to interfere with its distribution. But after twelve issues had appeared and the circulation had reached 40,000, the Soviet government decided to take energetic steps. On January 2, Krylenko, the Communist leader, appeared in the barracks of the Semenovsky regiment and called a general meeting of the soldiers. Krylenko was an excellent speaker. I had known him from the time he was a student at the University of St. Petersburg. Small, dynamic, dialectic, and superficial, he was effective in a demagogic way.

He spoke angrily and without control. He accused the regiment of giving support to "the enemy of the proletariat, to the obedient servants of international capitalism," meaning us. He called our newspaper "a dirty corrupt sheet which I would not even care to make use of in a water closet." He spoke with increasing bitterness, employing the usual expressions and expletives of the Communist propagandists. "Do you want to remain under the domination of blood-thirsty international bankers? If not, then close this anti-proletarian, filthy newspaper."

Krylenko had made a grave mistake. He threatened the regiment with severe punishment if they did not obey him. This produced violent indignation among his listeners, and his speech ended amid shouts and boos. "Enough! Enough!"

Then Boris Petroff, our editor, spoke up. He was no orator. He spoke very simply and without fire. He acknowledged that he was the editor in chief of *The Soldier's Capote*. He protested against the abusive words used by Krylenko. "Who are you, Mr. Krylenko," he said, "to teach us a lesson and threaten us? . . . You have usurped power. You have closed all newspapers but your own. From beginning to end, there is nothing but lies in all your claims and statements. You deny today what you said yesterday. You use slogans which can appeal only to completely ignorant people. Do you think we are ignorant creatures, Krylenko? What is this talk about international bankers and whatnot? Who is crazy . . . we or you? The issue between us is clear. For more than three months you demanded the immediate convocation of the Constituent Assembly, and your avowed purpose was to over-throw the provisional democratic government. It was under your direction, and may I say under your pressure, that the elections took place. I myself saw how your party members falsified the results in your favor. I know of rear-army de-tachments who claimed four times as many voters as they actually had. And, in spite of all your efforts, you lost the election. And now you are attacking the same Constituent Assembly elected by the people, and you are ready to dis-perse it by armed force, yes, by armed force. And because there are still a few courageous people in this regiment who are ready to defend their—yes, *their*—Assembly, and they publish a newspaper which prints nothing but the truth, you have the nerve to threaten us as if we were your slaves. Be ashamed, Krylenko!"

Unanimously, the Semenovsky regiment decided to continue the publication of *The Soldier's Capote* and to give it full armed protection.

Those nights in the printing shop, protected by machine guns against possible attack by the Communists, were exciting ones. Outside the frozen windows, three-foot-deep snow covered the square. It was very cold in the shop, for the only heat was furnished by a small fireplace. Consuming enormous amounts of hot tea, we were in high spirits as we discussed which editorials to publish, which cartoons were the most effective, and how to present the news items collected by our city editor.

"What do you think of this cartoon?" and Serge, the cartoonist, would show us Kamkoff, the left-winger, with a long tail and on four paws, licking the hand of Lenin, who was saying: "Go away, you dirty dog. . . . I don't need you anymore."

"Excellent. . . . Kamkoff will be furious."

At about four o'clock in the morning, the four-page sheet would be ready, fresh off the printing press. We would immediately awaken the soldiers who were guarding us and read the paper to them. We counted heavily on their reaction as a test of public response. For *The Soldier's Capote* was addressed not to the intellectuals but to the masses of people whose minds were poisoned by Communist propaganda. "*Khoroscho . . . khoroscho*" ("Good . . . good"), the soldiers would say. When we found that it "clicked" with them, we were ready to distribute the issue to the public.

The four weeks of feverish activity on the part of our commission were bearing fruit. Our plans for January 5 were almost ready. As the day of decision approached, our military commission became more optimistic than ever. On January 3, we reviewed the over-all picture as impartially and critically as it was possible to do. Power was in the hands of the Communist party, but this power was not altogether real. There was an element of hesitancy in their actions. True, they had received a large number of votes in the Petrograd district, but this did not mean that the voters were members of their party. Neither did it indicate that everyone who had voted for them was an enemy of the democratic Constituent Assembly. On the contrary, the majority of people had given them their votes because of the Communist slogans "Immediate peace" and "Immediate convocation of the Constituent Assembly."

The paradox of the situation was this, that even those who had voted for the Communists were wholeheartedly behind the Constituent Assembly. Large factories such as the Franco-Russian steel plant, and regiments such as the Ismailovsky and Litovsky organizations, which had given them many votes, were firmly against an armed assault on the Constituent Assembly. Every time a Communist speaker tried, even timidly, to attack the sovereignty of the Assembly, the audience shouted: "Don't touch the Constituent Assembly! Don't you dare attack it!" And our impression was unanimous that, except for the Red soldiers, numbering about 10,000, no one would make any attempt to disperse the convention.

What was the morale of the Communists? Many of them were preparing to leave the city in the event of a democratic victory. Documents showing the true situation in those days, later published in the Communist press, all confirm, although indirectly, the precariousness of their political situation and indicate their uncertain prospects in the fight for the Constituent Assembly. "Lenin is worried," wrote Dybenko.[5]

Our commission arrived at the conclusion that the chances were about equal. A victory for democracy, in our opinion, hung on the Assemblymen's firm conviction that the fight, however bloody, was justified and unavoidable. It was clear to us, as it was to everyone except the "parliamentarians" on Bolotnaia Street, that the final decision in the struggle between Communists and democrats would take place on the streets of Petrograd and not in the Tauride Palace.

We went carefully and in detail into the plans for January 5. As always, it was Demidoff who supplied the inside information on Communist plans.

"They realize," he explained, "the difficulties of their position. They are realists . . . are they not? They expect a demonstration of about two hundred thousand people in favor of the Constituent Assembly. They have decided to disperse it. But they have no armed forces to cope with this movement. So their plan is to mobilize all the armed forces on which they can depend completely—and there are no more than twelve or fifteen thousand men at their disposal— and to throw an armed cordon around the Tauride Palace. A very clever tactic. All streets surrounding the Palace will be filled with Red soldiers. Only members of the Constituent Assembly will be admitted through this circle. Do you see the cleverness of their plan?"

We saw it very clearly. They intended to isolate the All Russian Constituent Assembly from the rest of the city and thus render it harmless, and perhaps even to make it the prisoner of the Soviet government.

"That isn't all," Demidoff continued. "I learned that as

---

5. *The Rebels*, Krasnyi Novi, Gosizdat, Moscow, 1923, p. 108.

long as the people's demonstration is peaceful and unarmed, they hope to succeed. Lenin is exerting strong pressure on Tchernoff, through the left-wing Socialists, to forbid any armed demonstration on our part."

"I don't believe it," said Sourgoutscheff, a member of our defense commission.

"Anyhow, our plan is clear," Demidoff resumed. "Our immediate goal is to break their military cordon and penetrate to the vicinity of the Tauride Palace." We all agreed.

Our strategy was simple. The largest street leading to the Tauride Palace was Liteinyi Prospect, a splendid avenue. Our two regiments, both located near the Fontanka River, would form the spearhead of a huge crowd of anti-Communists. An armored division would help the regiments to break through the Red military outposts, smash them to pieces, and lead the anti-Communists to the Tauride Palace.

Many labor unions and professional and civic organizations willingly consented to take part in the procession. Once the Tauride Palace was reached and armed pressure by the Communists relieved, the convention could proceed in a much more normal and peaceful atmosphere, guided by the democratic majority of the Assembly.

We saw no flaw in our plans and were quite satisfied with our accomplishments.

While our military commission was trying to mobilize all possible military forces for the defense of the convention, life for the assemblymen on Bolotnaia Street went on uneventfully. One after another, bills were elaborated for presentation to the Convention's plenum. These bills, which would have become law if the Constituent Assembly had survived, were very progressive. An extensive plan for general education reform was offered. A bill considerably reshaping the ownership of land was worked out to the smallest possible detail. Considerable autonomy was planned for the various national areas of Russia. And it was assumed that from all these reforms a United States of Russia would gradually emerge which would contribute to the rapid progress of the nation as a whole. The right of private property was retained, and hopes were expressed that individual initiative would soon be able to develop a more extensive industry and commerce.

The assemblymen, engaged in the technicalities of law-making, showed little if any interest in what our commission was trying to achieve. They seemed wholly detached from the events which were fermenting in Petrograd.

We were in a high mood and hopeful of success when we gathered in Demidoff's apartment on the night of January 3. We delegated Sourgoutscheff to report our plans to the Assembly's bureau and obtain its final approval.

It was late at night when he returned. We could see at once that something had gone wrong. He was gloomy and silent.

"All is lost," he declared at last. "Demidoff was right. Tchernoff, the eternal appeaser, has agreed to sell us out, under pressure from Lenin. How naïve, how childishly naïve he is." And he explained that in the absence of the right-wing Socialists, who were in jail, Victor Tchernoff remained indisputable master of his party. He objected strongly to any armed demonstration on January 5. "We must avoid any provocative act which might anger the Bolsheviks," Tchernoff had declared. "We must show them that we want a peaceful settlement of the conflict. We must demonstrate our good intentions and our willingness to cooperate with the people. We are their representatives, and it is our task to carve out the future of Russia."

The majority in the bureau and in the national committee agreed with him. Some refused to believe or even admit the possibility that the Communists were conspiring against the high convention. "It's a dangerous adventure, this armed demonstration," argued Mark Vishnyak, the general secretary of the bureau.[6] "It might spoil all our chances of opening the convention and presenting our bills. We've been entrusted by our electors to introduce the laws according to which many generations of Russians will live."

Tchernoff stressed that he had received assurances from Lenin that no pressure, no assault would be made on the Constituent Assembly by the Communists.

"Who told you so?" Sourgoutscheff angrily inquired.

"Martov and Nathanson [left-wing Socialists] informed me of Lenin's attitude."

"Was this official?" insisted our delegate.

"Yes, more or less. And if you want to know, I myself asked them to discuss this matter with Lenin," admitted Tchernoff. "Lenin has no malicious intentions toward the Constituent Assembly. And any armed demonstration would bring us into conflict with the Soviet government. We must avoid this at any price."

---

6. Discussing my memoirs (see the *Archives of the Russian Revolution*) in his book *The All Russian Constituent Assembly,* Vishnyak admits that the position of his party bureau was to prevent civil war, by any means, until the Constituent Assembly should be dispersed by the Communists, in order to preserve the dignity of that institution (pp. 228-230). He considers those Assemblymen who wanted to enter into armed combat with the Communists to be "lovers of risk and adventure." Many Americans would find it difficult to understand the extreme idealism of the majority of the Assemblymen.

In vain, Sourgoutscheff defended our plans. He painted a grim picture of the situation in Petrograd. He pointed out the Communist campaign against the Constituent Assembly, the arrests of many assemblymen, the concentration of armed bands around Smolnii, the complete suppression of the opposition press. But all this argumentation failed to change the attitude of the Assembly's bureau. The decision was made. No armed demonstration was to be allowed. "Unarmed demonstration of soldiers and civilians is, of course, welcomed," Tchernoff concluded.

"You haven't learned a thing!" shouted Sourgoutscheff. "Well, you will have your bitter lesson the day after tomorrow. You're as blind as a mole who lives under the earth. Do you realize that the issue between the Bolsheviks and the democratic parties will be decided *not inside* the Tauride Palace, as you naïvely assume, but *outside*, on the streets of Petrograd, on convention day?" And he left the conference without saying good-bye.

We were crushed by the decision. It was incredible. There was no doubt in our minds but that the cause of democracy was already lost by this inexcusable and dangerous appeasing movement on the part of the Assembly's bureau. Nevertheless, we obeyed it. We had no choice.

The same evening, we informed the committees of the Semenovsky and Preobragensky regiments that the armed demonstration had been called off. *The Soldier's Capote* ceased to exist the next day. Its last issue, its last song for democracy was composed by us, without hope, without enthusiasm, in the dead and morose silence of despair. Half of the front page was made up of large letterheads:

"Long Live the ALL RUSSIAN CONSTITUENT ASSEMBLY."

"Damn the Usurpers of the People's Power."

"Damn the Bolsheviks."

Demidoff suggested adding: "Death to the Appeasers," but we voted against this. It would have been too obvious a self-accusation, directed toward the leaders of democracy.

Chapter 12

JANUARY FIFTH

THE day was cloudy and cold.[1] The city, covered with thick snow, was in a gloomy, angry mood. Nobody smiled. The faces of passers-by were troubled. Here and there small groups of people moved silently and slowly in the direction of the city's central artery, Nevsky Prospect. A group of workers and white-collar employees paraded with banners. All the banners bore the same words: "Long Live the All Russian Constituent Assembly." Among hundreds of banners, I was not able to find one favoring the dispersion of the Constituent Assembly. Many unarmed soldiers and sailors joined the parade, and people were shouting, "Down with the Bolsheviks!"

---

1. The events of January 5, as I recorded them in the *Archives*, and as they appear in this chapter, are told almost identically by Mark Vishnyak, who was Secretary-general of the Convention, in his book *The All Russian Constituent Assembly*, pp. 98-116.

As I came closer to the Nevsky, the streets became more crowded. The mood of the paraders was slowly mounting into anger. By eleven in the morning, enormous crowds filled Nevsky Prospect and all the streets leading to the Tauride Palace. Hundreds of banners demanding "Down with the Bolsheviks," "Away with the Tyrants" were slowly moving toward the Palace.

The vanguard of the demonstration reached the "Red guard" detachment stationed on Liteinyi Avenue. This detachment was very small, comprising not more than fifty armed Communists. They gave up in the face of the immense crowd moving upon them and disappeared. A hundred feet farther on, a larger detachment of a Latvian regiment barred the road. There were no barricades or wire entanglements between them and the crowd. Only twenty machine guns. A crowd of thirty thousand people faced five hundred Latvian soldiers imported by Lenin for the occasion.

When the distance between the Communist detachment and the throng became less than fifty feet, the Latvian soldiers opened fire into the crowd of demonstrators, aiming at those who carried the banners. A student from the Institute of Technology, leading a group of his colleagues, was killed instantly. Two workers from the Treougolnik factory fell, gravely wounded, still holding a banner that read: "Down with the Murderers of Democracy."

The crowd surged back in panic, leaving a dozen dead and wounded on the street. But new masses of shouting, angry people pouring from Nevsky Prospect pushed forward. The Latvian regiment, reinforced by a detachment of Red sailors, opened up with a murderous fire. This time, workers from the Oboukhov factory, known for their democratic tendencies, took terrible punishment. A well-known member of the workers' cooperative union, Loguinoff, was wounded in the chest, and about twenty other workers and bystanders were killed or wounded. This time the crowd was unable to withstand the fire. Slowly they fell back. Here and there one heard "To arms, citizens, to arms!" But there were no arms. An old worker in a peaked cap said to me, "Oh! if only a small detachment of our soldiers were here, we could easily crush these Latvian swine." But not even a company was available on the democratic side. The leaders of democracy had forbidden any armed demonstration.

I gave first aid to Loguinoff and helped carry him to the hallway of a private house nearby. He was still breathing, but he died soon after from an internal hemorrhage. I left him and stepped down into the street.

The distance between the Red Latvian soldiers and the throng of demonstrators was about two hundred feet. Both sides remained passive, as if expecting some new development in the situation, but on the other streets and avenues leading to the Tauride Palace, similar scenes were taking place. Democratic sympathizers were nowhere able to penetrate the military cordon installed around the Palace. From many people who observed these hopeless attempts to reach the convention and save it from the humiliation of an armed dispersion, I heard the same story. The balance of power oscillated between the two sides. More than two hundred thousand people participated in the demonstration, demanding the transfer of power into the hands of the Constituent Assembly. Against this huge, enraged mass, the Soviet government had only enough armed forces to prevent unarmed crowds from reaching the convention. One regiment would have been sufficient to throw the delicate balance of power in favor of democracy. This was admitted by many Communist leaders in private conversation. They were afraid, uncertain how violent the people's anger might become.

It was noon. The city was still in a convulsion of rage at being unable to achieve its goal and break through the armed opposition. But the climax of indignation had been reached. It began to decline. Subfreezing weather worked on Lenin's side. The streets, covered with ice and snow, were unpleasant ground for demonstrating. The throngs of people were still encircling the streets around the Palace, but apathy and hopelessness were gradually replacing the earlier fury. By now, it was clear to me that nothing could save the Constituent Assembly short of a miracle. Reluctantly, and only out of a sense of duty, I decided to go to the Tauride Palace. To be killed? I expected anything.

I approached the Red cordon and was promptly stopped by the Latvian soldiers. "What the hell do you want?" the sergeant rudely demanded. I was in my army doctor's uniform.

"I am a member of the Constituent Assembly."

"Let's see your card."

I took out the red card, with the signature of Uritsky, the Peoples' Commissar. The sergeant said nothing, and in silence he allowed me through the cordon.

Ideas have a magic power over the human mind. When a man believes in an idea, and this idea is strong, sincere, and deeply implanted in his mind, he loses some sense of reality. His faith in his idea enslaves him; it paralyzes the centers of perception and critical analysis. The idea of a democratic Constituent Assembly had dominated the life of the Russian intelligentsia for decades. The Constituent Assembly, elected on the basis of full participation by the people, was the goal of the stubborn, bloody fight that the democratic intelligentsia had waged for almost a century. And at last the goal was near. In a few hours, the All Russian Constituent Assembly would open its historic convention. In spite of all the distressing rumors and abnormal circumstances, deep in their hearts the members of the Assembly retained their faith in the mysterious power of this institution. They were the representatives of the people, elected according to democratic law. They lived in the humanitarian traditions of the Russian intelligentsia. They believed in man, in honest political disagreement, and in respect for other men's opinions. All in all, they were idealists, this group of three hundred men who gathered at noon, January 5, on Bolotnaia Street. They were ready for the worst, to die if necessary for the idea of the Constituent Assembly and democracy. However, they were not prepared for what they met in the Tauride Palace. The thought had never entered their minds that anyone would try to make fools out of them, or out of the idea of the Constituent Assembly. They did not know Lenin well enough.

The Tauride Palace looked like an armed camp. Everywhere were armed sailors, Latvian soldiers, and groups of civilians, with shotguns and machine guns. Several cannons were in readiness before the Palace. All doors were closed but one. Again a military detachment checked my ticket. I entered the reception hall of the Palace and another armed group asked for my identification card.

I went on into the great assembly hall, where the opening session was to be held. It was filled with Red sailors and Latvian soldiers. They wandered around, they occupied the galleries. The members of the convention also wandered around, asking one another in low voices, "Will the convention really open?" "Will they disperse it before the session even begins?"

The assembly hall was very cold.

The Communist faction was absent, holding a meeting somewhere. Hour after hour went by, and still no sign of it. Not until much later did we learn that Lenin had purposely

delayed the convention's opening in order to be assured of
the situation in the city. He knew of the possibility of demonstrators breaking through the military cordon and reaching
the Tauride Palace. And so it was on the streets of Petrograd
that the fate of the convention was actually being decided.

Not until about 4:00 P.M., four weary hours after the convention was to have opened, did signs of activity appear. By
that time, Lenin was assured that his armed forces had with-
stood the pressure of public indignation and that the crowd
had begun to disappear from the streets. It was the green
light for action. Now he was in a position to do as he pleased.

Lenin had already won the battle. Democracy was at his
mercy. However, to make his victory even more complete
in a moral sense, he decided to submit the Constituent Assembly to a maximum of humiliation. "No bloodshed," he
ordered; he did not want to make martyrs of the Assembly
members. But the behavior of his adherents and the conduct
of the soldiers and sailors chosen for admission to the session
fully indicated his intention of making a mockery of the convention.

The great assembly hall of the Palace was slowly filling.
The armchairs on the left were occupied by the Communist
faction; those in the center and on the right, by representatives of the democratic parties. Several leading Communists
took their places on the platform. Among them were
Dybenko—the colorful figure who some years later was "liquidated" by Stalin—and Stecloff. Lenin sat in a box on the left
of the platform. He was very pale and seemed nervous.[2] He
looked back and forth around the hall, observing the audi-

2. The Communist Bontch-Brouevitch writes: "Vladimir Ilyich . . .
   was nervous and deadly pale as never before. . . . He sat clutch-
   ing his hands convulsively." *On the Fighting Posts of the February
   and October Revolutions,* p. 256.

ence. From time to time, Stalin would approach him and, after receiving some instruction, would depart again. Trotsky was absent. He was discussing peace terms with the Germans somewhere on Russia's western front.

Before taking my seat, I mounted the stairs to the galleries. These were filled almost entirely by Red sailors and Latvian soldiers. Armed with rifles and automatic guns, they had been posted there to produce a psychological effect upon the convention. Many were young boys who had never seen war. Most of them looked like deserters. Some were drunk. Here and there a group was playing cards.

I asked of one group, "Are you men members of the Bolshevik party?"

"No."

"Why did you come here?"

"We were ordered by our committee to be here in case we were needed."

Their leader was a red-haired sailor from the battleship *Aurora*, and I listened as he addressed them. "When I raise my hand," he instructed them, "shout: 'Down with the bourgeois scoundrels.' You may threaten them with your rifles, but don't shoot. It is a strict order that no blood should be shed today. Do you understand?" And to some of the older sailors, he added, "Watch your comrades."

I tried to talk with some of them. "Do you realize what the convention has been called for?" I asked a young sailor with an open, friendly face.

"No," he murmured, somewhat confused and embarrassed by my question. "I don't know much about this convention. They sent me here, but I don't know why."

At ten minutes past four, a tall, graying man, Lorkipanidje, a representative from Georgia, proposed that the oldest member of the convention should open it. Sergei Schvezoff, a

Social-Revolutionary, with a white beard and long gray hair, rose and mounted the platform. He was greeted with hisses and calls from the gallery and from the Communist faction: "Usurper!" "Capitalist!"

Schvezoff rang for order, but in vain. He called for silence, in vain. The cries and general uproar continued for several minutes. Angered, Schvezoff shouted: "I declare the All Russian Constituent Assembly opened."

His words were drowned out by an organized uproar from the gallery. At that moment, Avanesoff, secretary of the Communist central committee, snatched the bell from Schvezoff's hand and gave it to Sverdloff, a Communist. The noise stopped at once, as if by magic. All was silence, followed immediately by applause from the gallery and the Communists. This continued for several minutes.

"Long live Lenin!" "Down with the capitalists!" "Down with the international bankers!" shouted the sailors from the gallery.

Finally, Sverdloff rang the bell and declared the convention opened. In his speech, which, as we now know, was written by Lenin, Sverdloff expressed hope that the Assembly would approve and accept without reservation all decrees and laws introduced by the Soviet of People's Commissars. What he called for amounted to a demand to recognize "the dictatorship of the proletariat," or, in other words, the dictatorship of the Communist party, and to renounce all aspirations for a democratic state and human rights.

He proposed, in effect, that the convention capitulate, that it serve as a sort of appendage to the Soviet of People's Commissars, in a consultative capacity. But even this offer was by no means sincere, nor did it reflect Lenin's true intentions. In presenting this declaration, Lenin was only preparing the ground for a new political slogan with which to impress the masses. A few days later he was to tell the Russian people that "the reactionary elements in the Constituent Assembly refused to accept the people's power and clung to their capitalistic friends"; that he was obliged to dissolve this "reactionary convention for the sake of the people."

While Sverdloff was reading his declaration, I observed that Lenin was writing a note. He sent this note to one of the leaders of his faction. Immediately after Sverdloff's speech, the leader rose and requested that the "Internationale" be sung. Again clever strategy on Lenin's part, for it put the convention in an embarrassing position. The request was accepted by the convention and, rising to their feet, the members of the assembly sang the "Internationale," some willingly, some unwillingly. Many remained silent.

Sverdloff's speech had ended with wild applause from the gallery—and shouts from the center and right: "Shame . . . shame!"

The election of the Assembly president followed. Victor Tchernoff, former Secretary of Agriculture in Kerensky's government, was elected by 244 votes to 151, with many abstentions. His opening speech, however, instead of being strongly anti-Communistic, was actually a speech of appeasement. Yet his words evoked neither sympathy nor even tolerance on their part. He spoke in an atmosphere of openly exaggerated hostility on the part of the gallery. His speech was repeatedly interrupted by shouts of "Bourgeois lackey," "Enough, windbag . . . enough, you old capitalistic reptile."

Again and again, Tchernoff called for silence, begging "respect for the dignity of the convention" and asking the public to leave the gallery. The only answer was an increase in the force and variety of noise. For minutes on end, not a word could be heard from the speaker. Only the movements of his mouth and the gesticulations of his hands told us that he was continuing his speech.

Although I was seated well up front, in the second row of armchairs, I was able to hear only a part of what Tchernoff said. He expressed the hope that a common language could be found among the various factions, that the birth of the All Russian Constituent Assembly meant an end of fighting among them.

But not only were the Communist-controlled galleries hostile; further than that, Tchernoff's speech was received with silent irritation on the part of the democratic majority. There was no room for appeasement, and everyone knew that the moment acutely required a firm moral position.

Bukharin, a close friend and collaborator of Lenin, spoke soon after and left no doubt about where his party stood. "There is an enormous chasm between you and us," he announced to the parties of the majority. "We want complete dictatorial power over all political functions in this country . . . and you are defending a scabbish parliamentary republic. . . ." And he ended with a strong, definite declaration: "From this platform, we proclaim mortal war to any and all democratic ideas." No stronger statement could have been made by Lenin's party. The Communists had signed the death warrant of the convention.

The most brilliant and impressive speech was spoken by Tzeretelli, a Social Democrat from Georgia. He was met by cries of: "Traitor!" "Kill him!" "Capitalistic hireling!" But his powerful speech commanded the attention of the whole assembly and even silenced the elements in the gallery.

"Members of the Constituent Assembly," he began, "today's events will have tragic consequences for democracy throughout the whole world. It is a tragic day for every freedom-loving nation. History will not forgive the disgrace of which we are witnesses, the ignominious and shameless conduct of the minority of this convention. Yes, I repeat," addressing the Communists, "your hateful and repellent conduct. There is no excuse for your conduct, no justification. . . . Nothing can warrant such insolence as we witness on the part of those who claim that they are the government of this country. They are not the government."

And, step by step, Tzeretelli described the insidious tactics of the Bolshevik party. "You all are elected by the people, you all are responsible before your electorates. . . . You, too, of the Bolshevik party were elected by the people to defend this high institution, not to conspire against it. You were sent here to write the laws of the country, the democratic laws, and not to try to establish the rule of a small minority. You are traitors not only before this high convention but before the people who elected you and who instructed you to work for democratic ideas." And he developed his point that even the Communist members of the Assembly were bound by their promise to write democratic laws. Had they not been elected according to free and general electoral law? Had they not assured the people that they would accelerate the assembling of this convention? And now what were they trying to do, they who had received only a minority position in the same convention? They were preparing a conspiracy, in the most bare-faced fashion.

"Who are you," Tzeretelli demanded, "who dare to raise your hand against the most sacred right of any nation . . . the right to dispose of its own fate, to write its own laws?" And he asked them what they could give to the people that this Assembly could not. "The Assembly," he said, "is ready to write extensive and far-reaching laws, which can put Russia on the road of progress and prosperity. There is no single field of social reform which will not be met with approval by the convention, except one important point, *the fundamental principles of democracy.* In this respect, and only in this respect, there lies an enormous difference between you and us."

He declared that what the party of the minority wanted was power, and nothing else. The decrees of the Soviet government were nothing but a batch of demagogic declarations, which were not worth the paper on which they were written. "If you want power, have the courage to say so." He accused them of misleading the people with all kinds of slogans and declarations which had no meaning and served only to deceive. "History will punish you sooner or later for this political fraudulence."

His speech was met with a long, warm ovation from the majority of the convention. The Communists remained subdued and morose during these few minutes of moral triumph for democracy.

Lenin had sat silent in his box, listening to Tzeretelli's speech. His face was expressionless, sphynxlike. If he disliked what he heard, he showed no sign of it. Tzeretelli was a political leader of spotless reputation, respected equally by political friends and enemies. He was a man of great moral courage, of unshakable honesty of opinion, and without a trace of demagogy. He could not easily be ignored.

Stalin approached Lenin's box and the two whispered together for several minutes. What orders Lenin gave his faithful assistant, I do not know. But from then on, the conduct of the armed gangs became even more insolent. Some of the sailors descended from the galleries and took away empty chairs designated for deputies. Not only was their conduct impudent, it was provocatively obstructive. Every time a majority member mounted the platform to deliver a speech, the noise would increase to such an extent that it was impossible to understand him. The cries of "Shoot him!", the clatter of arms, the aiming of rifles at the orators created an increasingly threatening atmosphere. It was psychological war, a war of nerves. It became evident to all that there was no longer a question of preserving the Assembly. It was doomed, we realized only too well. The only question was whether we would be able to protect the dignity of the convention and prevent its moral collapse. Anything was bearable but this slow torment of obstruction by wild young hoodlums. Some of us were on the verge of provoking bloodshed. Some were sincerely ready to be killed if it would stop this intolerable nuisance, the purpose of which was to mock the idea of a democratic convention.

As if to express our concealed feelings, a member of the assembly, Efremoff, suddenly mounted the platform. He was a simple peasant and spoke like a peasant. With a long beard and a face like Tolstoy's and a loud, slightly musical voice, he was an impressive figure. "Brothers," he said—and this appellation was so unexpected that silence fell—"Brothers," he repeated—and he was addressing not the convention but the galleries—"you are threatening us, your representatives. Your fathers and your brothers sent us to this sacred institution, now you are menacing us with shotguns and rifles. We aren't afraid. We are not afraid to die. Shoot if you have the courage. Shoot me," he cried almost hysterically, "I shall be glad to die for this convention which we have dreamed about for decades. Shoot, but don't insult us." For a moment the armed bands were silent. No one answered him. No one shot. But the silence did not last long.

It was 10:00 P.M. and the session was degenerating into even greater chaos. The chairs on the left, occupied by the Communist party, were almost empty. A few Red sailors with guns lounged in them, smoking and talking loudly among themselves. Some slept.

I mounted the stairs to the gallery. The scene I found there was even more disgusting. Many of the sailors were drunk and sleeping peacefully on the floor. Others played cards, paying no attention to the events going on in the assembly hall. The floor was thickly covered with cigarette butts and empty vodka and beer bottles. I searched for the young sailor with whom I had talked few hours before. I found him sitting with two of his friends and listening to the speeches. "Well," I asked him, "what do you think of this convention?" His face was troubled, and at first he hesitated to answer me, but his friend promptly responded to my query. He was as young and friendly looking as the first sailor.

"Something is wrong, *gospodin* [mister] doctor," he said. "We are quite disturbed . . . we are not happy."

"This old man who said to shoot him," injected the first sailor, "he is a good man. He is like my father. He spoke so simply we understood him easily."

"Yes, he spoke from his heart," the second sailor added.

"But who is wrong and who is right?" I pressed.

"We don't know for sure," the second sailor answered. "We feel that there is something right in the Assembly."

"They shouldn't have behaved so badly," the first sailor complained. "I mean our comrades here have behaved very badly."

"What will you tell your father when you see him, my friend?" I asked the first sailor.

"I don't know, honestly, I don't know. For sure, he will be very angry with me when I tell him I was sitting here so quietly," he replied.

"What do you mean, sitting quietly? What else could you do?"

"My father is a very straight man. He has no fear. He would have acted like the deputy who tore open his shirt and asked us to shoot him. My father will be very angry with me for not defending the Assembly." And he was close to tears as he spoke.

"Well, my boy," I said, "nothing is lost forever. Someday, sometime, the people of Russia will understand what they have missed this day. Give your father my regards. He must be a good fellow."

"Oh, yes, *gospodin* doctor, he is. Good-bye."

I descended to the assembly hall in slightly better humor. This conversation with the two sailors had produced a stimulating effect on me. Some hope . . . not for today, but for tomorrow. Democracy, I said to myself, can never die.

In spite of the continuing noise, the session went on. Member after member delivered his speech, full of hopes and wishes for democratic Russia. But the crisis seemed to be approaching. Any minute now we expected some action on the part of the Communists.

At about eleven that night, the Communist faction requested an intermission. They wanted to discuss among themselves the question of further participation in the convention. The interval was granted, and the Communist faction held a meeting in their room.

Lenin took the lead at that meeting. "The central committee of the party," he said, "proposes to leave the Constituent Assembly after making a special announcement to the convention."[3]

Gregory Pyatakoff expressed some doubt as to the wisdom of such an action. "The idea of the Constituent Assembly is

---

3. This scene was described by the Communist H. L. Metscherikoff in *The Press and the Revolution*, No. 4, 1924.

deeply locked in the heart of the nation, and our leaving the session before the end seems not very wise."

Bukharin spoke in defense of Lenin's suggestion. "There's not much sense remaining here," he insisted.

Others agreed, and it was decided to quit the convention.

Lenin suggested a declaration in which the Communist faction would proclaim the majority of the Constituent Assembly to be "enemies of the people . . . traitors of the revolution." The Communists' resignation from the convention was motivated, the declaration said, by their unwillingness to participate with counterrevolutionary parties who did not want to accept the dictatorship of the proletariat and the achievements of the Soviet government.

Raskolnikoff, a member of the Assembly, was chosen to present the declaration to the plenum of the convention. The Communists were preparing to return to the assembly hall. Lenin protested. "What, comrades?" he said. "Do you intend to go back to the session and then leave after Raskolnikoff reads his declaration?"

"Why not?" he was asked.

"That's hardly possible. Do you realize," Lenin asked, "that when our resolution is read and our faction quits the session, so strong an impression might be produced on the armed soldiers and sailors in the gallery that some shooting may occur? And I do not want any bloodshed."

"There's no harm in shooting a few Mensheviks and Social-Revolutionaries," remarked Avanosoff.

"But that's exactly what I don't want," angrily replied Lenin. "I don't want to make martyrs of the members of the Constituent Assembly."

"And many of them would like to be killed and become the saints of the revolution," Bukharin said, sustaining Lenin.

"The men in the galleries are in a state of complete demoralization," remarked Pyatakoff.

"An awful band of scoundrels," said Lenin irritably. "Where on earth did you get such a gang of deserters, Comrade Dybenko?"

"I did my best," answered Dybenko.

"Incidentally, Comrade Dybenko, I am informed that you ordered your gang to disperse the convention. Is that true?"

"Yes," admitted Dybenko. "I gave the order to Comrade Gelejnyakoff."

"Call Gelejnyakoff here," ordered Lenin.

A few minutes later, the sailor Gelejnyakoff entered the room. Lenin himself wrote and signed the following order, signed also by Uritsky, commandant of the Tauride Palace in charge of the convention: "I order the comrade sailors and soldiers not to allow any assault on the counterrevolutionary members of the Constituent Assembly and to permit them all to leave the Tauride Palace freely. Nobody should be admitted to the Palace without special permit." Besides this general order to the guard of the Tauride Palace, Lenin wrote Gelejnyakoff a note confirming his oral order: "The Constituent Assembly should not be dispersed till the end of the session. Tomorrow, from early morning, nobody should be admitted to the Tauride Palace." (This order was not obeyed by Gelejnyakoff.) [4]

Midnight had long since passed. We were sitting in the assembly hall, waiting for the Communists to return. Tension mounted with each minute. A man on trial awaiting the jury's verdict might feel as we did. I thought of the French Revolutionary Convention. How did we differ from them? Robes-

4. *The All Russian Constituent Assembly,* published by the Soviets in 1930, p. 207. The same episode was reported by Dybenko in *The Rebels,* p. 110.

pierre. Marat and the Girondists. There was much blood and cruelty and fighting then, but there were also some great dramatic moments, when death seemed attractive and glorious. And here, a band of politically ignorant, half-drunk youngsters. They knew nothing. They cared for nothing. The cruelty of ignorance! Whom must we fight? Who would hear our voices? We were isolated. There was no free press. There was no communication with the outside world. An iron curtain made all our speeches almost useless. A waste of time. Getting nowhere. Cold anger was brewing among us. With minutes passing so swiftly, action seemed the only solution for this unbearable impasse.

It was after one o'clock in the morning when the session was reopened. The Communist faction was absent. We knew now that they would not return. The chairs of the center and the right were still full.

Raskolnikoff read the Communist declaration. It was brief. It was clear. We were declared to be the enemies of the people. And, as such, we were outlawed at once. "Now it comes," we said to ourselves. "Now they will begin to mob us. They will be as cruel and vindictive as they know how."

They surrounded us from all sides. We were defenseless. Unarmed. We sat in tense silence while the gallery exploded with a fantastic roar. It was hell. The air was filled with words of insult that I had never heard in my life. "Patricides . . . bourgeois carrion . . . capitalistic bastards" were the mildest of the invectives used by Lenin's gang. Catcalls and hisses deafened us. Many of the sailors, it seems, were supplied with police whistles. Twenty or more whistles blowing at one time produced a paralyzing effect upon our hearing.

Some of the sailors descended the stairs, aiming rifles at the members of the convention. "Capitalistic murderers!" cried one of them. "Kill them!" "Hirelings of French capitalists . . . lackeys of Rothschild. . . . Shoot them!" It was a nightmare. We were sure the critical hour had arrived and that the gang would begin to massacre us.

But the noise stopped as suddenly as it had begun. And the session continued its work in a much calmer atmosphere than at any time before.

Soon the left-wing Socialist faction declared itself. The left-wingers had remained in the convention, although they had actually entered into full coalition with the Communists. Steinberg, their leader, read the statement. They were quitting the convention, he said, because the parties of the majority had refused to sign a separate peace treaty with Germany, a peace which they had promoted.

They left in silence, and their exit did not produce any explosion from the gallery. The role of the left-wing Socialists had been pathetic enough—and their fate was tragic. Although admitted to the Soviet of People's Commissars, in which they received a few seats, they were mercilessly liquidated as soon as their usefulness as appeasers had ended. Boris Kamkoff and many of their leaders, who had given so much help to the Communists during the October *coup d'état* and the days preceding the Constituent convention, were among the first victims of the Red terror.

For long hours the convention lived in expectation of bloody tragedy. Several times it looked as if the butchery of the democratic members was about to begin. But it never came. The climax was never reached, and, after hours of painful tension, prostration and fatigue began to permeate the convention.

The speeches continued in an atmosphere that lacked enthusiasm and ardor. We were tired, dead tired from the long, exhausting, passive struggle. It was psychological torture by exhaustion.

It was four o'clock in the morning. We had begun to discuss the land bill, which would have completely revised existing agrarian laws and provided the farm population with land they needed so badly, when a sailor slowly mounted the platform. There was nothing remarkable about him except his longish hair. Rather tall and broad-shouldered, he was not distinguishable from the other sailors who filled the galleries. He approached the president of the convention, Tchernoff, who was giving instructions about voting. The sailor waited a minute or two, then lightly touched Tchernoff's arm. We could not hear his words, which were spoken in a low voice. But we saw Tchernoff angrily shake his head.

The sailor repeated his demand in a louder voice. "I have instructions from Comrade Dybenko. You must all leave the assembly hall."

"I refuse to obey this order," Tchernoff answered. "Citizen sailor, the Constituent Assembly will be dissolved only if armed force is used."

"I must insist that you all leave the hall immediately," the sailor stubbornly repeated.

"I refuse, I refuse," Tchernoff said again and again. For a few minutes a heated discussion went on between the president and the sailor. Other members of the presidium joined in. It was decided that there was no sense in provoking a riot. Force was on the sailor's side.

The land bill was hurriedly voted on—in less than five minutes. The manifesto addressed to the Allied countries was hastily read and accepted unanimously. With this manifesto, the Constituent Assembly refused to accept a separate peace with Germany and confirmed its allegiance to the Allied cause. And, lastly, a special law was passed whereby Russia was declared a federative democratic republic.

While the convention was passing these bills, the sailor stood patiently on the platform. He said nothing.

This sailor was Gelejnyakoff, and he was the same to whom Lenin had given the order not to interfere with the Assembly's session. It happened that he was not a Communist. Not even a fellow traveler. He was an anarchist.[5]

At 4:42 on the morning of January 6, by the Russian calendar, the first session of the All Russian Constituent Assembly was announced as closed. It was decided to resume the session on the same day at 5:00 P.M., but no one believed that this Assembly would ever meet again.

In morose silence, we left the assembly hall, expecting at any moment to be assaulted by the armed men who came down from the gallery and followed us to the antechamber of the Palace. Turning my head, I saw behind me the three sailors with whom I had talked earlier in the evening. "What are you doing here?" I asked them.

"We came to protect you," one of them murmured to me. And, guarded by my friends, I left the Palace, but there proved to be no necessity for the precautions. Nobody was molested, and all members of the Constituent Assembly were permitted to leave the Palace and to go off into the darkness of the winter night.

A few evenings later, I went to Bolotnaia Street to say

---

5. "It was after four A.M. An unknown sailor ascended the estrade. . . . Gelejnyakoff touched the arm of the chairman [Tchernoff] and declared that according to the instructions he received from the commissar [Dybenko], all present must leave the hall." *The All Russian Constituent Assembly,* Mark Vishnyak, p. 115. The same scene was reported in *The All Russian Assembly,* published by the Soviets in 1930, p. 207, and in Paul Dybenko's *The Rebels,* p. 110. Anatolyi Gelejnyakoff was executed by the Soviets for "banditry" several years later, according to Vishnyak, *ibid.,* p. 100.

good-bye to my friends and colleagues there. Approaching the building where the assemblymen were lodged, I saw a crowd of by-standers. "What's going on?" I asked.

"The Bolsheviks have come to arrest the members of the Constituent Assembly," was the prompt answer.

Those who had been unable to hide or leave the city were sent to jail. And the All Russian Constituent Assembly, the century-old dream of the Russian intelligentsia, was dead.

The Soviet government ordered my arrest. I had expected it. The house I lived in had been under observation by two suspicious-looking men. The Red police were not yet properly organized and were far from efficient then. Before coming home, I had telephoned my mother, and she told me that she had seen the men from the window. "Michael [our janitor] learned that they were sent to arrest you. Don't come home," she warned me.

It was freezing cold, and a savage north wind blew mercilessly through the streets. "But I have nothing with me," I protested. "I have to come home and get money and other things."

"I'll send Natasha [my sister]. She can bring what you need."

"I don't want to involve her. It's dangerous."

"Well! I don't know what to do." My mother was distressed.

"I have an idea," I said. "It might work." We had two Dalmatian dogs, ferocious animals, that were quite unfriendly to strangers. "Ask Natasha to take the dogs out and walk them as close as possible to the men. Watch from the window and I'll call you in ten minutes or so."

When I called again, my mother was delighted.

"It worked," she announced, laughing. "The combination

of the growling dogs and the cold was too much for them.
They retreated to a beer hall on Sadovaia Street. You have,
my dear, thirty minutes or more to get your things."

"Keep the dogs on the street," I pleaded. In no time, I
reached home. I gathered up my things and left in a hurry,
hardly having time to kiss my mother and sisters good-bye.

The Institute of Science, with which I was associated, was
located on Angliskyi Prospect, only a few blocks from home.
I reached it safely. The six-story building was very large. Part
of the enormous basement was occupied by storage rooms
filled with anatomical preparations preserved in jars with
formalin. Specimens of liver, heart, and other organs of men
and animals, duplicates of the specimens exhibited in the
Museum, filled every corner. With the help of Martha, my
assistant, I found a place to sleep. She brought me blankets,
pillow, and sandwiches. She locked the door and I was alone.

The room was called "The Comparative Heart." Hearts
of all ages, beginning with that of a human embryo of two
months and ranging up to the heart of a man of 95, and of all
species, from fish to monkey, were stacked by the hundreds
on shelves and floor, a memorial to man's evolution.

Martha had a sense of humor. She had left Aristotle's
Natural History with me. "Useful reading in your condition,"
she said. Perhaps it was. The heart, asserted the Greek philosopher, is the center of man's mental activity. Perhaps it
was so, after all, I thought gloomily. Once the heart has
stopped beating and is placed in a formalin jar, all thinking
processes are terminated.

The room was filled with the smell of formalin, which
evoked in me a mood expressed by the Russian proverb
"Soueta souet," which, in exact translation means, "Vanity of
vanities." After ten days in "The Comparative Heart," I was
partly convinced that there was a definite meaning to this

proverb, and at night I carried on long discussions on the subject with the heart of the 95-year-old man.

One evening, after two weeks of hiding, I decided that it was time for me to leave Petrograd. I reached the railroad station without incident and took a train, overcrowded with demobilized servicemen, for Kiev. There was no room in the third-class cars, or in any cars. Bag over shoulder, I elbowed my way into a narrow space in a compartment. My presence produced an unexpected effect. My closest neighbors moved as far from me as they could, leaving me all the room I needed. Some even left the compartment. I was perplexed. What was wrong?"

"Are you from a hospital?" a man asked.

"From a hospital?"

"You smell like hell, Comrade." And he hastily left. Only then did I realize that I had become "formalinized" during my stay in "The Comparative Heart." "*Net chuda bes dobra,*" a Russian proverb says, which means, "There is always some good in anything bad."

The front was quiet. The war was actually over. Trotsky was in Brest-Litovsk, signing the peace between the Kaiser's Germany and the Soviet government. Only a skeleton of the army remained, and soldiers were deserting by the thousands. They were almost all peasants, anxious to return to their villages and take part in the distribution of the land-lords' estates. To them, the Soviet regime symbolized the popular slogan: "Land for everyone." It took them only a few years to find out that the Communists brought them not land but the collectivization of it, and actually deprived them of all their possessions.

Ilya, my orderly, met me in Rovno. In gloomy silence we reached the hospital, exchanging only a word or two.

"When are you leaving, Ilya?" I inquired.

"I'm in no hurry, Chief. The old woman and my daughter take good care of my little farm. I'd like to stay with you as long as you need me." And he asked, "Is it bad?"

"Very bad."

There were few patients at the hospital; occasional cases of mild infection or other minor ailments. The personnel took their jobs easy and played bridge from early afternoon till late at night.

Soon an order came to me to move my unit to Kiev for demobilization. The night before we left, I went to the old church. It was early spring. Through the bombed-out ceiling I saw the sky, dark blue, covered with stars, calm in its immense, unreachable distance. I was exhausted. And slightly bitter. The Russian intelligentsia were defeated, betrayed, sold down the river by their own brothers to the reactionary forces of pseudocommunism. Yet, who dares to accuse them for their idealism, which they had been nursing so tenderly for almost a hundred years, the idealism which brought them defeat and the annihilation of all that they believed and dreamed of.

Chapter 13

LOVE ISN'T EVERYTHING

The spring of 1918. I was in Kiev, the capital of the free Ukraine. The nationalistic movement was in full swing. The Russian language was forbidden in public institutions, and everyone was trying to learn the Ukrainian dialect. I had no plans for the future, a demobilized physician without a job and unable to find any because of my Russian name. I made a pathetic attempt to return to my scientific work and started in at the Institute of Bacteriology of the University of Kiev. The work progressed slowly, if at all. My mind and thoughts were far away from the *Trichomonas* I was studying. My country was suffering the most painful convulsions, bleeding profusely and growling like a wounded bear.

At one of the scientific meetings of the Institute, I made the acquaintance of a young physician who was in a state of mind similar to mine. Dr. Leonid Krentovsky, a graduate of the University of Moscow, was an instructor in pathology at the time he was mobilized and had been sent to the north-western front. Twice wounded there, he took an active part in the fight against the Communists, was arrested by them, but succeeded in escaping to Kiev. He impressed me as a man of strong personality and considerable courage. He was anxious to return to Moscow, if only for a few days. He told me that he was in love with a girl, a talented poetess, Mariette S.

"An extraordinary creature, my Mariette," he said. "She writes beautiful poems, as beautiful as she is herself. A fine girl. I must see her at any cost."

He had not seen her in more than a year. "She wrote me regularly till the October trouble. Afterward—not a word from her. We are engaged, and we planned to be married as soon as the war was over."

As the days went by, he became more and more restless. He stopped his work at the Institute, lost weight and became careless in his appearance, going unshaven for two or three days.

One day I met him in the hall of the Institute. He looked different. Gay and talkative. "I'm leaving for Moscow to-night," he announced.

"That's a dangerous business," I said.

"Who cares! I can't live without Mariette."

"Good luck!" I said, and we shook hands.

For two months I had no news of him. Then, by a peculiar coincidence, I met him on a boat sailing down the river Volga. I was on my way to Ufa, a town in the Ural Mountains.

In the late spring of 1918, I had been informed that the Czechoslovakian legions, organized by Kerensky's government from cadres of former prisoners of war, had revolted against the Soviet regime and were forming a new front along the Volga. The democratic leaders, scattered to all parts of Russia after the tragic days of January 5, had been summoned to Ufa to attend the convention of the Constituent Assembly. For members of the Assembly, like myself, who lived in Kiev and other cities of the Ukraine, the trip was not so simple. We were faced with the problem of crossing central Russia, where the Red terror reigned unabated, where the jails were filled with political prisoners and thousands were liquidated daily. The borders were guarded by military police, and every suspicious-looking man or woman was arrested on the spot.

For a few days I hesitated to plunge into this new adventure. The chances of reaching Ufa safely were slim indeed. Several members of the Assembly who had made the attempt were caught at the borders and immediately put to death.

Furthermore, prospects for the convention were not bright. I had no illusions about its future. And yet, somewhere in my heart, I felt an obligation toward the voters who had elected me. I had no right to evade participating in the attempt to revive the All Russian Constituent Assembly on territory free from Communist domination.

Together with two colleagues, I set out on the dangerous enterprise. I decided to be bold and travel under my own name, as a demobilized physician returning to his native town near the Volga. Dr. Maidansky of the Army Medical Corps supplied me with demobilization papers. Whether I was crossing the frontier or traveling through cities occupied by the Communists, I went directly to the local Cheka, requesting a permit to continue travel.

We arrived in Moscow without complications and from

there we took the train to Pensa, a town about eighty miles from the front line.

The closer we came to the front, the greater was the danger of arrest. We left the train and continued by horse-drawn coach, changing horses from time to time. At last, we had come to within ten miles of the Czechoslovakian lines. Red army patrols were blocking all roads. The situation was desperate, but a sudden offensive by the Czechoslovakian army brought us into no man's land and safety. We were among welcoming friends. The next day, we took the boat down the Volga River.

I was resting on the deck when I noticed a man in a dirty uniform. Hair long, beard unkempt, toes protruding from his shoes, he looked like a beggar. He was sitting on the floor and writing on a piece of paper. He turned his head in my direction and calmly said, "A nice day, isn't it?" It was Dr. Krentovsky.

Resting on the deck and eating watermelon, the specialty of the Volga region, we talked about my trip and the Ufa convention.

"Have you seen Mariette?" I asked.

He smiled sadly. "Yes, I've seen her."

"And . . . ?" I was quite curious.

"Love isn't everything," he replied, and he told me the story of his trip.

He walked with firm, measured step, looking neither to the right nor to the left. His hands were buried deep in the pockets of his military topcoat. He wanted to create the appearance of a man who belonged to the Red regime. Only once, while he was walking along a street in Moscow, was he stopped. Two Communists approached him.

"Comrade, where do you come from?"

One of the men, a big fellow with a round face, laid his hand upon his shoulder. In reply, Krentovsky took out his leather cigarette case and started to smoke. Slowly, deliberately, through clenched teeth he snarled: "Get out of here, you wretch!"

Respectfully, the two retreated. And with long, slow strides he continued on his way. He came to Mariette's house. The steps, which had known neither broom nor water for many weeks, were poorly lighted, by a smoking kerosene lamp. The doorbell refused to ring. He tapped on the door. It opened.

"*You!*"

She was stunningly beautiful, more so than ever before. Yet he was disappointed. For her long, heavy black hair, which had fascinated him, had been cut short and there was sternness and even hardness in her eyes. Her dress was different too. A red leather belt and a carefully adjusted dark-red tie gave a touch of the schoolmistress.

She blinked her eyes. His coming was a shock to her. Recovering, she smiled, took his hands in her own, and drew him to her. He kissed her hands, one after the other, and whispered, as if talking to himself.

"I've dreamed about this moment." He noticed the engagement ring, his present, on her finger. "You are still wearing the ring? You still love me?"

She kissed him instead of answering.

The room was warm. The furniture was the same—soft couches and armchairs. Yet there had been a change. In place of the pictures by old Italian artists, large portraits of Lenin and Trotsky hung on the walls.

"What does this mean?" The question was on the tip of his tongue, but he restrained himself from asking it. He was hungry, tired, and in love with her.

The following morning they quarreled. She accused him of "capitalistic trends." She admitted she was a Communist, that she had joined the party shortly after the February revolution.

"Communism is what our country needs," she said. And she explained that the Russian intelligentsia were suffering from a deep inner conflict. They were seeking the answers to their own problems from others. The others couldn't even solve their own problems. Communism relieved them from schizophrenic aberrations. "It has solved all their problems once and forever. All they have to do now is to follow the directives of the party, the orders of our great leaders Lenin and Trotsky."

"What nonsense!" he cried angrily.

"Darling, you are full of bourgeois prejudices. Try to be objective and you will find much truth in what I say."

"Do you mean that we must give up our personalities, our opinions, our judgments, and follow party lines? And this, for you, is the greatest value of communism?"

"Of course, darling. Look at our intelligentsia. What they were. Groundless idealists, engorged in discussions about the eternal problems of life and death. They were tormented souls, full of contradictions and confusion. Now everything is clear. Everything is like two and two are four. No more doubts, no intellectual imbecility. A gigantic mass of people united in uniform thoughts and actions."

"With Lenin and Trotsky your gods?"

"Don't be sarcastic, darling. . . . Please try to understand the bigness of this revolution. Man is free at last from all his doubts, his split personality. . . ."

"And his individuality!"

"Yes! And his individuality, which was nothing but a killing burden."

He lost his temper. He walked to the wall and took down the pictures of Lenin and Trotsky. He smashed them and threw the small pieces into the garbage can.

"How dare you touch them!" she cried angrily, and rushed into her bedroom, slamming the door.

He listened. She was calling someone on the telephone. "Well!" Krentovsky took a seat in the armchair and lit a cigarette. She returned to the living room, looking docile and amiable, and apologized for her conduct.

"Darling, I love you more than my own life. Let's not talk about politics. We all have our own opinions."

The two nights they spent together, Krentovsky acknowledged to me, were worth the trip to Moscow.

In the morning, she was very restless and disturbed. "My love, you must leave my apartment at once."

"Why?"

She avoided his eyes.

"Believe me, you must go at once. Go quickly. It's already 8:00 o'clock."

"I don't want to go away." He stubbornly refused to obey her. "And why should I? Unless you tell me why."

"I . . . I expect some party members here any minute."

"You mean the Chekists."

"Yes . . . yes!" she was hysterical now. "Please, I beg you to go away. Go, if you love me."

"Mariette, my girl. I will not leave. I know you called the Cheka and told them about me."

She was crying. "I did, I did. It was my duty to report your presence here. . . . But I love you. I swear that I love you more than anything else."

"Mariette, my dear. I love you too. And that's why I'm staying here. If I leave, they might arrest you for helping me to escape."

"But you will be killed!"

A knock on the door. She hurried to the kitchen, sobbing bitterly. "Come in," Krentovsky said. He was arrested and taken to jail.

He remained in solitary confinement for two weeks. One day, twelve prisoners, including Krentovsky, were gathered into the little office of Dubianky Prison. The silence was broken from time to time by an old woman prisoner, whose gray hair was covered by a silk handkerchief, a relic of the past.

"Oh, Lord, my Lord, protect me and save me!" she cried.

It seemed as if the dark, filthy walls were going to close in upon their victims. The dusty lamp was covered with soot. A faint light came in through the small window, like a last glimpse of departing life.

"Oh, Lord, my Lord, save your poor servant!'"

Krentovsky wanted to shout at the woman to keep quiet. Krentovsky's name was called.

"Take him out for execution," the warden ordered a short guard with a long beard. "Be careful that he doesn't escape."

"How could he? I do this every day."

They left the prison.

It was a calm, warm night in July. A truck stood at the door, waiting to take the condemned man to the place of execution.

The bearded guard whistled and beckoned to Krentovsky. "Hey, you! Hurry up!" he shouted.

The streets were deserted. The dark, silent houses seemed to vibrate with life. The windows, in the moonlight, looked like smiling eyes which refused to close in sleep. "A beautiful night, Comrade," Krentovsky said.

"Shut up!" was the answer.

The guard, sitting with the prisoner in the back of the

truck, opened his tobacco pouch and started rolling a cigarette. The prisoner stealthily crept up on him. He moved in suddenly and sent the guard to the floor with a heavy blow. He jumped on him, closed his hands around the guard's throat, and in a fit of animal passion strangled him to death. He robbed the dead man of gun, overcoat, and cap, and after having carefully secreted the papers which he found in his pockets, jumped off the truck, which continued on its way.

Krentovsky walked toward the boulevards. In a few minutes, he turned into a short, narrow alley. He stopped, took a tobacco pouch from his coat, rolled a cigarette, and started to smoke.

"It tasted good, that cigarette," Krentovsky said to me, ending his story.

"And your love for Mariette?" I asked.

"Oh, I love her as much as ever. But I've learned that love isn't everything. That's what I wrote in my letter to her."

I never met him again. But an English pathologist told me that he had met Dr. Krentovsky in Saigon and that he was attached to a hospital unit as a pathologist, somewhere in the Far East.

The All Russian Constituent Assembly opened in Ufa under unfavorable circumstances. The Red army was on the offensive, pushing the Czechoslovakian legions to the Ural Mountains. The railroads and highways leading to Siberia were crowded with refugees, troops, and wounded. On the day of the convention, September 8, 1918, the advance guards of the Red army were in the vicinity of Ufa. The fall of the town was expected momentarily.

Victor Tchernoff presided. Instead of discussing practical measures for fighting the approaching Communist troops, he plunged into a long discourse about the defects of Soviet doctrine. We sat in a gloomy mood, listening patiently. A new manifesto condemning the Communist party for its betrayal of democratic principles was voted. There still was a note of appeasement in Tchernoff's speech and a hope that coexistence between Communist and democratic parties might be reached. The convention was adjourned late in the evening, in an atmosphere of doom.

It was a cold, rainy night. Depressed and in despair, I walked through the muddy streets of Ufa, unwilling to return to my hotel and see my colleagues again. A large sign appeared on the wall of a house. In red printed letters, it said: "APPEASEMENT." It disappeared the next second. It was a visional reflection of my thoughts. I was amazed by the human brain's ability to transform thoughts into visions.

The next morning I took the train for Omsk, in Siberia, from where, in the spring of 1919, I left for France, by way of Japan and China. The revival of the Constituent Assembly in Ufa was a complete failure.

Chapter 14

THE KNIGHT OF POETS

IT was early summer. Paris, excited by victory, enchanted by dreams of lasting peace, with the Peace Conference in full swing, was blooming with flowers. Life was gay, carefree, nonchalant. I had just arrived from Siberia, after witnessing the disastrous attempt by the democratic parties to revive the All Russian Constituent Assembly in Ufa.

From the dullness of life in Siberia, I suddenly found myself in the center of international political activity. Through my friend Albert Thomas, I met Émile Vandervelde, Belgian delegate to the Peace Conference, Dr. Edward Beneš of newly formed Czechoslovakia, and many other leaders of democratic countries. The defunct Russian democratic government was unofficially represented at the Conference by Kerensky and other former government members. The Soviet government was not recognized. Not yet.

One day, I invited Adolf Berle, at that time a first lieutenant in the U. S. Army attached to the Slavic section of the American delegation, to my small apartment at the Rue de Fleuris to meet Kerensky and other democratic Russian leaders.

Kerensky had not changed, either in appearance or in his attitude toward the tragic events of his premiership. Dynamic in speech, restless as ever, he was not ready to accept the defeat of democracy. He believed, in fact he was sure, that the Soviet regime would be overthrown. Joseph Minor, the former mayor of Moscow, a wise old man with whom I had traveled from Siberia through China and Japan to France, was much less optimistic. He was cognizant, as I was, of the handicaps of democracy in its fight against communism. But Kerensky still remained the incorrigible idealist, the dreamer, the child of St. Petersburg's white nights, with their call for detachment from the realities of life.

Berle spoke very little but apparently was impressed by Kerensky's unbounded enthusiasm, his passionate belief in the victory of democracy over "the dark forces of reaction," as he termed the Communist movement.

"Where is your family, Mr. Kerensky?" Berle inquired.

"They remain in Petrograd, hostages of the Communists," gloomily answered Kerensky.

"Are they in danger?"

"Of course, they are."

The same night I took a stroll through Montparnasse. Fresh from the calmness of Siberian towns and villages, I enjoyed the stimulating rhythm of Parisian life. The loud talk of passers-by, their gay laughter and absorption in their own affairs, their earthiness were in striking contrast with the character of life in Petrograd. Here, in Paris, they lived for today, taking from life all that was offered to them, slightly cynical, utterly realistic, yet full of instinctive optimism. The eternal problems of life and death which preoccupied the people of Petrograd had no place in modern Paris. One must live as fully as possible—this was written on the face of everyone I met, everyone I saw in the streets, in cafés, at parties. Yet it was in Paris that Roger Bacon had lived and passionately searched for the truth, as we did in our city. But Roger Bacon had been dead for more than seven hundred years, forgotten by the French of today, a peculiar stranger to them, a crazy old man who spent twenty years in prison for his attempts to solve the destiny of the human race.

I stopped at the "Causerie de Lillas," a café on Montparnasse, the meeting place of French poets and writers. As usual, Paul Faure, the "prince of Parisian poets," was surrounded by younger poets listening to the old maestro and sipping their apéritifs. Faure was glad to see me and invited me to join the group. They discussed trends in modern poetry and recited their poems.

"*Mon vieux,*" Faure addressed me, "who is the Russian poet who promotes acmeism? I forget his name. He was in Paris several months ago and read his poems to us. These Russian names! *Parbleu,* how ever can one remember them?"

"Acmeism?" I hesitated. "It couldn't be Gumileff?"

"*C'est lui* . . . Gumileff."

"But what brings him to Paris?" I asked, perplexed. "The last I heard, he was in the army, on the Russian front."

"Yes. He told us. He was sent to the Turkish front but never got there. He stayed in Paris instead."

"Is he here now?"

"No, he returned to Russia a few months ago."

"To Soviet Russia?" I was astonished.

"Yes!" roared Faure. "He gave us a farewell party. He

told us that he had killed many lions and tigers and other wild animals in Africa but had never met the new specimens of human savagery, the Bolsheviks. 'I want to meet them,' he proclaimed. *Un drôle garçon! Il est fou."*

I agreed with Faure.

I did not like him the first time I met him. In fact, I even disliked him when I attended a children's party at Tsarskoye Selo, a suburb of St. Petersburg. He was fifteen then, four or five years older than I. A play was performed, some of the children put on musical and dramatic numbers. He was a star of the party, reciting his own poems. He read them poorly, and I grew tired of listening to his not-very-pleasant voice. He was ugly, or appeared so to me at the time. With his long, egg-shaped head and narrow forehead, he irritated me, young as I was, with his arrogant self-assurance. I didn't catch his name.

My attention was focused on a very pretty girl of eleven, who also read her own poems. She read them with much expression and emotion. Very thin, with large, brown eyes and long, dark hair, in a red dress, she impressed me so deeply that I applauded her violently. Overcoming my shyness, I asked her after the performance:

"What is your name?"

"Anna Gorenko."

She did not ask my name. Paradoxically, hers stayed in my memory for many years to come.

When I was a student at medical school, one of my colleagues invited me to one of the "Wednesdays" at the "Tower," the residence of the poet Vyatcheslav Ivanoff, which attracted the flower of St. Petersburg's literary world. "Nicholas Gumileff and his wife, Anna Akhmatova, will read some new poems. They do some striking work." Busy with my clinical work though I was, I hesitated to decline the opportunity of meeting them. Both were celebrities of the time. Gumileff, the fearless adventurer recently returned from hunting lions in the African jungles, represented the new trends in poetry and was head of the Academy of Verse. She, just married to him, was less well known, yet much admired by the public for the originality and simplicity of her writing.

I took the evening off from my studies and accepted the invitation.

Gumileff retained the same appearance of arrogant superiority that was so repellent to me when he was a boy. Yet he had an enormous strength and vitality that impressed his listeners. He stepped up to the platform. Straight and haughty, in white tie and tails, a picture of elegance foreign to the other guests, he read the manifesto of the group he had organized, the acmeists.

"Our new movement, acmeism, will take the place of symbolism. . . . The word 'acme' means the highest degree of anything. . . . This movement might also be called 'adamism,' a manly, firm, clear outlook on life. . . . We demand a greater balance of form and a more exact knowledge of the relationship between subject and object than was the case with symbolism. . . . All in all, one must fight for a lyricism of faultless words, and fight for it in one's own way."

He recited several of his poems, from which I remember only a few lines:

> *I teach them how not to fear,*
> *Not to fear and do what one must.*
> *And when a woman with a beautiful face*
> *The dearest face in the whole universe*
> *Will say "I do not love you,"*

I teach them how to smile
And to go away, never to redeem.

Anna Akhmatova came after Gumileff. I gasped. She was the same little girl I had seen some years before, Anna Gorenko. She was stunning. Calm and detached, her voice vibrant and penetrating, she seemed utterly monastic. One could hardly believe her when she said, with all the sincerity in her nature, "Saint Antonin can confirm that I was never able to conquer my flesh." One would never have suspected that she liked night gatherings in bars and clubs and often remained there till early morning.

I have been deceived by fate
That sheds neither faith nor rue.

That evening, she read a new poem.

I approached her after the performance and reminded her of our meeting as children.

"What does your husband think of your writing?" I asked her.

She smiled painfully. "He looks upon my poetry as fancy. He does not take it seriously."

Two years later, they were separated. On one occasion, when I met her again, she complained to me that Gumileff "loves love but not women." She, in turn, fell in love with another poet, Alexander Blok. Once more, I was present at a literary party. The star performers were Blok and Akhmatova.

Blok read:

We are revelers, sinners here,
Who can be gay in secret shrouds?
The birds are flowers on the walls
Longing for the freedom of the clouds.

Akhmatova answered him:

> *You don't love, you don't wish to look!*
> *How beautiful, damned, you are!*
> *And I cannot leave my nook*
> *Though since youth I could win afar.*

Her romance with Blok was soon ended, according to rumor. I met her several years later in St. Petersburg, when it had become Red Petrograd, in "The Cave of the Wandering Dog." She was thinner and paler than ever, and even more monastic looking.[1]

The end of 1916. There was a lull on the front after some bloody battles with the Germans. I took this opportunity to go to Lutzk and visit friends. Walking on the main street, I almost collided with a cavalry officer. He was twice decorated with the Cross of Saint George, which was the highest military mark of honor, given for exceptional bravery. I did not recognize him at first and let him pass.

Something made me look again. "Gumileff!" I shouted. He stopped and turned back.

"Yes?" he answered politely.

"You don't remember me!" And I reminded him of the children's party in Tsarskoye Selo.

"I remember the party," he said with a smile. "But forgive me, I don't remember you."

I invited him to have dinner with me. I was anxious to hear about his doings and, most of all, about his wife.

He told me that he had enlisted in the Fifth Hussar Regiment, the day war was declared.

"I enjoyed the war, every moment of it," he remarked.

---

1. See p. 137.

"Were you wounded?"

Twice Saint George has touched the breast.
Which was untouched by any bullets,

he declaimed.

He was in good humor.

"War and the danger of death seems to excite my soul," he said. "It was thrilling to tempt fate. My friends, my comrades in arms were killed or gravely wounded. Only a few of the original regimental staff remained alive, and I wasn't even scratched. Amazing, truly amazing! But, then again, I was sure I wouldn't be wounded or killed. Of course, any premonition might be wrong, though, mightn't it?"

I agreed.

"Perhaps I'm a gambler by nature, even if I never play cards. I always liked to play for high stakes—my own life, for instance. Shortly before the war, I went to Abyssinia to hunt lions. One day, I was told that a ferocious lion, which had devoured several villagers, had returned to the nearby hills. His roars could still be heard, and the natives hid in their huts in panic. Not one of my guides wanted to go with me, so I went alone. Believe me, it was the most exciting moment in my life, facing this wild beast."

"And . . . ?"

"I killed him with the third bullet when he was just a few feet from me. My first shot missed. The second shot wounded him."

Our conversation turned to his work. He talked about his review, *Apollon*, and the future of Russian poetry.

"Every man is a poet in his soul. Every man can create poetry if he works hard on style and technique. Poetry is like music, and a poet is like a pianist who has to work every day on his technique if he wants to be perfect." He told me that while he was at the front, he had written a poem called "Gondsla." He recited it to me. It was his best piece of work.

"I can hardly believe that you could write such a splendid piece here at the front."

He smiled proudly.

"I need excitement to stimulate my creative power. Danger gives me the incitement I need."

"Where's your wife?"

"My wife?" He seemed puzzled.

"Anna Akhmatova."

"Oh, Anna." His voice was dull. "She's in Petrograd. I hear from her once in a while. She sends me her poems from time to time. She doesn't write too badly."

Four years passed. I was in Petrograd after spending four months in Moscow's Boutyrki Prison. In spite of the oppression of the Soviet regime, the literary life there was quite active. I learned that Gumileff had organized "The House of Poets," where he lectured regularly and taught youth "the true poetry." He devoted much of his time to "World Literature," the publishing enterprise founded by Maxim Gorky and himself. He often was called upon to read his poetry or give courses on literature in the "Workers' Clubs," a Communist organization. I was quite anxious to meet him again and find to what extent he had accepted the new regime. One night, I went to "The House of Poets." It was full of youngsters who listened to his discourse with warm attention.

I was somewhat disturbed by the frankness of what he said. "Creative writing needs freedom. Otherwise, it is a mockery of the basic laws of creation. You must write what you think and believe, not what you are ordered to write."

A dangerous attitude, I thought, in a country where the

Communist police dominated all phases of men's lives.

Gumileff was glad to see me. He introduced me to several of his students, who obviously admired him. He was in a gay and enchanted mood.

"You are not very prudent, Gumileff," I said, as we walked together to his house.

"Prudent? When was I ever prudent? I've lived dangerously all my life, and I don't intend to change my habits."

"Dangerous excitement again?"

He laughed. "Do I look scared?" He did not.

"They are more dangerous than the Abyssinian lions and German bullets," I remarked gloomily.

"Who cares? I simply ignore them! I remain myself. And that's that."

"How long will this last?"

"I don't know. I do know that creative writing, and poetry as the purest form of it, is incompatible with this regime of brute force and ignorance and suppression. If creative writing has to be strangled and die, then I'll die too."

On August 25, 1921, Gumileff was returning home after a meeting at "The House of Poets." Several students accompanied him through Nevsky Prospect to the river Moika. He was very gay and joked a good deal as he discussed the poetry of ancient Greece.

A car was parked near his house. He paid no attention to it, and stayed with the students another fifteen minutes in front of his house, exchanging anecdotes. They decided to meet again the next day in "The House of Poets." He entered his apartment, and just as he was turning on the light, two police agents, Chekists, walked up the steps and took him by the arms. They ordered him to follow them. He knew what to expect. He took with him the New Testament and Homer's *Iliad*.

From prison, he wrote a brief note to his second wife, A. H. Engelgardt. "Don't worry. I'm well. I'm writing a new poem and playing chess."

On August 27, he was executed. It was said that he smiled when he faced the firing squad. He was hastily buried by the Communists somewhere outside the city. His grave was never discovered, despite every effort on the part of his admirers.

Was he thinking, during his last moments, of Anna Akhmatova, his childhood sweetheart, his former wife,[2] the great poetess? We don't know. She remained alive for many years after Gumileff's death.

Talking with Faure in the "Causerie de Lillas" about Gumileff and his writings, I suddenly was seized by acute nostalgia, a desire to go back to Russia and my old city of St. Petersburg. Perhaps Gumileff's return to his native country, in spite of his revulsion toward the Communists, was responsible for my decision to visit Russia again. Three weeks later, in October 1919, I joined a Red Cross hospital which was to be sent to North Russia, still in the hands of anti-Communistic elements. I sailed with other hospital personnel to Archangel, by way of Norway and Murmansk. Subconsciously, I hoped to be in my city again, the city of white nights and unrealizable dreams.

---

2. They were divorced in 1918, three years before he died.

Chapter 15

INSTEAD OF CONCLUSION

THE polar night was calm, bright, and starry.[1] A thick padding of snow covered the streets and houses of Archangel. Freezing cold made breathing difficult, and the frost burned face and lips. Now and then, a pedestrian, bearlike in Eskimo fur coat, could be seen wandering alone through the streets.

It was on such a night that the evacuation of the northern front was decided upon. The Red army was closing in on the city of Archangel.

In February 1920, the Red army, increased in strength, had begun exerting strong pressure upon the armies of North Russia. By the middle of the month it became evident that North Russia had to be evacuated. The decision was made

---

1. The events described in this chapter were reported by me in the article "The Fall of North Russia," published in the *Archives of the Russian Revolution*, v. 9, Berlin, 1923, pp. 5-90.

on the eighteenth. Some troops moved overland to Finland and Norway, while the army staff, the wounded, hospital personnel, and the government, including myself, were embarked on the *Minin*. The captain of the cutter was Commander Tchaplin. By the night of February 20, sailing with considerable difficulty through the frozen sea, we came upon the small cutter *Rousanov,* imprisoned in ice. I was attending the wounded on the *Minin,* with the assistance of a nurse, when a young navy officer informed me that Commander Tchaplin requested my presence. I went to the upper deck.

Tchaplin was very brief: "Dr. Sokoloff, General Miller has ordered your transfer to the cutter *Rousanov.*"

"Isn't the *Rousanov* immobilized by ice, without a chance of reaching Norway?" I inquired.

"Yes," he quietly admitted. "We do not want you to go to Norway."

"Do you realize," I said, trying to remain calm, "that you are deliberately condemning me to death at the hands of the Communists?"

"I have my orders and you must obey."

"May I take my belongings?" I asked.

"I don't think it's necessary."

In silence, I followed the young officer down the ladder to the *Rousanov.* There, I found Sergeev, an army captain, who had been assigned to me as aide when I was nominated a member of the government. Much later I was to learn that a group of archmonarchist naval officers had requested General Miller, acting head of the North Russian government, to "deliver Sokoloff into the hands of the Communists," on the ground that I was "a friend of Kerensky."

The skipper of the *Rousanov* met us in a friendly spirit. He was sympathetic but did not try to give us any hope. The

White Sea, he informed us, was full of icebergs too large for his ship to cut through. Furthermore, Tchaplin had taken a large part of the coal and foodstuffs from the cutter. "Sooner or later," the skipper consoled us, "if the northeast wind frees the sea of ice, we should reach land." He advised us to be patient and to become accustomed to a diet of seal meat.

I paced the deck through the rest of the night. General Miller's outrageous act had no justification whatever. But I accepted it fatalistically, and I was quite certain that every thing would end well. The picture from the deck made my heart beat faster. Mountains of ice kept charging our ship like living beings. They crept up on deck, broke deafeningly, and fell back into the sea. The cutter creaked and groaned under their assaults.

The days passed slowly. Held fast by the ice, we were carried through the White Sea, helpless against the power of the wild and willful icebergs. After ten days or so, our food supplies were reduced to almost nothing.

Then the seal hunting began. At that time of year, the seals give birth to their funny, red-eyed babies. As the little creatures slid awkwardly over the ice, the hunters killed them by hitting them on the nose with sticks. I refused to take any part in the slaughter. But I liked the sweetish seal meat, and it was well that I did, for soon it constituted our sole diet.

Many more days had passed in the monotony of seal hunting, when at last a south wind brought us to the western shore of the White Sea. There, around a small harbor, lay a village which bore the curious name of Iokhonka. It was hundreds of miles from the nearest settlement.

On a bare cliff, Allied troops had built a camp for Communists, fellow travelers, and other political prisoners. Several hundred, a few of them innocent, others under strong suspicion, and the rest clearly guilty, had been exiled to Iokhonka by the military authorities. When the news reached them that the Red army had taken Archangel, the prisoners mutinied, killed the commandant and guards, and elected a local soviet from among their own numbers. Then they settled down to wait—with what impatience!—for a ship to come to their harbor. And as fate or the wind had willed it, the first ship to arrive at Iokhonka, whose population was filled with desire for revenge and thirsting for the blood of its enemies, was our little cutter, which carried a member of the government which they hated.

The whole settlement came running to meet us, fully armed. They were almost incredulous when they discovered my presence on the cutter. "Sokoloff, the government minister!" they cried. About a hundred of them surrounded me, and each insisted upon touching me, as though to make sure that I was alive and real and not a mirage. Amidst wild shouting—which had none too friendly a sound—I was marched along the settlement's only street to the House of the Soviets.

The crowd cried: "A trial . . . a revolutionary trial . . . at once!"

A court chosen from among members of the soviet, all Communists, was formed without delay. I was permitted to speak in my own defense. What could I say to justify myself?

I stood in a large room, filled with people. Five or six judges sat at a table. Through the frozen window I could survey the sea, filled with ice and bathed in the bright polar sunlight.

For a moment I had a curious feeling of great inner freedom. My time among the living was short. There was no doubt of that. The crowd was raging. They were quite capable of tearing me to pieces without bothering to wait for a trial. There was not a chance in a hundred thousand of my coming through alive. I must accept the inevitable. I became calm, and a little sad. For my own sake? Possibly. I remembered, for some reason, the unfinished research I had been doing on tuberculosis. I thought too of the baby seals with red eyes.

I began to speak, as slowly and amicably as I could.

"Yes, I admit I am an enemy of the Soviet government and an incorrigible opponent of communism. . . ."

"Kill him!" they shouted.

"I was brought up in the faith that man is born to be free. Russia has suffered too long from oppression and despotism, and Lenin has brought it back to the Russian people. . . ."

"Shoot him!"

The court deliberated for not more than five minutes. It pronounced a sentence of capital punishment for me and my friend Sergeev.

The crowd met the verdict with wild cries of approval.

Once again we were led along the street. There was an icy northeaster blowing now. The shouts of the mob mingled with the howls of the wind. "Kill them. . . ."

But still, strange to say, I was convinced that I would not die—although there was reason enough to suppose that my hours were numbered.

We were taken to a little house and locked in a semidark room. Our three guards were on the other side of the wall from us, and we could hear every word they spoke. We, the condemned men, hung on their words, hoping against hope to catch some hint that might give us a chance to survive.

It was a typical polar night, black and bitterly cold, and a snowstorm was raging.

"The doctor has nice boots," we heard from the other room.

"The chief will take them," another replied, with an audible yawn.

We fell into a doze.

Soon after sunrise, a new guard appeared—ten soldiers with rifles. They surrounded us and marched us along the street, which was covered with newly fallen snow. It was bright and sunny, the storm long over. Flocks of seagulls were wheeling over the sea, which was almost free of ice. We walked in oppressive silence, and the numbness in my feet increased with every step.

"To the cliff." We were headed for that snowy cliff, which seemed so far and yet was so dreadfully near. How many minutes of the march to death are left, I wondered. Again I remembered the pink-eyed baby seals and I felt suddenly sorry that we had killed them, those naïve and trusting creatures.

"Stop! Hey, there, stop!"

We turned around. A bearded Communist was running after us, plunging through the deep snowdrifts.

"Hold on! The execution is postponed. . . . I have orders to send them to Moscow for further interrogation. . . . I've been speaking with Moscow over the telephone."

We were saved from death—for the time being.

The trip to Moscow was long and not very comfortable.

We embarked on the same cutter, the *Rousanov,* but I was placed in a dark storage room instead of a cabin. The cutter sailed north to Murmansk, where I was separated from Sergeev. I never learned what became of him. In Murmansk, I sawed wood for ten days in the City Square before a crowd which enjoyed the political spectacle tremendously. Apparently, I did my work well, for it met with the approval of my audience.

One night, I was again taken on board an ice-cutter. This

time they put me in a deep coal pit. Bread and water were handed to me through a hole in the ceiling. In no time, I was black all over from coal. I couldn't tell the difference between day and night—it was so dark.

I was taken one day and marched to a deck cabin. A Red army captain was seated there. When he saw me, he smiled feebly. "You don't look very handsome."

I turned to a mirror and saw a black man with wild eyes, blackish beard and hair, and in the dirtiest possible British officer's khaki uniform. I agreed that my appearance was far from attractive.

"You are a medical doctor?" the captain asked. I nodded.

"We have on board a regiment under my command going to the South. An influenza epidemic started as soon as we left Murmansk. Ten men have died already. I have no doctor with me and no drugs. You will be in charge of this epidemic. But I warn you, if a single man dies, you will follow him at once."

I made a brief tour of examination and found about a hundred men affected with the same viral influenza that in three years had killed more than two million in Europe and America. Many soldiers were in grave condition, with fevers up to 105°. The only medicines on the ship were a bottle of aspirin and some iodine. The situation seemed as hopeless as my sojourn in the coal pit. But on going through the storage rooms, I came across several large cases marked with the Red Cross stamp. I opened them up and discovered sixty gallons of rum.

I acted promptly. I prescribed four glasses of rum per day, one every four hours, to every patient. I should hesitate to claim that the rum helped my patients' influenza, but by sheer coincidence not a man died during the next five days. This therapy was exceedingly popular with my patients, and on our arrival at Archangel, they all signed a petition requesting my freedom. This petition, of course, had no effect on the Cheka, and I was sent to Moscow by train. There, after long and not-very-pleasant interrogations by the Cheka, I was confined to Boutyrki, the famous Moscow political prison.

I was with twenty other men expecting death. Some of us slept on the floor, some had cots, and life was not altogether grim. We talked, we ate, we read books borrowed from the prison library. We discussed almost everything—excepting the approaching end of our lives. Our tensest moments were those which we passed awaiting the commandant's call, which usually came at ten o'clock at night. Sometimes he didn't arrive till midnight, sometimes not till the small hours of the morning. There were days when he didn't appear at all, and those were the most anxious and terrible. "Is he going to come?" we would ask ourselves, and we could find no sleep. It was impossible to read or talk during these expectant hours; our thoughts flowed on without order or meaning. Trivial details would come to mind: a lost button, a favorite passage of verse, a stupid aphorism read long ago in some newspaper. At such times, the men imprisoned in that cell composed a unit, a single soul. The cell was transformed into one enormous ear.

Suddenly, from a distance, comes the noise or marching feet. First in the prison courtyard, then in the lower corridor. The marching stops for a moment. Somewhere, far below us, a cell door is opened and shut. *They are only on the first floor.*

We catch every sound, count every second. The stamping feet come nearer. They reach the second floor, then the third. Now we begin to hear words. The stamping becomes unbearably loud. The feet stop outside our cell, number 17. Fingers fumble noisily, the key is turned in the door. The warden enters, and calls out the names of those to be put to death. The unfortunates are led away. And so for one hundred and twenty-two days . . .

Paradoxically, I was in the midst of left-wingers. Out of twenty men in Cell 17, fourteen were men who only two years before had ardently promoted and defended communism. Two were maximalist Socialists, two Social-Democrats, six Left Socialists, two followers of Tchernoff, and two fellow-traveling Liberals. All were filled with hatred for the Soviet government. They claimed they had been betrayed, in the most outrageous manner, by Lenin and his comrades. "Without us," they reiterated, over and over, "the Communists would never have been able to overthrow Kerensky's government or disperse the Constituent Assembly. We believed them. We trusted their honesty, their integrity, their promises to adhere to democratic principles and respect freedom. We realize now that it was all a fraud. We realize now that they wanted power and nothing but power." Again and again, they discussed among themselves the ignominy of their own conduct, which had helped to bring disaster to their country.

The first to die were the two Liberals. Called by the warden soon after I arrived at Boutyrki, they walked out of the cell crying, "Damn the Communists." Next, one after another, the Left Socialists were taken. They went forth with murder on their lips, cursing their former comrades and associates the Communists.

Sitting in that Boutyrki cell and waiting to be sent away for execution, we freely discussed the question: "Why did so many Russian intellectuals give support to the Communist cause?" Why were so many of them fooled by Lenin and his followers? Why the fatally appeasing attitude in democratic circles, which basically were strongly anti-Communistic?

My position and that of several other cell mates was perfectly clear. From beginning to end I had been uncompromisingly opposed to communism. I had had no illusions. I fought it because I believed in democratic ideals and principles, in freedom, in the development of man's individual personality. Progressive and liberal as I had been from early youth, I recognized at the outset, without any reservations, the peril which Lenin's movement was bringing to Russian democracy. I fought communism in the name of democratic ideals. I lost the fight. I was in prison, condemned to death. I accepted my fate, without bitterness, as the logical consequence of a lost cause.

Nicholas Mikhailov, one of my cell mates, was outspokenly frank. Highly esteemed in labor circles, president of the Steel Workers' Union, a maximalist Socialist, he did not hesitate to admit that he had been "fooled" and "betrayed" by the Communists.

"I called upon the members of our union to support their cause," he said grimly. "They followed my call."

"Why did you do this?" I asked.

"Why? It isn't easy to define my motives. I was impressed by the Communists' energy. They were men of action. This pleased me. They promised a heaven on earth. They were quite convincing."

"Did you not know their past records, their tactics?"

"Of course, I knew. For ten years they had tried to capture my union. They used all their dirty tricks to get it in their hands. They insinuated against me, they accused me of 'reactionary and capitalistic' motives, they falsified votes. I threw them out of the union several years ago."

"And yet?"

"And yet . . . Lenin is very clever in his slogans," Mikhailov continued. "His cleverest slogan is that the one who attacks or even mildly criticizes him is a hopeless reactionary, a 'lackey' of capitalism."

"Why should this bother you?"

"My friend, what man wants his reputation as a progressive or Socialist or Liberal to be smeared? Believe me, their propaganda is so persistent and so effective that even my union members were half inclined to believe that I was a reactionary and had sold out to the capitalists."

My other cell mates warmly agreed with him. "No one likes to be called a 'blackguard' and a 'reactionary,'" they said.

I protested. I pointed out that I had never hesitated and many other progressive Russians had never hesitated to be openly critical and actively opposed to communism.

"A true liberal should have the courage of his convictions," I insisted. "The trouble with you, Mikhailov, and with your friends was that you weren't realistic. One must be an idealist, but a realistic one. You and your friends actually were fooled by Lenin and his followers because you had no sense of reality."

Boutyrki Prison, with more than three thousand political prisoners, was badly understaffed with medical personnel, and I was asked to help. Thus I gained relative freedom of movement inside the walls. Visiting the sick in the various cells, I was impressed by the fact that almost all the political prisoners belonged to the intelligentsia. Teachers, students, lawyers, white-collar employees, labor-union leaders, and skilled workmen were there. Only a few were of aristocratic origin. Many prisoners did not know the reason for their arrest and apparently had been jailed for purely preventive reasons. Some had been in Boutyrki for months without ever having been interrogated, their files lost or altogether absent.

There was a spirit of comradeship among the prisoners. The left-wingers who had helped to overthrow Kerensky's government received food parcels from relatives and shared them with the men and women who had defended the democratic government. All were united by a common hatred of communism. I made many friends in Boutyrki. Some of my patients needed moral support more than drugs or medication. And in spite of the fact that I was expecting to be executed any day, I remember my time in Boutyrki with a deep sense of satisfaction. I hope that I rendered some comfort to my unfortunate prison mates.

One day in July, shortly after luncheon, I was unexpectedly called in by the warden. I was ordered to bring my belong ings. Sometimes a summons of this sort meant, in the language of the prison, either "an invitation to execution" or a transfer to another political prison.[2] It was a beautiful sunlit day. I walked slowly, following the assistant warden and holding all my worldly possessions: two shirts, a piece of soap, and a spoon. When news of this development reached the prisoners, my jail mates on all four floors rushed to the windows to watch me leave through the prison courtyard. Thousands of them cried words of goodwill, words of friendship from their windows, and suddenly they started to sing the popular Russian song of political prisoners:

"Be brave, friend, be brave, in struggle you obtain your rights."

For the first time in the years of my adventurous political

---

2. A political prisoner called for execution was as a rule first transferred to Cheka headquarters. In 1920 there were so many prisoners whose cases were not yet passed on by the Cheka that every prison in Moscow and other cities was filled with men who were to be executed.

life, I was unable to control my emotions, and I cried.

The warden met me with a friendly smile. "You are free, Doctor." I almost fainted; possibly I did faint. I was speechless for a long minute. Was this a joke? I was the last man in Boutyrki to expect freedom.

"There must be some mistake," I stuttered.

The warden, who was not a Communist, smiled. "We are all glad that you leave us in good health." He shook my hand and gave me back my passport and money. I walked out of Boutyrki in a daze. Was this a dream? It seemed like one.

Moscow was in full summer. I walked for hours in the streets, enjoying my freedom, my unexpected new lease on life.

In Petrograd, where I arrived the next day, I learned the reason for my release. Nicholas Morosoff, President of the University of Lesgaft, had personally intervened in my case and begged Lenin to "save the life of a promising young scientist." Morosoff, a noted writer, poet, and scientist, was one of the few men to survive twenty years of solitary confinement in Shlissenburg Fortress. As a young man, he had been arrested for fighting the Czarist government and had received a life sentence. Although an anti-Communist, he was respected by Lenin, and his request for my freedom was granted against the advice of the Cheka.

I returned to my scientific activity and was soon nominated head of the Department of Experimental Medicine at the Institute of Science. I was free—free to walk in the streets, to perform my experiments, to look into the microscope, to operate on rats and mice. But it was not long before I realized that, for a man with my aspirations, with my passionate love for democratic freedom, with my individualistic inclinations, Soviet Russia was no place to live.

Shortly after my arrival, I was invited to give a lecture at the Academy of Sciences on my experiences in Paris during the Peace Conference. I was perfectly frank and said what I thought. I did not mince words. Only democracy, I said, would be able to bring lasting peace to the world. Only free nations, composed of sincere believers in democracy, want peace and work for it. Dictatorship, any dictatorship, means war.

The audience of academicians and scientists was apparently pleased with my lecture but refrained from comment or discussion. The next day, I was informed by Morosoff that I had overstepped the laws of Soviet Russia and might be arrested if I continued to express my opinions too freely.

A few weeks passed before I arrived at the conclusion that the only place where there was freedom of speech and thought in Communist Russia was in prison. There, we had discussed all topics freely, without fear of arrest.

I tried to plunge into research and ignore the things that were happening and the political atmosphere in which I lived. I tried, as many of my colleagues did, to readjust myself to the detached conditions of scientific work. I didn't succeed. The totalitarian regime of the Communists was becoming more and more intolerable. The absence of a free press, the necessity of watching one's every step, the ever-increasing severity of police regimentation, all led me to the unavoidable decision to escape to free Europe. The task would not be easy. All the boundaries of Soviet Russia were well guarded, and anyone who tried to cross, whether to Finland or to Poland, was shot at once.

As the days and weeks went by and I found no practical plan for escape, I became restless. Then, one day, waiting for my weekly ration in the House of Scientists, I noticed a woman in the lobby, poorly dressed and very pale, whose face seemed very familiar. A secretary dispelled my doubts. "Of course," he said, "she's the wife of Kerensky. She's in the most distressing circumstances. She has two sick sons and is actually a hostage of the Communists. She's under constant surveillance by the Cheka. She might be sent to Siberia at any time. We try to help her as much as we can. We give her rations now and then, but we're not supposed to."

I made up my mind at once. Going up to her, I reminded her that we had met on several occasions when she was the First Lady of democratic Russia. Quite boldly, I told her that she must escape from Russia, and with little delay.

But her spirit was completely broken. "This is an impossibility . . ." was the only answer she would give me.

"We shall escape," I told her.

Although the problem of leaving Russia with her and her two boys was much more complicated than it had been for myself, alone, my determination to escape was only increased in force.

At that time, in 1920, the Baltic states still were free and independent under their democratic governments. The Soviets, slowly consolidating their power over the Russian people, pretended to be ready and even eager for their small neighbors to live according to their respective governing patterns. To show their bona fides, the Soviet government had agreed to permit Estonian citizens to leave Russia and go back to their native country. A train was scheduled once a month to carry the Estonian refugees from Petrograd to Revel. They were, of course carefully scrutinized by the Cheka, and only those who were above suspicion were allowed to cross the boundary a few miles from the Narva River.

Dr. K., a friend of mine, was the Estonian representative in Petrograd and was in charge of the evacuation. I went to him and explained frankly my case and that of Kerensky's family. He hesitated, but not for long. "I hate to be involved in your adventure," he said, "but I'm soon leaving for Revel also. I owe much to the Russian intelligentsia. I am a part of it." Dr. K. wrote a certificate declaring that Hans Osolin, his wife Milda, and two children were natives of Estonia and were entitled to be returned there. "From now on," he told me, "you are on your own responsibility. This certificate means nothing without the approval of the Cheka. And their examination is very difficult to pass. The slightest suspicion on their part, and you and your friend will be thrown in jail. But if you want to take this risk and gamble on your life, it is up to you."

Neither I nor Mrs. Kerensky spoke a word of Estonian. In fact, we didn't even look like Estonians, who are, as a rule, fair and blond, whereas we were brunette.

"You must get a blond wig," I said to her. We're going to risk our lives, and we start tomorrow."

Everyone in Petrograd knew Mrs. Kerensky. For months her picture had been on the front pages. She found a blond wig—of very poor quality. It was too small and would slide back, showing a lock of dark hair. She looked so suspicious, she trembled so with nervousness, and her oversize glasses were so awkward on her finely molded nose that I hesitated for a moment to enter the Cheka building. She will surely betray herself, I thought. But our decision had been made, and we entered the office of the chief clerk of the Cheka.

I seated Mrs. Kerensky on a stool as far from the examiner as possible and did all the talking. He paid no attention to this foolish-looking woman. "My wife," I said, "is not well mentally. I would like to take her to her parents in Revel."

Fortunately, he did not speak Estonian. He asked me endless questions in Russian about my past and about my future plans. After twenty long minutes, he apparently was satisfied and put his stamp of approval on our certificates for evacuation to Estonia.

It was precisely at this moment that my premonition began. When I was walking away from the desk, I noticed a bearded man sitting at the other desk. He was young and had long hair and vivid eyes. He observed us with a distinctly suspicious look on his face. However, he didn't say a word, and we left the Cheka office with a promptness not surprising, considering our state of mind.

"I nearly fainted in there," Mrs. Kerensky confessed to me. "My heart was running so fast that it ached."

Our departure was scheduled to take place in two weeks, hence our visit to the Cheka. "It was a miracle," admitted my friend the Estonian consul. "But the worst is still ahead. On the Russian-Estonian frontier they scrutinize refugees even more carefully," he warned me.

During the next two weeks, I saw the face of the bearded Chekist in my dreams. He would enter my room and search my closet and traveling bags. He would point out to me something he had found there, a pen or a toothbrush. He became an obsession with me during this interlude. Mrs. Kerensky, on the other hand, claimed that she slept better than she had slept at any time since her husband's escape from Russia three years before.

The day of departure came at last. It was a sunny autumn morning when some three hundred refugees embarked on the train, without incident. But the moment the train left, whom should I see but the Chekist of my dreams, walking through our car. It was a bad sign. As he passed our seats, he slowed his pace. He glanced sharply at the Kerensky family and me, as if contemplating talking with us. He did not, however, and soon he disappeared into the next car.

We saw him again when the train stopped a few miles from

the Estonian frontier and the refugees were ordered to leave, with all their belongings. We unpacked our bags and waited in a field of wet grass for the inspection. In a few moments the bearded Communist appeared. He examined my bags superficially and stamped my paper.

Quite different was his attitude toward Mrs. Kerensky. He searched her bags meticulously. He found a few French books. "Oh," he said, "you read French?" At the bottom of her bag, he uncovered a gold pencil. It was a beautiful pencil and bore the inscription: "To Alexander Kerensky from his admirers."

"The foolish woman," I said to myself bitterly. "Now all is lost."

The Chekist read the inscription carefully and looked at her. Trembling and in despair, she made an involuntary movement of her head and the wig slid down, revealing her dark hair. "Madame," the bearded man said, "your hair-do has slipped. . . ." He remained silent for two long minutes, then murmured: "You may get back on the train. . . . But I will keep this pencil as a souvenir. . . ." He put his stamp on her certificate and was off. I never learned who this man was, but I guessed he was an underground anti-Communist working in the Cheka.

The train was on the move again. Mrs. Kerensky was sobbing hysterically.

In about an hour we crossed the frontier. We were in the free, democratic state of Estonia.

"You may take your wig off now," I said to her, rather sharply. I was still very tense from the encounter with the Chekist, and the untidiness of her wig irritated me. Mrs. Kerensky obediently took it off and handed it to me. I threw it into the river we were crossing.

Our trip was over. Kerensky met his family in Revel and took them to England, where they remained for many years. I spent another ten days or more in the camp for repatriates until, at last, a visa for England was granted to me.

I soon received an invitation from the University of Brussels to work on cancer there. With my arrival in Brussels, my adventurous political life was terminated. But, paradoxically enough, for my first six months in the quiet atmosphere of Brussels I was unable to sleep. I had acute insomnia. Traveling through Soviet Russia, crossing frontiers, languishing in the coal pit of the Arctic ice-cutter or in Boutyrki Prison, I had slept like a child and remained in perfect health. But in Brussels the aftereffects of my dangerous existence manifested themselves in grave form.

It has often been said that the success of the Russian Communist movement has depended on the poverty of the masses. This is true to some extent. An illiterate, impoverished, politically ignorant man joins the Communist party because it promises him everything he does not have. Yet the fact remains that the Communists, in conspiring to overthrow a democratic government, have never relied on the "masses." The *coup d'état* of 1917 was accomplished, as later in other countries, chiefly with the help of fellow travelers and intellectuals.

A careful analysis of every Communist victory, whether in Russia, Poland, or in the countries of Asia or Central Europe, gives us the same picture. The masses serve only as the substratum. Economic and political conditions are merely a source of effective slogans and propaganda. But the actual conspiratorial work has always been done by the intellectuals. In Russia, all the efforts of Lenin and his followers were directed toward forming a powerful nucleus of fellow travelers, by whom the destruction of democratic unity could be accomplished.

The pattern of Communist strategy has remained unchanged during the decades since the revolution. In every country of the globe, the fellow travelers work among, appeal to, and organize not the masses, not the politically and intellectually inept layers of the population, but the intellectuals, or intelligentsia. And a substantial part of the intelligentsia responds to their call. When a man of intelligence, of cultural background, of intellectual and humanitarian inclinations joins the ranks of the Communist party or actively helps it, he is acting in a manner totally contradictory to his principles.

Russian communism is generally considered to be fighting capitalism—whose defeat is its prime goal. Actually, of course, the Soviet regime, being an extreme form of state capitalism, is fighting not capitalism as such but only private initiative in industry and commerce. But much more important is the fact that neocommunism is a movement directed against individualization and toward the standardizing of all man's activities. It is the farthest-reaching attempt ever made in this direction. Steadily and persistently, the Soviet regime is driving toward its ultimate goal: *control of human behavior*. It states officially that man can transcend his heredity and transform his environment and so achieve full uniformity of behavior. In this gigantic social and biological experiment, carried out largely through the education of children and youth, the Soviets are using the conditioned-reflex mechanism on a large scale. They openly declare that this is essential to their purpose, that through such standardization a complete hold over their subjugated peoples can be attained.

The benevolent and often enthusiastic attitude of many intellectuals toward Russian communism is so incredible that one wonders if, in their case, there is not actually a psychological or even a psychiatric problem involved. For *only an emotional instability, a subconscious appreciation of a brutal primitive force such as Russian communism, a craving for submission to it, and an instinctive desire to escape from one's inner conflicts can explain the paradoxical fact that the intellectuals, who are extreme individualists, give admiring support to an utterly anti-intellectual and anti-individualistic movement such as Russian communism.*

They did so in 1917, they do it now, in spite of all the evidence available on the true nature of this movement.

Because of the benevolent attitude of certain groups of intellectuals toward Russian communism during the forty years of its existence, its whole history is actually a painful story of appeasement on the part of democracy, which always has ended in victory for communism. Since 1903–1904, the pattern of their strategy has been open and well defined. Victory over Kerensky's democratic government was a pathetic case of appeasement; the Communists were enabled to seize power in a country in which they were a small, insignificant minority. Their conquest of Latvia, Estonia, Lithuania, and other neighboring countries was only a minor example of their ability to exploit the psychological weakness of democracy. Their accomplishments in Teheran, Yalta, and Potsdam were miracles of political strategy, for there the democratic countries lost World War II and made communism what it is now, an irresistible military force.

These tragic mistakes on the part of the leaders of democracy were all made in a sincere attempt to find a peaceful solution to world affairs. The democracies naïvely believed that cooperation with communism was possible, despite all the cynical records of this movement.

The attitude of appeasement is still alive and still a factor in the national and international politics of America, Europe, and Asia. Influential intellectual circles in the United States and abroad continue under the spell of Russian communism and promote its cause, sometimes openly, often knowingly or unwittingly under cover of "progressive," "liberal," or "humanitarian" movements and organizations. Western leaders join in Soviet-inspired "peace talks" to find a peaceful way of preventing the forthcoming war. They do not realize, even yet, that the only thing which might stop the triumphal march of communism is a firm, unyielding stand backed by military might. Lenin's postulate has never been abandoned by the Communists or even slightly modified: *"Those who are not with us are our mortal enemies."* There is no room for neutrality in the fight against Russian communism. *One is either with it or against it.*

Future historians will be perplexed by this "illness of appeasement," which for so long has kept so powerful a hold on democracy, which has paralyzed counteractivity, caused ineptness and confusion, and brought communism one victory after another.